PAN-ORGANIZATIONAL
SUMMIT
ON THE U.S. SCIENCE AND
ENGINEERING WORKFORCE

MEETING SUMMARY

Marye Anne Fox
Government-University-Industry Research Roundtable

NATIONAL ACADEMY OF SCIENCES
NATIONAL ACADEMY OF ENGINEERING
INSTITUTE OF MEDICINE
OF THE NATIONAL ACADEMIES

THE NATIONAL ACADEMIES PRESS
Washington, DC
www.nap.edu

THE NATIONAL ACADEMIES PRESS   500 Fifth Street, N.W.   Washington, DC 20001

This study was supported by Contract/Grant No. N00014-01-1-0903 between the National Academy of Sciences and DOD, Contract/Grant No. NASW-99037, TO109 between the National Academy of Sciences and NASA, Contract/Grant No. DE-FG02-00ER30309/99-558-05 between the National Academy of Sciences and DOE, Contract/Grant No. N01-oD-4-2139, TO29/00-150-02 between the National Academy of Sciences and NIH, Contract/Grant No. 5B1341-02W-1510 between the National Academy of Sciences and NIST, and Contract/Grant No. 2002-38840-01973 between the National Academy of Sciences and USDA.

Any opinions, findings, conclusions, or recommendations expressed in this publication are those of the author(s) and do not necessarily reflect the views of the organizations or agencies that provided support for the project.

International Standard Book Number 0-309-08960-3 (Book)
International Standard Book Number 0-309-52530-6 (PDF)

Additional copies of this report are available from the National Academies Press, 500 Fifth Street, N.W., Lockbox 285, Washington, DC 20055; (800) 62-6242 or (202) 334-3313 (in the Washington metropolitan area); Internet, http://www.nap.edu

Printed in the United States of America

THE NATIONAL ACADEMIES
Advisers to the Nation on Science, Engineering, and Medicine

The **National Academy of Sciences** is a private, nonprofit, self-perpetuating society of distinguished scholars engaged in scientific and engineering research, dedicated to the furtherance of science and technology and to their use for the general welfare. Upon the authority of the charter granted to it by the Congress in 1863, the Academy has a mandate that requires it to advise the federal government on scientific and technical matters. Dr. Bruce M. Alberts is president of the National Academy of Sciences.

The **National Academy of Engineering** was established in 1964, under the charter of the National Academy of Sciences, as a parallel organization of outstanding engineers. It is autonomous in its administration and in the selection of its members, sharing with the National Academy of Sciences the responsibility for advising the federal government. The National Academy of Engineering also sponsors engineering programs aimed at meeting national needs, encourages education and research, and recognizes the superior achievements of engineers. Dr. Wm. A. Wulf is president of the National Academy of Engineering.

The **Institute of Medicine** was established in 1970 by the National Academy of Sciences to secure the services of eminent members of appropriate professions in the examination of policy matters pertaining to the health of the public. The Institute acts under the responsibility given to the National Academy of Sciences by its congressional charter to be an adviser to the federal government and, upon its own initiative, to identify issues of medical care, research, and education. Dr. Harvey V. Fineberg is president of the Institute of Medicine.

The **National Research Council** was organized by the National Academy of Sciences in 1916 to associate the broad community of science and technology with the Academy's purposes of furthering knowledge and advising the federal government. Functioning in accordance with general policies determined by the Academy, the Council has become the principal operating agency of both the National Academy of Sciences and the National Academy of Engineering in providing services to the government, the public, and the scientific and engineering communities. The Council is administered jointly by both Academies and the Institute of Medicine. Dr. Bruce M. Alberts and Dr. Wm. A. Wulf are chair and vice chair, respectively, of the National Research Council.

www.national-academies.org

Preface

Each of the 31 nonprofit organizations that contributed a presentation to the Pan-Organizational Summit on the Science and Engineering Workforce (November 11-12, 2002; The National Academies, Washington, DC) was invited to issue a corresponding position paper to be reproduced in this volume. The bulk of this document comprises these papers. In addition, Shirley Jackson and Joseph Toole, two of the keynote speakers, have included their remarks.

The most remarkable aspect of the summit was the spontaneous self-assembly of the contributing organizations into working groups. Groups focused on gathering a critical mass with which to drive the issues voiced at the meeting. This is both a credit to the passion of the community, and recognition of the gravitas of the issues at hand.

PRESENTERS' SUGGESTIONS FOR POLICY ACTIONS

This paper documents areas in which multiple organizations' interests and directions coincide. Each topical area is listed with its most frequently suggested policy solutions, followed by the names of the organizations that support those solutions. Many of the suggestions are taken directly from the position papers while others took shape from the dialogue that ensued at the summit itself.

The views expressed do not represent an official policy statement of the Government-University-Industry Research Roundtable nor of its sponsoring organizations nor the National Academies. Findings from reports of the National

Academies are not included here but may be found in a number of documents listed in Appendix D.

National Leadership: Develop a coordinated, multiorganizational, multisectored effort to address why there is a lack of development of U.S.-born S&E talent and ensure that effort has national leadership.[1] Key focus areas would include some or all of the issues below.

K-12 Teacher Training: Examine the reasons why domestic K-12 students are turning away from science, technology, engineering, and math (STEM)[2] and use those findings to develop novel approaches to attract students to STEM.[3] As a part of that effort, support pre-service training and in-service STEM teacher development to meet content knowledge needs of teachers.[4] Work with governmental science agencies and industry to provide professional development opportunities for teachers through summer fellowship programs[5] and long-term support relationships between federal agencies' (DOE, NASA, etc.) scientists, mathematicians, and engineers, and pre-college math and science educators.[6]

Financial Aid: Target financial aid for those wishing to major in S&E.[7] For financially disadvantaged S&E students, make financial aid readily available in the form of grants or loan forgiveness, rather than loans.[8] If a comprehensive national plan cannot be developed readily, some first steps might be taken—e.g., develop a plan for all federal agencies and National Laboratories to incorporate undergraduate and graduate loan forgiveness as part of their postdoctoral appointments.[9]

Undergraduate Curriculum and Pedagogy Reforms: Continue the efforts to transform the S&E undergraduate learning experience, expanding and building on what has been learned over the past decade about how to engage students with content/pedagogical approaches so that they are motivated to pursue careers in STEM fields.[10]

Effort/Reward Ratio: Address the poor effort/reward ratio of careers in science and engineering, for both practitioners[11] and K-12 teachers in the U.S.[12] Key issues are time to degree,[13] time to start of career,[14] lack of positions commensurate with training (for certain subfields),[15] impact of the global S&E labor force on U.S. salaries (for practitioners),[16] and lost earnings relative to other career paths and professions.[17]

Agility in S&E Education: Conceptualize and implement an infrastructure of interconnecting career pathways and educational resources that allows S&E students to readily migrate to and along the S&E pipeline.[18] As an example, more articulation agreements between universities and community colleges would address the needs of those who do not start their careers in four-year, baccalaureate-granting institutions.[19]

Agility in the S&E Workforce: To give S&E workers the exceptional agility their careers demand, ensure that there is national support of life-long learning.[20] As a first and necessary step, retool H-1B visa fees to support the retraining of highly skilled S&E workers rather than only the initial training of lower-skilled workers.[21]

Minority/Women Participation: Increase participation by women and minorities in S&E disciplines and careers.[22] As a part of that effort, investigate cultural differeces (e.g., in Asian families) that seem to encourage involvement in S&E.[23]*

A Systems Approach to Understanding the Problem: Develop a more comprehensive national database,[24] more extensive education research,[25] and the beginnings of a workable system model[26] of S&E education and workforce pathways. These resources are necessary to understand the factors that lead to changes in both supply and demand of S&E workers; i.e., to guide intelligent policymaking.[27]

The National Academies has conducted numerous studies on the state of the science and engineering workforce, and the educational pipeline that supplies that workforce (see Appendix D). In contrast, this volume is a snapshot in time of the deeply held policy opinions of various community groups, professional societies, and other not-for-profit organizations that work on the issue area of S&E education and workforce. We have reproduced those opinions faithfully, so that policy leaders and the organizations themselves can use this volume to assess the boundaries of a potential political consensus on this critical issue.

Marye Anne Fox, Chancellor
North Carolina State University

NOTES

[1]Supported by BEST, Business-Higher Education Forum, Commission on Professionals in Science & Technology (CPST), GEM Consortium, Industrial Research Institute (IRI), Information Technology Association of America (ITAA), National Society of Black Physicists, RAND, SACNAS, Sigma Xi, and WEPAN

[2]Supported by ASEE, BEST, Business-Higher Education Forum, IRI, ITAA, RAND, SACNAS, Sigma Xi, and WEPAN

[3]Supported by ASEE, BEST, Business-Higher Education Forum, GEM Consortium, IRI, ITAA, RAND, SACNAS, Sigma Xi, and WEPAN

[4]Supported by BEST, Business-Higher Education Forum, IRI, ITAA, RAND, SACNAS, Sigma Xi, and WEPAN

[5]Supported by BEST, Business-Higher Education Forum, IRI, ITAA, National Society of Black Physicists, RAND, SACNAS, Sigma Xi, and WEPAN

[6]Supported by BEST, Business-Higher Education Forum, CPST, IRI, ITAA, SACNAS, RAND, Sigma Xi, and WEPAN

[7]Supported by BEST, ITAA, NACME, National Society of Black Physicists, RAND, SACNAS, and Sigma Xi

[8]Supported by BEST, ITAA, NACME, National Society of Black Physicists, RAND, SACNAS, and Sigma Xi

[9]Supported by BEST, ITAA, NACME, GEM Consortium, National Society of Black Physicists, RAND, SACNAS, and Sigma Xi[22]Supported by ASEE, BEST, Business-Higher Education Forum, CPST, GEM Consortium, ITAA, NACME, National Society of Black Physicists, RAND, SACNAS, Sigma Xi, and WEPAN

[10]Supported by ASEE, BEST, Business-Higher Education Forum, ITAA, NACME, Project Kaleidoscope, RAND, SACNAS, Sigma Xi, and WEPAN

[11]Supported by BEST, Business-Higher Education Forum, ITAA, NACME, National Society of Black Physicists, RAND, SACNAS, Sigma Xi, and WEPAN

[12]Supported by BEST, ITAA, NACME, RAND, SACNAS, Sigma Xi, and WEPAN

[13]Supported by BEST, GEM Consortium, ITAA, RAND, SACNAS, Sigma Xi, and WEPAN

[14]Supported by BEST, GEM Consortium, ITAA, RAND, SACNAS, Sigma Xi, and WEPAN

[15]Supported by BEST, GEM Consortium, ITAA, National Society of Black Physicists, RAND, SACNAS, Sigma Xi, and WEPAN

[16]Supported by BEST, GEM Consortium, ITAA, NACME, National Society of Black Physicists, RAND, SACNAS, Sigma Xi, and WEPAN

[17]Supported by BEST, ITAA, NACME, National Society of Black Physicists, RAND, SACNAS, Sigma Xi, and WEPAN

[18]Supported by BEST, Business-Higher Education Forum, ITAA, GEM Consortium, NACME, National Society of Black Physicists, RAND, SACNAS, and Sigma Xi

[19]Supported by BEST, Business-Higher Education Forum, ITAA, NACME, National Society of Black Physicists, RAND, SACNAS, and Sigma Xi

[20]Supported by BEST, Business-Higher Education Forum, CPST, ITAA, National Society of Black Physicists, RAND, and Sigma Xi

[21]Supported by BEST, Business-Higher Education Forum, ITAA, National Society of Black Physicists, RAND, and Sigma Xi

[22]Supported by ASEE, BEST, Business-Higher Education Forum, CPST, GEM Consortium, ITAA, NACME, National Society of Black Physicists, RAND, SACNAS, Sigma Xi, and WEPAN

[23]Supported by ASEE, BEST, Business-Higher Education Forum, ITAA, GEM Consortium, RAND, SACNAS, Sigma Xi, and WEPAN

[24]Supported by BEST, Business-Higher Education Forum, CPST, GEM Consortium, ITAA, NACME, RAND, SACNAS, Sigma Xi, and WEPAN

[25]Supported by BEST, Business-Higher Education Forum, ITAA, RAND, SACNAS, Sigma Xi, and WEPAN

[26]Supported by BEST, Business-Higher Education Forum, CPST, ITAA, RAND, SACNAS, Sigma Xi, and WEPAN

[27]Supported by BEST, Business-Higher Education Forum, CPST, GEM Consortium, ITAA, NACME, RAND, SACNAS, Sigma Xi, and WEPAN

*Note: While addressed here as a separate concern, the issues concerning women and underrepresented minorities should also be incorporated into the other groups to provide adequate focus and ensure integration.

Contents

The U.S. Science and Engineering Workforce: An Unconventional Portrait

Michael S. Teitelbaum[1]
Program Director
Alfred P. Sloan Foundation, New York

NO SHORTAGE OF SHORTAGES

For much of the past 10-15 years, it has been a commonplace in many academic and public advocacy settings to emphasize current or prospective "shortages" or "shortfalls" (or sometimes "inadequate skills") in the U.S. science and engineering workforce. Beginning in the late 1980s, the then leadership of the National Science Foundation (NSF) and of a few top research universities argued that a "looming shortfall" of scientists and engineers emerging between the mid-1980s and 2006 could be discerned.[2] Their arguments were based upon projections produced by the NSF's late Division of Policy Research and Analysis.[3]

When, only a few years later, it became apparent that the trend was in the opposite direction to that of the forecasted "shortfall," i.e., a growing surplus of scientists and engineers, the NSF as a whole was subjected to the embarrassment of an investigation by the staff of the Subcommittee on Investigations and Oversight of the House Committee on Science, Space, and Technology, followed by an investigative hearing. In his opening remarks at the latter, the subcommittee's chairman Rep. Howard Wolpe stated that the "credibility of the [National Science] Foundation is seriously damaged when it is so careless about its own product." The subcommittee's ranking minority member (and now chairman of the full Science Committee), Rep. Sherwood Boehlert, stated that the NSF director's shortfall prediction, "delivered up in the context of growing concerns about our nation's competitive standing, was the equivalent to shouting 'Fire' in a crowded theater. . . . Today we will hear that number was based on very tenuous data and analysis. . . . In short, a mistake was made, let's figure out how to avoid similar mistakes and then move on."[4]

Notwithstanding this unfortunate recent history, in September 2002 a new report issued by a year-old entity called Building Engineering and Science Talent (BEST), established by the Council on Competitiveness to focus on admirable concerns about underrepresentation of women and some minority groups in science and engineering, pointed to a "Quiet Crisis" of insufficient production of scientists and engineers in the U.S.[5]

Moreover, only one month earlier, the administrator of the National Aeronautics and Space Administration (NASA) testified before the House Science Committee about NASA's hiring problems. He reported that "[e]ven utilizing all the tools at hand we are at a disadvantage when competing with the private sector," but then went well beyond NASA's own particular competitive problems to claim a general "lack of scientists and engineers":

> *NASA is not alone in its search for enthusiastic and qualified employees. Throughout the federal government, as well as the private sector, the challenge faced by a lack of scientists and engineers is real and is growing by the day.*

He pointed to NSF statistics showing that graduate enrollment in engineering, physical and earth sciences, and math showed declines between 1993 and 2000, and from the mid-1990s to 2000, engineering and physics doctorates declined by 15 percent and 22 percent, respectively.[6]

Thus it would appear that "shortages" or "shortfalls," whether current or impending, have become the hardy perennials of public discourse on these issues. Suffice it to say that there is no credible quantitative evidence of such shortages. All available evidence suggests that overall labor markets for scientists and engineers are relatively slack, with considerable variation by field and over time. This generalization is quite consistent with the existence of very tight labor markets in some areas that are new or growing rapidly (e.g., bioinformatics). Meanwhile, in other areas there appear to be substantial surpluses, with special problems in previous boom sectors such as telecommunications, computing, software, etc. This is not surprising, given that the broader U.S. economy is in a period of economic downturn, and especially given the recent collapse of the dot-com bubble and the deep crises in the telecommunications industry.[7] Labor market projections that go very far into the future are notoriously problematic: no one can know what the U.S. economy and its science and technology sectors will look like in 2012. Certainly there are no credible projections of future "shortages" on which sensible policy responses might be based.

CONTRADICTORY CONCERNS

When concerns about current or forecast shortages are invoked, the trends described typically are attributed to:

1. The failings of the U.S. K-12 education system, especially its inadequacies in science and mathematics.

2. A declining level of interest in such fields among U.S. students, especially among the "best and brightest," in part because of the relative difficulty of science and mathematics as fields of study.

3. Inadequate knowledge among younger U.S. cohorts of science and engineering fields as careers, or in the alternative of the science and math prerequisites required to pursue them at university level.

4. For women and minorities, a lack of role models in these fields, suggesting to younger cohorts that such fields are "not for me."

Others with knowledge of science and engineering labor markets have expressed equally energetic concerns about the increasingly unattractive career experiences of newly minted scientists and (to a lesser extent) engineers. Numerous reports and pronouncements in this direction have emanated from scientific and engineering societies, from Congress, and from the press. A prominent example is the report by a National Research Council (NRC) committee chaired by Shirley Tilghman that pointed to serious career problems facing young biomedical scientists in the second half of the 1990s.[8] Yet recent data reported by the National Institutes of Health (NIH) indicate that key indicators of such career problems have continued to deteriorate since then. *Science* magazine (4 October 2002) reported as follows on an interview with Tilghman (now president of Princeton University) about the new NIH data:

> *It's appalling. The data reviewed by the panel in 1994 looked "bad," but compared to today, they actually look pretty good.*[9]

AN UNCONVENTIONAL PORTRAIT

The main message of this brief note is that the two apparently contradictory concerns above are in fact closely linked to one another. To state the message succinctly: *those who are concerned about whether the production of U.S. scientists and engineers is sufficient for national needs must pay serious attention to whether careers in science and engineering are attractive relative to other career opportunities available to U.S. students.*

As noted, this is not the conventional picture, but it is one that I believe warrants thoughtful assessment and discussion. It begins with the acknowledgment that pursuit of the qualifications required for careers in engineering and in science (especially) requires large personal investments. The direct financial costs of the higher education required for entry into such careers can be very high, depending in part on the family financial circumstances of undergraduates (where financial aid is often need based), whether the institution attended is private or public, whether post-baccalaureate education is required, and, if so, whether such education is lengthy and/or highly subsidized.

Engineering and science differ substantially in these characteristics. For engineering, only the baccalaureate is normally required for entry into the profession, for which educational subsidies are available for those in financial need. In contrast, for professional careers in the sciences the conventional entry-level degree is the Ph.D. and increasingly a subsequent postdoc, the direct financial costs of which are typically heavily subsidized by both government and institutions. Yet even with such subsidies, the personal costs of the required Ph.D. can be quite high—less in the form of direct financial expenditures and more in the time required to attain the qualifications needed.

The extreme case is that of the biosciences. In this large domain of science, which comprises a large fraction of all Ph.D.'s awarded, an average of 10-12 years postbaccalaureate are now required for initial entry as an independent professional: first a 7-8 year Ph.D. program, and then 2-5 years spent in postdoctoral status that has become a virtual requirement for career initiation. In career terms, this implies that most young bioscientists are now unable to initiate their careers as full-fledged professionals until they are in their early thirties, and those in academic positions are not generally eligible for tenure until their late thirties. As noted by Wendy Baldwin, deputy director of Extramural Research for NIH, this is a source of concern to NIH because of "the long-held observation that a lot of people who do stunning work do it early in their careers."[10] Such a pattern, in which career initiation is delayed until one's thirties, is also a source of inherent conflict with the social and biological patterns of marriage and family-building.

There are also significant economic effects of this 10-12 year period in a student or apprentice position: a substantial fraction of annual income that would otherwise be earned[11] must be forgone—what economists term "opportunity costs." A recent study of this subject concludes that bioscientists experience a "huge lifetime economic disadvantage": on the order of $400,000 in earnings discounted at 3 percent compared to Ph.D. fields such as engineering, and about $1 million in lifetime earnings compared with medicine. When expected lifetime earnings of bioscientists are compared with those of MBA recipients from the same university, the study estimated a conservative lifetime difference in earnings of $1.0 million exclusive of stock options, and perhaps double that if stock options are included.[12]

In smaller scientific fields such as physics and chemistry, where times to Ph.D. are shorter and lengthy postdocs less universal, the differentials are smaller but still substantial. Given these significant personal investments of direct expenditures or forgone income, careers in science and engineering must offer commensurate attractions relative to other career paths available to U.S. students. The key words in the preceding sentence are "relative to other career paths available to U.S. students." If U.S. students perceive careers in science and engineering to be increasingly unattractive in relative terms, they have numerous options for career choice in other domains. College graduates who have demonstrated that they are talented and interested in scientific and mathematical domains can choose to go to medical school, law school, or business school, or they can enter the workforce without graduate degrees.

The options available to most non-U.S. students (at least for those from low-income countries) are profoundly different. Attendance at U.S. medical or law schools is not a realistic opportunity, due to the very high costs involved and the absence of subsidies. Meanwhile, it is well known that science Ph.D. programs at many U.S. universities actively recruit and subsidize graduate students from China, India, and elsewhere.

There are, of course, many significant noneconomic rewards (or "psychic income") associated with careers in science and engineering: the wonderful intellectual challenge of research and discovery; the life of the mind in which fundamental puzzles of nature and the cosmos can be addressed; the potential to develop exciting and useful new technologies. For many, these attractions make science and engineering careers worthy of real sacrifices— "callings" analogous to those of the religious ministry or artistic expression. Happily, some fraction of talented U.S. students will decide out of such personal values and commitments to pursue graduate degrees and careers in science or engineering, even with full knowledge that the career paths may be unattractive in relative terms.

Yet it is also true that others with strong scientific and mathematical talents will decide that a better course for their lives would be law school, business school, medical school, or other directions. The following simple questions may usefully be posed regarding the relative attractiveness of careers in science and engineering fields:

1. Does the career path offer a reasonable likelihood that those who have made the sacrifices needed to attain the entry-level degree (B.S. in

engineering, Ph.D. in science) will have predictable access to the "practice" of their chosen profession? In other words, is there known to be sufficient demand in the labor market to provide reasonable career opportunities for most newly qualified engineers and scientists?

2. Can those contemplating a career in science or engineering realistically aspire to a middle-class life style, roughly parallel (even if somewhat less remunerative) to those experienced in other professions?

3. Is the trajectory of a career in science or engineering compatible with a typical adult "life"? That is, does the career path fit realistically with marriage, family-building, and the biological constraints of human reproduction?

SUMMARY

There is a general consensus on the importance of attracting significant numbers of outstanding young U.S. citizens to science/engineering careers. Yet it appears that a variety of forces have conspired—with no one intending this outcome—to a relative deterioration of such careers when compared with those available in medicine, law, and business.

The main negative forces involved seem to differ for engineering and for science. For prospective engineers, the primary deterrents at present may be the visible instability of career paths and the increasing exposure to competition with engineers from low-income countries who are prepared to work for small fractions of prevailing U.S. living standards—a situation not generally experienced by other professionals such as lawyers and physicians. For would-be scientists (with considerable variation by field), the deterrents seem to include the lengthening time to degree and in postdoc/apprenticeship roles, coupled with increasing uncertainty as to the possibility of being able to "practice" as a professional scientist once this lengthy postgraduate apprenticeship period has been completed.

As previously noted, those who are concerned about whether the production of U.S. scientists and engineers is sufficient for national needs must pay serious attention to the relative attractiveness of careers in science and engineering, when compared with other career opportunities available to U.S. students. It would therefore be judicious to exercise caution in again invoking the hardy perennials of prospective "shortages" of scientists and engineers, lest these prophecies prove to be self-fulfilling—leading to actions that cause further deterioration in the relative attractiveness of such careers, thereby exacerbating the very problems they seek to resolve.

NOTES

[1]The views expressed are those of the author, and not necessarily of the Alfred P. Sloan Foundation.

[2]Accessible reports on these materials may be found in, e.g., Constance Holden, "Wanted: 675,000 Future Scientists and Engineers," *Science*, 30 June 1989, pp. 1536-1537; testimony of Erich Bloch, director, National Science Foundation, before U.S. Senate, Committee on Commerce, Science and Transportation, Subcommittee on Science, Technology, and Space, *Hearing on Shortage of Engineers and Scientists*, May 8, 1990, p. 25.

[3]This was a small staff office located within the NSF director's office. The 1992 congressional investigation described below uncovered extensive documentary evidence, reproduced in the subcommittee report, that NSF's own professional experts on the science and engineering workforce had expressed strong skepticism about the validity of the shortfall projections.

[4]U.S. House of Representatives, Committee on Science, Space, and Technology, Subcommittee on Investigations and Oversight, *Projecting Science and Engineering Personnel Requirements for the 1990s: How Good Are the Numbers?* Washington, DC: U.S. Government Printing Office, 1993, pp. 1-10.

[5]See Shirley Ann Jackson, *The Quiet Crisis: Falling Short in Producing American Scientific and Technical Talent*, BEST (Building Engineering and Science Talent), Washington, DC, September 2002.

[6]"Hearing Details Concerns over Future of NASA's S&T Workforce." *APS News*, October 2002; pg. 7.

[7]On October 11, 2002, Lucent announced that a further $1 billion restructuring charge in the quarter will involve cuts of 10,000 jobs during the current fiscal year, which ends in September 2003. These cuts would bring Lucent employment down to 35,000, 22 percent lower than its previously expected total of 45,000 at the end of calendar year 2002. The company employed 106,000 in 2001. (Reuters News Wire, October 11, 2002).

[8]National Research Council, Committee on Dimensions, Causes, and Implicatons of Recent Trends in the Careers of Life Scientists, *Trends in the Early Careers of Life Scientists* (Washington, DC: National Academy Press, 1998).

[9]Erica Goldman and Eliot Marshall, "NIH Grantees: Where Have All The Young Ones Gone?" *Science, 298*, 4 October 2002, p. 40.

[10]Ibid., p. 40.

[11]Plus deferred benefits such as pension contributions, which with tax-free accumulation can become very significant sums over time.

[12]Richard Freeman, Eric Weinstein, Elizabeth Marincola, Janet Rosenbaum, Frank Solomon, "Careers and Rewards in Bio Sciences: The Disconnect between Scientific Progress and Career Progression," American Society for Cell Biology, ms., September 2001, pp. 10-12.

Position Paper on the U.S. Science and Engineering Workforce

Mary L. Good, Chairman
Alliance for Science and Technology Research
in America (ASTRA)

INTRODUCTION

ASTRA is a newly established policy research collaboration comprising 48 of America's leading science and technology companies, associations, professional societies, universities, and research institutions. ASTRA's underlying companies and institutions in turn represent hundreds of thousands of science and technology professionals across dozens of scientific disciplines through their workplaces, professional organizations, and academic institutions. ASTRA's mission is quite simple: we strive to increase public funding for basic research in the physical, mathematical, and engineering sciences based upon overwhelming evidence that underfunding and imbalance in the current federal research portfolio has reached crisis proportions.

Finding 1: Federal funding of basic research in the physical, mathematical, and engineering sciences is in long-term decline and needs to be significantly increased over time.

This decline is long term and began in the late 1980s. By any measurement, it is part of a persistent and long-standing pattern. For example, the share of federal R&D as a percentage of gross domestic product (GDP) has now reached an all-time low (see Figure 1). The decline in federal R&D as a percentage of GDP is a good index to cite because it reflects long-term swings in public and political support for science funding and demonstrates that these swings are not attributable to par-

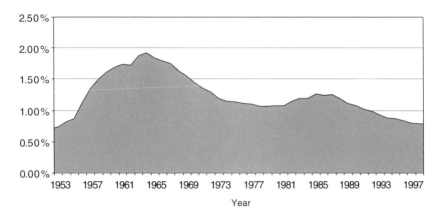

FIGURE 1 Federal R&D as percentage of GDP 1953-2000. *Source:* National Science Foundation, *Science and Engineering Indicators 2000.*

tisan differences, but rather competing policy priorities between 1953 and the present.

ASTRA believes the recent decline is due to several factors, including: the Cold War "build down," which left a gap in defense science budgets, the overall need to redress chronic budget deficits by a succession of administrations and Congresses, and a strongly supported policy decision to increase research funding for the life sciences in the mid-1990s.

Underfunding creates imbalance in the scientific research portfolio, disrupts academic recruiting and grant making, stymies faculty development, and thwarts infrastructure investment. This in turn hampers the traditional educational "pipeline," which is tasked with creating new science and engineering (S&E) workers for industry, academe, and other research institutions.

The consequences of such underfunding have been the subject of many public and private studies, perhaps the most compelling of which was the prescient February 2001 *Report of the U.S. Commission on National Security* (Hart-Rudman Commission), whose assessment has been borne out by painful loss. The commission called for a doubling of federal science and technology (S&T) funding across the board over the next decade.

The Hart-Rudman report details the need for "recapitalizing" America's science and technology educational structure, and it suggests many excellent steps for averting future crises in the areas of U.S. industrial competitiveness, national security, and technological leadership.

Similarly, the July 2001 *Report of the Committee on Trends in Federal Spending on Scientific and Engineering Research of the Board on Science, Technology, and Economic Policy (STEP)* of the National Research Council detailed alarming erosion of federal funding in specific disciplines and made very worthwhile recommendations on improvements.

While it may be difficult to assess why individual students choose their particular courses of study, there is a clear correlation between student degree choice and federal research funding for the mathematical, engineering, and physical sciences (MEPS). Moreover, the percentage of students entering into the life sciences as opposed to other disciplines has reached an extreme point, as demonstrated in Figure 2.

Finding 2: Dysfunction in the S&E educational "pipeline" is closely related to lack of consistent federal support beginning in the late 1980s.

U.S. bachelor's degree production in non-life sciences and engineering continues its long-term decline. The graduation rates for different disciplines between 1975 and 1998 are shown in Figure 2. From these data, ASTRA has calculated the peak year of undergraduate enrollment and the increase or decrease since that time. Only the "life sciences" category has increased during the period 1975-1998. This comes at a time when Asia and Europe are increasing their number of overall science degrees significantly (see Figure 3).

Perhaps more disconcerting, participation by foreign students in U.S. S&E doctoral degree production is now essential. Depending upon the scientific discipline being measured, anywhere from about 35 percent of doctoral degrees in the natural sciences to about 48 percent of doctorates awarded in engineering are being awarded to non-U.S. citizens (see Fig-

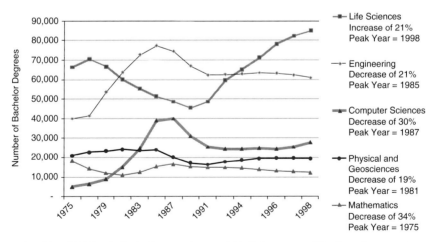

FIGURE 2 U.S. bachelor's degrees in non-Life Sciences and Engineering continue long-term decline 1975-1998. *Source*: National Science Foundation, *Science and Engineering Indicators 2002* and ASTRA.

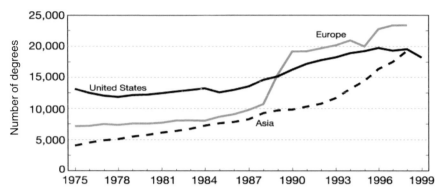

FIGURE 3 U.S. Natural Science and Engineering doctoral degrees 1975-2000 compared with global competitors. Degree totals for U.S. include foreign nationals enrolled in U.S. academic institutions. *Source:* National Science Foundation, *Science and Engineering Indicators 2002.*

ure 4). The significant immigration of foreign-born S&E workers over the past two generations has allowed the U.S. to sustain its long dominance of most scientific and technological fields.

Reliance upon foreign student matriculation has profound implications for the federal S&E workforce in particular. It is estimated that more than 50 percent of federal S&E workers will elect to retire from the workforce over the next 10 years. Because restrictions on non-U.S. citizen employment within the federal S&E workforce apply to many sensitive areas of federal research, and science degree conferral upon U.S. residents continues to drop, no solution is in sight if demand continues at past levels.

Failure of U.S. students to undertake science training and possible reasons for this state of affairs have been analyzed by others. Many factors are at play, and they may include cultural, gender-based, economic, and educational disincentives for science education and the relative attractiveness (money, prestige, ease of learning) of other professions to our brightest students. The teaching of mathematics—the language of science—also presents special problems throughout the educational continuum.

Finding 3: Serious imbalance in the federal R&D portfolio threatens the availability, quality, and preparedness of the U.S. scientific and technology workforce.

Finding 4: Student choice of science discipline correlates strongly with the availability of federal funding for science research.

Viewed in light of Figure 5, Figure 6 demonstrates, through cross analysis of different data sets, an incontrovertible relationship between

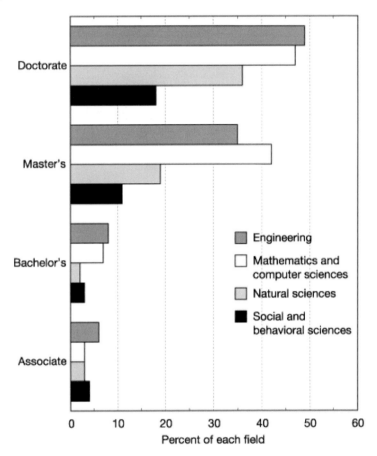

FIGURE 4 Foreign students now constitute nearly a majority of graduates in key scientific disciplines. *Source:* National Science Foundation, *Science and Engineering Indicators 2002.*

federal science funding and student degree choice for MEPS. This pattern is particularly pronounced at the B.S. level, where initial career decisions tend to be made by individuals.

Analysis of these data also seems to demonstrate that individual choice of science discipline is affected less by actual labor market demand and more by the availability of grants and stipends for particular scientific disciplines, such as in the life sciences.

Finding 5: "Basic" research funding is a government responsibility, and the federal science research budget needs to be more focused on basic scientific research.

One unfortunate consequence of mergers, consolidations and the slow recovery in the high-technology sector is that Wall Street and the invest-

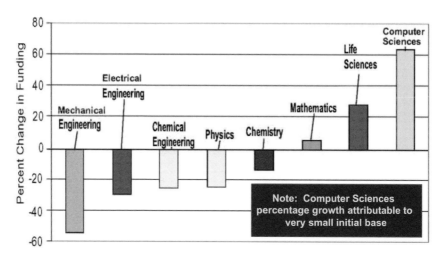

FIGURE 5 Percentage change in federal research funding by discipline 1993–1999. *Source:* National Research Council, *Trends in Federal Support of Research and Graduate Education,* 2001.

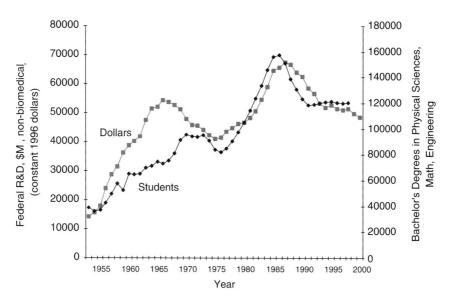

FIGURE 6 Student choice of scientific discipline (U.S. degrees) follows federal R&D funding patterns 1950–2000. *Source:* Mayo, Bruggeman, and Sargent, 2002 (unpublished).

ment community generally disfavor companies that cannot show near-term and consistent profitability. ASTRA's industry members tell us that the accelerating shift by industry away from pure research makes the federal government's role in *basic* scientific research all the more important.

Only the federal government can afford some of the massive investment in infrastructure and equipment needed to keep U.S. science competitive. And this is all the more necessary when viewed in context with an increasingly sophisticated global research community. Unfortunately, government's role in basic research is lagging other types of research. Basic research now constitutes 41 percent of nondefense R&D and only 3 percent of defense R&D (see Figure 7).

Finding 6: Of all citations in U.S. industry patents, 73 percent originate from research conducted through publicly supported institutions (universities, colleges, certain nonprofit research institutions)—about five citations per patent. Paradoxically, U.S. industry performs less "directed basic research" now than in the past, due in part to market demands for immediate profitability.

Figures 8, 9, 10, and 11, prepared by Dr. Gregory Tassey, senior economist at the National Institute of Standards & Technology (NIST) analyze current industry trends in basic research investment and risk reduction over the technology life cycle and suggest possible policy options available:

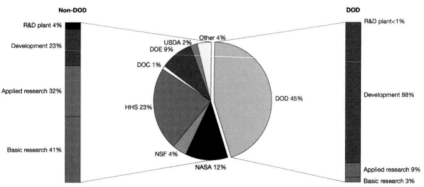

DOC = Department of Commerce; DOE = Department of Energy; DOD = Department of Defense; HHS = Department of Health and Human Services; NSF = National Science Foundation; NASA = National Aeronautics and Space Administration; USDA = U.S. Department of Agriculture

FIGURE 7 Projected federal obligations for R&D and R&D plant, by agency and character of work: FY 2001. *Source:* National Science Foundation, *Science and Engineering Indicators 2002.*

IRI "Sea Change" Index:
Member Firms' Annual Planned Investments in
Directed Basic Research

Year	Percent Planning Increase (> 5%)	Percent Planning Decrease	Sea Change Index
1993	14	40	-26
1994	13	39	-26
1995	8	27	-19
1996	17	23	-6
1997	15	41	-26
1998	14	28	-14
1999	14	37	-23
2000	17	26	-9
2001	17	38	-21
2002	12	25	-13

FIGURE 8 Industrial Research Institute (IRI) member firms' annual planned investments in directed basic research. *Source:* IRI as reported by Gregory Tassey, National Institute of Standards & Technology (NIST).

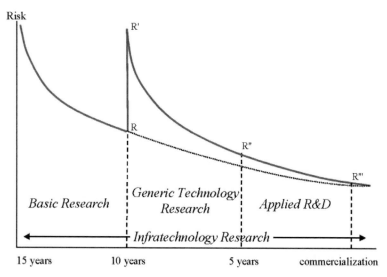

FIGURE 9 Risk reduction over a technology life cycle. *Source:* Gregory Tassey, National Institute of Standards & Technology (NIST).

R&D Policy Options

How much R&D?

- If all manufacturing industries invested at the same rate as the high-tech segment, this sector's R&D would increase from $130B to roughly $400B

- If the Federal Government spent as much on all areas of science combined as it does just on health research, its R&D budget would increase by roughly $11B

- One recent economic study (Jones and Williams) estimated that national R&D should be increased by a factor of four

FIGURE 10 Various scenarios for setting the level of federally funded R&D. *Source:* Gregory Tassey, National Institute of Standards & Technology (NIST).

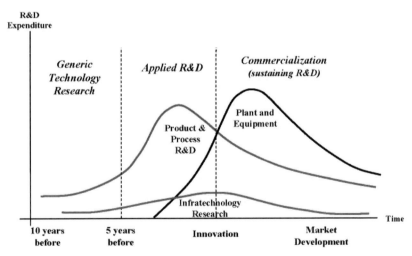

FIGURE 11 Relative expenditures by phase of R&D over technology life cycle. *Source:* Gregory Tassey, National Institute of Standards & Technology (NIST).

RECOMMENDATION

A sustained, multiyear increase in science research budgets must be undertaken immediately. ASTRA advocates a doubling of all budgets in the physical sciences, engineering, and mathematics as a first step toward addressing past neglect and to stanch the flow of talent out of core scientific disciplines.

CONCLUSIONS

ASTRA appreciates the opportunity to review S&E funding in light of the prolonged decline in federal investment in the physical sciences, mathematics, and engineering.

We firmly believe that the most critical step at this point in time is to change the trend, fund all science agencies adequately, and develop a long-range vision of the outcomes we as a nation need from our strong commitment to public science. The imperative to renew this commitment is urgent.

Position Paper on the U.S. Science and Engineering Workforce

Shirley M. Malcom, **Director**
Directorate for Education and Human Resources (EHR) Programs
American Association for the Advancement of Science (AAAS)

INTRODUCTION

Founded in 1848, the American Association for the Advancement of Science (AAAS) is the world's largest federation of scientific and engineering societies, with over 270 affiliated organizations. AAAS members include more than 138,000 scientists, engineers, science educators, policymakers, and interested citizens.

AAAS seeks to "advance science and innovation throughout the world for the benefits of all people." To fulfill this mission, the AAAS Board has set the following broad goals:

- Foster communication among scientists, engineers, and the public
- Enhance international cooperation in science and its applications
- Promote the responsible conduct and use of science and technology
- Foster education in science and technology for everyone
- Enhance the science and technology workforce and infrastructure
- Increase public understanding and appreciation of science and technology
- Strengthen support for the science and technology enterprise

Although stated as a separate goal, building and maintaining a strong U.S. science and engineering (S&E) workforce is integral to all the other AAAS goals. Overall, these goals foster lifelong learning skills in research, technology, ethics, communications, and international collaborations. Through our weekly journal, *Science*, AAAS provides S&E professionals with cutting-edge knowledge and research findings.

Today the United States is the world leader in the global S&E enterprise, but other countries stand ready to challenge this economic strength. One of the main reasons is a shortage of U.S. workers to fill S&E positions. Technically skilled workers on H-1B visas (guest workers) are now making up for the U.S. worker shortfall. This supply of talent could dwindle in the near future as other nations take steps to increase their own S&E productivity. Add to this the following:

• The percentage of white non-Hispanic men in the U.S. workforce is shrinking; this population group represents the majority of the current U.S. S&E workforce. Further educational and employment data indicate that women, African-Americans, Hispanic Americans, American Indians, and persons with disabilities provide an untapped reservoir of talent that could be used to fill S&E jobs (OSTP, 2000).

• The S&E profession competes with other professions, such as law, medicine, and business, for the "best and the brightest" (Teitelbaum, M., 2001).

• The S&E career path is not fully understood and is often filled with obstacles.

A well trained and supported science and technology workforce is essential to the continued vitality of the S&E enterprise and its contributions to society. To maintain the quality of that workforce over time requires sustained efforts at all levels, including attention to transition points along the educational and career continuum. Toward this end, AAAS focuses its efforts on high-quality preparation in science, mathematics, and technology (SMT), as well as recruitment and retention of students and professionals in S&E. Strategies include involving experts and stakeholders in the development of tools that guide educational policies, programs, and practices; development of S&E career resources; and evaluation and research on S&E human resources development.

LESSONS LEARNED

From studies and policy forums with scientists, educators, policymakers, and students, AAAS staff members have identified factors, along the educational and career continuum, that facilitate or limit progression in S&E. Factors that facilitate progression include:

• Taking high-intensity and high-quality SMT high school courses, including physics, and chemistry, algebra II, and calculus (Adelman, C., 1999)

- Pre-college programs that include enhanced SMT courses, college admissions test preparation, and early exposure to S&E research and career information (Commission on the Advancement of Women and Minorities in Science, Engineering and Technology Development, 2000)
- Undergraduate academic support programs and peer networks, particularly in calculus, physics, and chemistry (Campbell, G. et al, 2000)
- Financial aid that reduces debt burden (Rapoport, A. 1999)
- S&E pre-graduate school bridge programs that increase enrollment in doctoral programs (Orfield and Kurlaender, 2001).

Factors that limit progression into S&E careers include:

- K-12 educational policies, practices, and allocation of funds that hinder implementation of high-quality K-12 SMT standards, as well as selection of high-quality curriculum and assessment materials
- College admissions criteria that do not take into account all assets of applicants (Orfield and Kurlaender, 2001)
- The poor quality of science and mathematics education in many teacher preparation programs (National Center for Education and Statistics)
- High school SMT teaching that often lacks rigor and mentoring toward S&E careers
- College and university SMT teaching that often does not take into account the learning styles of students, as well as a lack of faculty mentoring toward S&E doctoral careers
- Community college SMT curricula that may not be aligned with curricula in bachelor of science degree-granting institutions
- Undergraduate SMT curricula that may not have the depth and breadth to prepare students for success in S&E doctoral programs
- College and university departmental policies, practices, and cultures that may slow degree completion or affect the retention of all students (especially underrepresented groups) in S&E, particularly for those in pursuit of doctorate degrees and participation in the professoriate (George, Yolanda, et al., 2001)
- Institutional policies and practices related to S&E postdoc status, including classifications, compensation, career and professional development, and duration of postdocs (AAU, 1998).

RECOMMENDATIONS

Given lessons learned about education and training, as well as knowledge about existing programs to develop and sustain a strong U.S. S&E workforce, AAAS urges all decision makers to coordinate and leverage resources to make sustainable changes in both the S&E workforce preparation and environments in which preparation and work take place. Efforts to make any sustainable changes must take into account the complex social, economic, and political forces that have combined in the past to discourage groups such as women, African-Americans, Hispanic Americans, American Indians, and persons with disabilities from pursuing S&E careers.

Specifically, AAAS urges policymakers, government agencies, businesses, educational institutions, labor unions, and professional societies to work collaboratively to support the following:

• **An increase in attention, resources, and accountability related to S&E career development in existing SMT educational reform programs**. Many initiatives are already in place to bring about structural reforms in educational institutions that prepare and train the S&E workforce, including reforms related to pre-college, undergraduate, and graduate education, as well as postdoc training and the professoriate. As a part of these reform efforts, greater attention and increased resources must be given to career mentoring and transitions along the S&E education and career continuum, including providing career resources and high school and undergraduate research experiences.

• **Research on S&E workforce development.** While there is a thrust on research on teaching and learning, less attention is being paid to research on S&E workforce development. In particular, we need to better understand how to identify, attract, mentor, and retain talent and produce leaders in S&E (AAU, 1998). In addition, we urge increased federal support for the National Science Foundation to continue to provide educational and employment S&E indicators that are disaggregated by race / ethnicity and gender and disability, so critical to monitoring the state of the S&E workforce.

• **Talent development in all S&E disciplines.** Due to the integration of research and education in our higher-education institutions, as well as the interdisciplinary nature of research, it is important for the federal research budget to support balanced increases in all the sciences. New inventions and innovations in health, defense, and technology, as well as in other areas, are codependent on talent development in all the sciences, including biology, chemistry, physics, mathematics, and engineering.

REFERENCES

AAAS Science and Technology Policy Yearbook 2002. Washington, DC: American Association for the Advancement of Science.

The Association of American Universities, Committee on Postdoctoral Education, Reports and Recommendations. (1998). Available online: http://www.aau.edu/reports/PostdocRpt.html.

Adelman, Clifford. (1999). Answers in the tool box: Academic intensity, attendance patterns, and bachelor's degree attainment. Washington, DC: U.S. Department of Education, Office of Educational Research and Improvement.

Campbell, George Jr., Denes, Ronni, & Morrison, Catherine (eds.). (2000). Access denied: Race, ethnicity, and the scientific enterprise. New York: Oxford University Press.

Commission on the Advancement of Women and Minorities in Science, Engineering and Technology Development. (2000). Land of plenty: Diversity as America's competitive edge in science, engineering and technology. Arlington, Va.: National Science Foundation.

George, Yolanda S., Neale, David, Van Horne, Virginia, and Malcom, Shirley M. (2001). In pursuit of a diverse science, technology, engineering, and mathematics workforce: Recommended research priorities to enhance participation by underrepresented minorities. Washington, DC: American Association for the Advancement of Science; and New career paths for students with disabilities: Opportunities in science, technology, engineering, and mathematics (2002). Washington, DC: American Association for the Advancement of Science.

Teitelbaum, Michael. (2001). How we (unintentionally) make science careers unattractive. In Daryl Chubin & Willie Pearson (eds.), Scientists and engineers for the new millennium: Renewing the human resource. Washington, DC: Commission on Professionals in Science and Technology; and Chubin, Daryl E. (2002). Who is doing science—and who will? In Albert Teich, Stephen D. Nelson, & Stephen J. Lita (eds.),

National Center for Education and Statistics. Contexts for elementary and secondary education: International comparison of teacher preparation in 8th grade mathematics and science. Available online: http://nces.ed.gov/programs/coe/2001/section4/indicator43.asp.

Rapoport, Alan I. (1999, April 16). Does the educational debt burden of science and engineering doctorates differ by race/ethnicity and sex? National Science Foundation. Available online: http://www.nsf.gov/sbe/srs/issuebrf/sib99341.htm.

U.S. Office of Science and Technology Policy. National Science and Technology Council. (2000). Ensuring a strong U.S. scientific, technical, and engineering workforce in the 21st century. Washington, DC.

Orfield, Gary and Kurlaender, Michael. (2001). Diversity challenged. Cambridge, MA: The Harvard Education Publishing Group.

Statement on Workforce Issues

Dianne Dorland, President-Elect
American Institute of Chemical Engineers (AIChE)

The American Institute of Chemical Engineers (AIChE) is pleased to submit comments on educational and societal forces that affect the engineering workforce in the United States. Our purpose today is to share data and ideas related to chemical engineering workforce issues that are important to potential policy development.

WHO IS AIChE?

The American Institute of Chemical Engineers, founded in 1908, is a professional association of more than 50,000 chemical engineers worldwide. AIChE fosters and disseminates chemical engineering knowledge, supports the professional and personal growth of its members, and applies the expertise of its members to address societal needs and improve the quality of life.

Chemical engineers are creative problem solvers who perform research and develop processes and products utilizing the principles of engineering, physics, chemistry, biology, and mathematics. They play key roles in such diverse industries as energy, chemicals, biotechnology, food, electronics, and pharmaceuticals. Chemical engineers are also leaders in environmental health, safety, and sustainability. They endeavor to improve the quality of life for people the world over.

COMMITMENT TO DIVERSITY

The AIChE Board of Directors announced the following AIChE Statement on Diversity in 2000 and strives to encourage the development of a diverse profession and professional society:

Diversity means, on a global basis, creating an environment in the Institute and the profession in which all members, regardless of their sex, race, religion, age, physical condition, sexual orientation or nationality, are valued equitably for their skills and abilities, and respected for their unique perspectives and experiences.

The Institute has placed an emphasis on better understanding the needs of its diverse membership and other stakeholder populations. Research is being conducted in order to better serve underrepresented minority, physically challenged, and female stakeholders of the Institute.

A survey of member and nonmember populations focused on underrepresented minority and female chemical engineers has been completed. The results of this survey are currently being evaluated and an action plan is being developed to implement results to address the following major areas:

- Review the past and present status of diversity within the Institute and the profession, including a review of statistics describing undergraduate and graduate students
  - Assess future professional needs of chemical engineers
  - Assess future professional diversity needs of the profession
  - Recommend long- and short-term strategies to meet such needs

Here is what we know so far with respect to gender:

In light of the number of undergraduate chemical engineering degrees earned by women, chemical engineering is often described as a "female friendly" discipline. In 2000, 36 percent of B.S. degrees in ChemE were awarded to women; in 1990 that statistic was 33 percent, which was up from 29 percent in 1985.

In 1996, specific initiatives implemented by the Institute were aimed at capitalizing on the fact that women choose chemical engineering in unusual numbers. These initiatives were designed to ensure the entry, retention, and full participation of women within the profession.

One such initiative, a Women's Initiatives Committee, was established in 1997 as a standing committee of the Institute. This group presents relevant programming at national meetings, hosts networking luncheons and receptions for women chemical engineers, sponsors career sessions during the Annual Student Conference, and maintains a listserv and Web site for cross talk among women engineers. The Committee serves as a vital representative of women's concerns within the Institute. It has provided leaders for highly visible volunteer assignments within the organization. Additional programs and assessments will continue to be conducted. For example, in collaboration with the Commit-

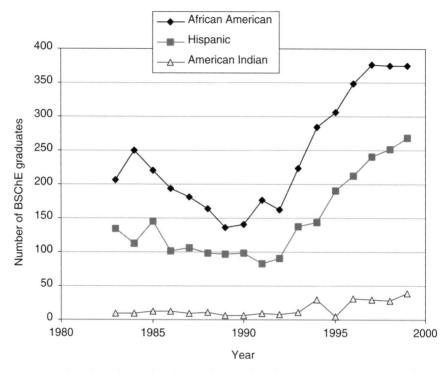

FIGURE 1 Number of B.S.ChE degrees by year by ethnicity. *Source:* Data from the National Action Council for Minorities in Engineering, (NACME).

tee on the Advancement of Women Chemists (COACh), AIChE is hosting specialized advanced training for women university faculty at each annual meeting.

Although data on other segments are still being analyzed, the numbers are not as encouraging for minority chemical engineers. As can be seen in Figure 1, increases in the number of African-American and Hispanic chemical engineering graduates have been recorded since 1990, but the relative numbers are still very low.

TRENDS IN INDUSTRY

Trends in industry are occurring that significantly affect the employment of chemical engineers. Mergers, acquisitions, and globalization continue to have a considerable impact on the opportunities for the workforce in the traditional chemical processing industry. For example, many chemical engineers working in areas of technology development have had their jobs eliminated. The 2002 AIChE Salary Survey demonstrates that there is

TABLE 1 Unemployment Rates for Engineering Disciplines

Field	2001 Annual (%)	2002 Q2 (%)
All engineers	2.3	4.0
Aerospace engineers	2.1	5.2
Chemical engineers	3.8	5.1
Civil engineers	1.1	1.6
Electrical engineers	2.0	4.8
Mechanical engineers	2.6	3.7

Source: Bureau of Labor Statistics (unpublished) compiled by the Institute of Electrical and Electronics Engineers (IEEE-USA).

now less optimism among chemical engineers for advancement and job security.

Changes in opportunities for chemical engineers are occurring. New graduates are moving toward life sciences and business industries, and flatter organizations are eliminating promotional and management tracks. Furthermore, the unemployment rate of new graduates is beginning to rise.

Bureau of Labor Statistics (BLS) data for the various engineering disciplines are described in Table 1. As you can see, unemployment rates for chemical engineers, along with aerospace engineers and electrical engineers, are worse than the other engineering disciplines. Please note, however, that these BLS numbers are projected based on surveys, not on actual unemployment filings, and that sample sizes are relatively small when broken out for the disciplines.

The chemical engineering workforce is aging, and our recent salary and employment survey indicates that it is taking longer for older workers to return to the workforce, and that those in older age groups are more likely to be under- or unemployed. Compared to those age 45 or younger, under/unemployment is about twice as likely for those ages 50-55, four times as likely for those ages 56-60, and seven times as likely for those ages 61-65.

Issues such as how to retrain workers and the role of the government, universities, and professional societies in helping older workers are important to consider.

WHAT CAN BE DONE?

Bringing more women and underrepresented minorities into the profession and maintaining opportunities for older workers will help to ensure an adequate workforce. Promoting greater diversity within the profession requires a consistent, long-term effort focused on the education, recruitment, retention, and advancement of all groups. This approach requires the combined participation of businesses, government, professional societies, and the education community. AIChE will continue to address the promotion and education of a diverse workforce.

AIChE supports public and private programs that improve the science and mathematics achievements of the nation's pre-college students and motivates them—with special attention to women and minorities—to pursue engineering and scientific careers. Challenging young children with high-quality math and science programs will motivate them to learn and will provide the opportunity to pursue high-wage engineering careers.

AIChE encourages the interaction of engineering colleges, industry, national laboratories, and federal agencies, including the National Science Foundation (NSF). For example, in an effort to raise the public's awareness of the engineering profession and the specific roles that women and minorities play in it, AIChE along with Girl Scouts, USA, developed engineering kits to be used in conjunction with Girl Scout troops.

To help encourage the understanding of engineering at the high school level AIChE, in partnership with NSF and others, is developing a new high school chemistry curriculum, "Active Chemistry," which presents sciences in the context of open-ended challenges. Engineering approaches and problem solving are the key to this new curriculum, which also includes challenges related to using science and engineering to address sustainable development issues of providing adequate food and water for our world's population.

AIChE encourages policy that will help fund innovative programs such as these and will help provide for the continuing education of our workforce.

We respectfully submit the following options for consideration and study:

• Continued establishment of public-private partnerships to ensure equality of opportunity and diversity in mathematics, science, and engineering at all levels. These partnerships would involve government, industry, relevant associations, and individuals.

• Increased funding of the NSF Math and Science Partnerships Initiative. The Partnerships bring local school districts, university departments of math and science, engineering schools, and other interested parties together. The focus of the Partnerships Initiative is on both the teachers and the students, with an emphasis placed on encouraging younger students to pursue their interests in science and mathematics.

• Additional studies on retraining displaced workers to reenter the workforce are merited. Moreover, employer understanding of the portability of engineering skills transferable among various industry sectors should also be studied.

In conclusion, AIChE looks forward to developing programs that ensure a well-educated engineering workforce that is broadly utilized as we seek to address world problems.

The Physics-Educated Workforce

James Stith and Roman Czujko
American Institute of Physics (AIP)

INTRODUCTION

The science and engineering workforce is essential to technological innovation, which in turn drives economic development and enables advances in national security, medicine, education, transportation, energy, and other components of the standard of living in the United States. Physics-educated workers are a critical part of the S&E workforce.

This paper will not attempt to address all aspects of the physics-educated workforce, such as the role of physics in the scientific literacy of the general public or the contributions of the experienced physics workforce. Instead, this paper focuses on physics undergraduate education and the central role it plays in preparing the S&E workforce.

PHYSICS UNDERGRADUATE EDUCATION

What are we trying to accomplish? In general, an undergraduate degree in physics encompasses four general goals: knowledge of the discipline, cognitive skills, technical skills, and traits important for a good scientist.

Knowledge of physics is, obviously, a defining characteristic of a physics education. However, it is not the only defining characteristic. Physics students develop cognitive skills such as critical thinking, analytical thinking, and problem solving, including how to identify the set of likely solutions from the universe of possible solutions to a problem. In addition, physics students acquire a variety of technical skills, often through undergraduate research experiences. These can include advanced mathematics, modeling and simulations, use of computer hardware, and the ability to manipulate sophisticated lab equipment. Finally, a physics education helps students develop traits that are important for good scientists such as being meticulous, hard working, and tenacious.

It should, of course, be noted that the above are general goals. Undergraduate education is not a single, unified system. It consists of thousands of students earning bachelor's degrees from nearly 770 physics departments. Thus, individual physics students develop different profiles of the knowledge and skills that we commonly associate with a physics education.

Role of physics in undergraduate education

Physics is a comparatively small field. During academic year 2000-2001, nearly 4,100 physics bachelors were awarded. That same year, over 1.2 million bachelor's degrees were awarded across all fields in the United States. Thus, out of every 1,000 bachelor's degrees awarded each year, only about 3.4 are in physics.

Beyond the number of bachelor's degrees awarded, physics also plays an important role in higher education more generally. By way of example, 900,000 students took physics in high schools in academic year 2000, and about a half million students took introductory-level physics in 4- and 2-year colleges. Clearly, physics plays an essential role in the education of engineering and physical science majors, most of whom are required to take several physics courses. However, the impact of physics is even broader. By way of example, recent studies by the U.S. Department of Education indicate that most bachelor's degree recipients in the United States have taken physics in high school, college, or both.

What do physics bachelors do?

Physics bachelors commonly pursue remarkably diverse educational and career paths. There are three predominant paths immediately pursuant to obtaining the bachelor's degree: attend graduate school in physics (32 percent), attend graduate school in other fields (20 percent), and enter the workforce (48 percent). These are general trends, although they differ by type of institution that physics students attend. For example, physics bachelors who earned their degrees from a department with a graduate program are more likely to pursue advanced degrees in physics than are those who earned their bachelor's from an undergraduate institution. Also, the rates fluctuate slightly, in part, in response to perceived opportunities and economic conditions. In addition, the first few years post-bachelor's degree are characterized by change. Thus, within seven years, two-thirds of physics bachelors have earned an advanced degree or are full-time students pursuing an advanced degree.

A physics education has value as a foundation from which people can react to changes in demand. However, the diversity of educational and career paths is neither a recent phenomenon nor simply a reaction to economic conditions. It also reflects the varied interests of physics bachelor's degree recipients. One indicator of these varied interests is the fact that over one third of physics bachelors graduate with two bachelor's degrees. The other degree is typically in mathematics, engineering, or one of the physical sciences, but a broader spectrum is also common, including life sciences, philosophy, education, history, music, anthropology, psychology, etc.

In summary, a physics education is not monolithic; it prepares students for more than a narrow set of careers. Similarly, physics students are not homogeneous. They have varied interests, and their physics education provides them with the knowledge and skills to pursue a broad range of educational and career paths.

The job market for physics bachelors

Most physics bachelors who enter the workforce find employment in the private sector. However, unlike in the fields of chemistry and engineering, there is no physics industry. Nevertheless, about 85 percent of physics bachelors find employment within the science and engineering enterprise. This rate varies by a few percentage points depending upon economic conditions. About half of those students who work outside of the technical workforce report that their decisions were based on a change in interests and personal preferences.

The dominant types of technical positions vary depending on economic conditions and the contemporary demands of the workforce. Engineering and technical positions often predominate, but during the Internet-driven economy of the late 1990s, software-related positions dominated. As is described in *The Early Careers of Physics Bachelors* (Ivie and Stowe, 2002), the knowledge and skills that physics bachelors possess allow them to react to changes in demand.

PHYSICS GRADUATE STUDY

An undergraduate education in physics uniquely prepares students for graduate study in physics. Historically, about one third of physics bachelors go to graduate school in physics. However, only one in six physics bachelors earn a Ph.D. in physics. Some students leave programs before earning their Ph.D.'s, and others directly enter programs that offer a master's as the highest degree.

Ph.D. physicists play important roles throughout the economy. On average, physics Ph.D.'s spend 38 years in the workforce. They enter the workforce with a unique profile of knowledge, skills, and interests, which change and evolve over time. Some add to the knowledge base through basic research, some teach, some create innovation, and others react to the constantly changing opportunities in the workforce.

Physics master's degree recipients participate in the economy in ways that are qualitatively different from either physics bachelors or physics Ph.D.'s. There has been a growing interest in many sectors of the economy for employees with a master's-level background. Simultaneously, in part due to the efforts of the Alfred P. Sloan Foundation, there has been a recent increase in the number of professional master's degree programs. Professional master's degree programs are intended to provide the knowledge base that individuals will be able to draw upon during their decades in the labor force combined with a set of educational experiences that have direct and immediate relevance to the contemporary needs of the workforce.

OTHER GRADUATE STUDY

About one-third of physics bachelors use their undergraduate education as a base for pursuing advanced degrees in other fields. In fact, more physics bachelors earn master's degrees in other fields than earn a master's in physics. Many earn master's degrees in engineering, but a broad spectrum of fields is common, including other physical sciences, business, and education. Some earn Ph.D.'s in chemistry, materials science, or engineering and related fields, and a few go on to earn professional degrees such as M.D.'s.

Where these individuals work and what they do are related to both the level of their highest degree and the field of degree. While occupational diversity persists, physics bachelors who earn advanced degrees in other fields report that their undergraduate physics education has enduring value. The vast majority note that their undergraduate physics knowledge and analytical and problem-solving skills had a dramatic and positive effect on their subsequent educational and career choices.

SUPPLY VERSUS DEMAND

One of the underlying issues that this conference is intended to address is the relationship between supply and demand. In our particular case, how many physics bachelors are in demand? How do we know how many physics-educated workers the United States needs? These are important questions and, as is often the case, the most important questions can be the most difficult to answer.

While we have had modest success projecting degree production several years into the future, none of us has succeeded in projecting future demand. In part, this is because demand is affected by economic and political events in both national and international arenas. In part, demand is difficult to project because it is not discipline-specific but, rather, reflects a complex system. Degree recipients from a specific field change their field of work with time and changing opportunities and interests. Conversely, changes in demand draw people at different experience levels. Even when the demand is focused largely in a specific area, it is seldom exclusively in one narrow disciple. By way of example, if the personal computer revolution of 1980 were dependent on discipline-specific degree production, it may not have occurred until 1985 or later. It occurred when it did because the economy had computer scientists, physicists, electrical engineers, materials scientists, etc. who had the knowledge and skills to create the innovations or were in a position to take advantage of those opportunities.

CONCLUDING REMARKS

Undergraduate study in physics is not just preparation for a Ph.D. Physics graduate study is an important choice, and an undergraduate physics education is an essential preparation for those who pursue this option. However, they are in the minority of all physics bachelors. Departments need to be aware of the varied educational and career paths pursued by their graduates and to develop curricular offerings that address their students' needs. However, this is not unique to physics. The kinds of knowledge, skills, and educational experiences that are useful to physics graduates are also useful to physical scientists and engineers.

The authors of this paper do not believe it is appropriate for them to state whether the nation needs 4,000, 6,000, or 8,000 physics bachelors each year. Rather the number of physics bachelor's degrees awarded nationally should be driven by informed decisions made locally by individual physics departments. It is the responsibility of each department to assess both whether its graduates are well prepared to pursue their career goals and whether the number of graduates it produces matches the demands of the workforce and of graduate programs in both physics and related fields.

RECOMMENDATIONS

- Leverage the traditional strengths of physics
- Link physics education to student goals and expectations

- Develop a feedback loop between physics education and workforce needs
  - Focus on the professional development of students
  - Strengthen the connection between physics and society

Historically, undergraduate physics education has served students and the nation well. However, as knowledge, technology, and the challenges facing the United States continue to evolve, it is time for physics departments to examine whether their curricula are meeting the goals and expectations of contemporary students as well as addressing the demands and opportunities in the S&E workforce.

At the present time, this vital feedback loop is inadequate in most departments. Each department should track its own graduates as one way of ensuring that the curriculum it provides is meeting the needs of its students. In addition, each department should develop connections with the employers of its graduates. If most of a department's graduates enter the workforce, then that department should contact those employers to learn how prepared its graduates were for their positions. Similarly, a department whose bachelors tend to enter graduate programs should open a dialogue with those departments to learn how well prepared its graduates were for advanced study.

Master's degree recipients have value and satisfy a unique need within the economy. They fill positions that are qualitatively different from those filled by either bachelors or Ph.D.'s. Thus their preparation should be different from that of a Ph.D. program. The recent emphasis on professional master's degree programs is timely and has a great deal of promise. Physics departments are encouraged to examine whether such programs would build on their strengths and help them address the opportunities available to the physics-educated workforce.

Foreign Scientists Seen Essential to U.S. Biotechnology

Stephen Dahms
American Society for Biochemistry and
Molecular Biology (ASBMB)

The scarcity of skilled technicians is seen by the biotechnology industry in the U.S. and Canada as one of its most serious challenges. The success of this industry is dependent on the quality of its workforce, and the skills and talents of highly trained people are recognized as one of the most vital and dynamic sources of competitive advantage.

The U.S. biotechnology industry workforce has been growing 14 to 17 percent annually over the last six years and is now over 190,000 and conservatively estimated to reach 500,000 by 2012. Despite efforts by the industry to encourage U.S. institutions to increase the production of needed specialists, a continual shortfall in the needed expertise requires access to foreign workers. Foreign workers with unique skills that are scarce in the U.S. can get permission to stay in the U.S. for up to six years under the H-1B classification, after which they can apply for permanent resident status. There are currently over 600,000 foreign workers in this category across all industries, and they are critical to the success and global competitiveness of this nation. Of these H-1B visa holders, 46 percent are from India and 10 percent are from China, followed in descending order by Canada, Philippines, Taiwan, Korea, Japan, U.K., Pakistan, and the Russian Federation.

Our annual national surveys have demonstrated that between 6 and 10 percent of the biotechnology workforce have H-1B visas. The constant shortfall in specialized technical workers that has been experienced by the biotechnology industry over the past six years has been partially alleviated by access to talented individuals from other nations. However, the industry's need is sufficient to justify a 25 percent increase in H-1Bs in 2004.

Biotechnology industry H-1B visa holders are mainly in highly sought after areas such as analytical chemistry, instrumentation specialization, organic synthesis, product safety and surveillance, clinical research/bio-statistics, bio/pharm quality, medicinal chemistry, product scale-up, bioinformatics and applied genomics, computer science, cheminformatics, pharmacokinetics, and pharmacodynamics.

Forty percent of H-1B foreign workers are at the Ph.D. level, 35 percent M.S., 20 percent B.S., and 5 percent M.D. In comparison, the U.S. biotechnology industry technical workforce is estimated to be 19 percent Ph.D., 17 percent M.S., 50 percent B.S., and 14 percent combined voc-ed/community college trained. These and other survey data by industry human resource groups clearly show that the H-1B worker skills match the most pressing employment needs of the biotechnology industry. The data demonstrate that maintaining a reasonably-sized H-1B cap is critical to the industry. Although the national annual H-1B visa cap was raised from 115,000 to 195,000 in the 106th Congress via S. 2045, the cap has already been exceeded. The increased cap remains in effect until 2003 and efforts are under way to ensure that it remains high.

The Third Annual National Survey of H-1Bs in the biotechnology industry found that 80 percent are from U.S. universities, and 85 percent of those eventually get green cards. Companies now spend, on average, $10,200 in processing fees and legal expenses to obtain each green card, an estimated cost to the industry of more than $150 million over the past 5 years.

In the wake of the 9/11 World Trade Center attacks, debate has been focused on more restrictions on foreign students, a development that would have a severe impact upon the competitiveness of the U.S. biotechnology industry. Clearly, the H-1B route provides a temporary solution to shortages in the national and domestic biotechnology labor pools, shortages mirroring the inadequate production of appropriately trained U.S. nationals by U.S. institutions of higher learning. The reality is that universities have inadequate resources for expanding the training pipeline, particularly in the specialized areas of the research phase of company product development. Efforts should be directed toward influencing greater congressional and federal agency attention to these important topics.

The author of this article, A. Stephen Dahms, is executive director of the California State University System Biotechnology Program (CSUPERB); chair of the Workforce Committee, Biotechnology Industry Organization; and a member of the ASBMB Education and Professional Development Committee. Statistical data are from surveys conducted by CSUPERB, as an activity of the Biotechnology Industry Organization's Workforce Committee; and for Canada, from Statistics Canada.

Academic Prerequisites for Licensure and Professional Practice

Thomas Lenox, Senior Managing Director of Education,
Geographic Services, & Diversity
American Society of Civil Engineers (ASCE)

POLICY

The American Society of Civil Engineers (ASCE) supports the concept of the master's degree or equivalent as a prerequisite for licensure and the practice of civil engineering at a professional level.

ASCE encourages institutions of higher education, governmental units, employers, civil engineers, and other appropriate organizations to endorse, support, and promote the concept of mandatory postbaccalaureate education for the practice of civil engineering at a professional level. The implementation of this effort should occur through establishing appropriate curricula in the formal education experience, appropriate recognition and compensation in the workplace, and congruent standards for licensure.

ISSUE

The practice of civil engineering at the professional level means practice as a licensed professional engineer. Admission to the practice of civil engineering at the professional level means professional engineering licensing, which requires:

- A body of specialized knowledge as reflected by a combination of a baccalaureate degree and a master's or equivalent
- Appropriate experience
- Commitment to lifelong learning

The required body of specialized knowledge includes a technical core, technical electives, a nontechnical core, and technical and nontechnical courses to support individual career objectives. The current baccalaureate civil engineering degree is an entry-level degree that may no longer be adequate preparation for the practice of civil engineering at the professional level.

The civil engineering profession is undergoing significant, rapid, and revolutionary changes that have increased the body of knowledge required of the profession. These changes include the following:

- Globalization has challenged the worldwide geographic boundaries normally recognized in the past, primarily as a result of enhanced communication systems.
- Information technology has made, and continues to make, more information available; however, the analysis and application of this information is becoming more challenging.
- The diversity of society is challenging our traditional views and people skills.
- New technologies in engineering and construction are emerging at an accelerating rate.
- Enhanced public awareness of technical issues is creating more informed inquiry by the public of the technical, environmental, societal, political, legal, aesthetic, and financial implications of engineering projects.
- Civil infrastructure systems within the United States are rapidly changing from decades of development and operation to the renewal, maintenance, and improvement of these systems.

These changes have created a market requiring civil engineers to have simultaneously greater breadth of capability and specialized technical competence than that required of previous generations. For example, many civil engineers must increasingly assume a different primary role from that of designer to that of team leader. The knowledge required to support this new market is found in the combination of an appropriate baccalaureate education and the completion of postgraduate courses sufficient to attain a master's degree or its equivalent.

RATIONALE

Requiring education beyond the baccalaureate degree for the practice of civil engineering at the professional level is consistent with other learned professions. The body of knowledge gained and the skills developed in the formal civil engineering education process are not significantly less than the comparable knowledge and skills required in these other professions. It is not reasonable in such complex and rapidly changing times to think that we can impart the specialized body of knowledge and skills required of professional engineers in 4 years of formal schooling while other learned professions take 7 or 8 years. Four years of formal schooling were considered the standard for three professions (medicine, law, and engineering) 100 years ago, and, whereas medicine and law education lengthened with the growing demands of their respective professions, engineering education did not. Perhaps this retention of a 4-year undergraduate engineering education has contributed to the lowered esteem of engineering in the eyes of society, and the commensurate decline in compensation of engineers relative to medical doctors and lawyers.

Current baccalaureate programs, while constantly undergoing review and revisions, still retain a nominal 4-year education process. This length of time limits the ability of these programs to provide a formal education consistent with the increasing demands of the practice of civil engineering at the professional level. There are diametrically opposed forces trying to squeeze more content into the baccalaureate curriculum while at the same time reducing the credit hours necessary for the baccalaureate degree. The result is a production-line baccalaureate civil engineering (BSCE) degree that is satisfactory for an entry-level position but which may be inadequate for the professional practice of civil engineering. The 4-year internship period (engineer-in-training) after receipt of the BSCE degree cannot make up for the formal educational material that would be gained from a master's degree or equivalent program.

This concept will not be implemented overnight. Although ASCE cannot mandate that it be done in a specified time period or manner, ASCE will be an active partner with other groups and organizations to institute this policy. The ultimate full implementation may not occur for 20 or more years. Appropriate grandfathering for existing registered and degreed engineers would be a part of the implementation process. This concept is a legacy for future generations of civil engineers. However, perhaps the most important aspect of the implementation of this policy is already in place. Within the U.S. system of higher education, high-quality, innovative, and diverse master's degree programs currently exist in colleges and universities to support this concept. A growing number of organizations now offer high-quality on-site and distance learning educational opportunities. The active support of this policy by all of the stakeholders in this process, such as the educational institutions, the registration boards, and the various employers of civil engineers, will be required to develop and promote the elements necessary to eventually implement this concept.

Engineering Education and the Science and Engineering Workforce

David Wormley, Dean of Engineering
Pennsylvania State University
Chair, Engineering Deans Council
American Society for Engineering Education (ASEE)

ENGINEERING EDUCATION AND THE NATIONAL INTEREST

A vibrant engineering education enterprise benefits civic, economic, and intellectual activity in this country. Engineering graduates learn to integrate scientific and engineering principles to develop products and processes that contribute to economic growth, advances in medical care, enhanced national security systems, ecologically sound resource management, and many other beneficial areas. As a result, students who graduate with engineering degrees bring highly prized skills into a wide spectrum of sectors in the American workforce. Some conduct research that results in socially or economically valuable technological applications. Others produce and manage the technological innovations said to account for one third to one half of growth in the American economy. Still more bring advanced analytical abilities and knowledge of high technology to fields as diverse as health care, financial services, law, and government. Within all of these groups, the diversity of engineering graduates' backgrounds and viewpoints contributes to their ability to achieve the advances in innovation, productivity, and effectiveness that make them valuable contributors to the American workplace.

THE IMPORTANCE OF TECHNICAL COMPETENCIES

At a time when technological innovations are intrinsically coupled with virtually every aspect of society, it is imperative to develop a scientific and technically literate society. However, broad indicators of shortcomings in developing technical competencies within the U.S. population at large indicate the scale of the challenge at hand. In 2001, companies spent over $57 billion on training, much of which paid for workers' training in basic skills that should have been learned in school.[1] Meanwhile, the United States' poor performance in teaching math and science—shown in results from the Third International Mathematics and Science Study and the National Assessment of Educational Progress—eliminates many of the best and brightest schoolchildren from the ranks of future scientists and engineers. With little chance to learn in school how science and math skills might translate into professionally useful knowledge, students are unable to make informed choices about further education and work options. As a result, some unprepared students undertake science and engineering studies in college, only to drop out; other, potentially capable, students never consider these subjects in the first place. In both cases, precious human and institutional resources are squandered.

An increasingly large share of the workforce consists of women and minorities. The 2000 report of the Commission on the Advancement of Women & Minorities in Science, Engineering, and Technology notes that, although African-Americans and Hispanics represent 3 percent each of the technical workforce, they are each 15 percent of the school-age population. Demographic projections only reinforce this point: by 2035, these students will rise from about 30 percent to nearly 50 percent of the nation's schoolchildren.[2] Twenty years of improvements in math and science achievement have brought girls near parity with boys on National Assessment of Educational Progress tests. However, as they move through middle and high school, girls' interest in math and science wanes, as teacher, parent, peer, and media influences work in complex, often unconscious, ways to discourage their pursuit of these subjects. As a result, women represent only 19 percent of the technical workforce, although they represent 46 percent of all American workers. Success in encouraging and retaining women and underrepresented minorities throughout their pre-college, college, and postgraduate years must be a core component of enhancing the U.S. science and engineering workforce.

A curriculum framework based on connecting science and mathematics to the world around them can also impart habits of mind to students that yield benefits beyond workplace productivity and career advancement. At the simplest level, the imperatives of good citizenship increasingly require acquaintance with fundamental principles of scientific knowledge. Taking a problem-based approach to learning, engineering

[1]*Training Magazine,* "Industry Report 2001," Minneapolis: Bil Communications.

[2]Commission on the Advancement of Women and Minorities in Science, Engineering and Technology Development (2000). *Land of Plenty: Diversity as America's Competitive Edge in Science and Technology.*

education asks students to integrate knowledge and practices from the sciences, economics, language, and creative arts. Thus, elements of science and engineering education are important contributors to developing fully literate citizens.

ENGINEERING EDUCATION DEMOGRAPHICS[3]

In 2001, just over 65,000 students earned engineering bachelor's degrees. While this is almost 3,000 more than in 1999, the total represents a decrease from the mid-1980s, when about 85,000 students a year graduated with engineering degrees. Nearly 386,000 students were enrolled in undergraduate engineering programs last year; however, the national attrition rate is high, and at least 40 percent of students who start engineering programs do not finish them.

Graduate enrollments increased approximately 5 percent in 2001, with approximately 79,000 master's degree students and 41,500 doctoral students. Within these groups, 43 percent of master's degrees and 54 percent of doctorates were awarded to foreign-born students, and these trends have been increasing. Meanwhile, U.S. engineering graduates incur near-term financial penalties for choosing grad school—with its modest stipends and delayed rewards—over immediate employment at some of the highest salary levels among college graduates. Foreign-born students bring a wealth of diversity and energy to U.S. campuses, but they also have an increasing inclination to return to their home countries after graduating, taking with them expertise and potential achievement that would otherwise enhance the strength of the U. S. science and engineering workforce.

In 2001, 19.9 percent of bachelor's degrees in engineering were awarded to women, 5.3 percent to African-Americans and 6.4 percent to Hispanics. For women and African-Americans, these percentages represent slight but perceptible decreases from recent years. And indeed, when understood in the context of recent increases in overall undergraduate enrollments, these dwindling percentages indicate even more clearly that engineering is failing to attract the diversity of students needed to draw on the full extent of abilities available in an increasingly diverse American society.

Engineering programs' faculties have comparably low representations of women and underserved minorities. Women make up about 9 percent of tenured and tenure-track faculty members, although they account for 17.5 percent of assistant professors. African-Americans and Hispanics make up less than 3 percent of tenured and tenure-track faculties, although they also

---

[3]American Society for Engineering Education (2001). *Profiles of Engineering and Engineering Colleges*. Washington, DC.

represent a higher percentage of the entry faculty levels. If women and minority faculty continue to increase at the entry levels, their presence could increase in the future. In light of the trends in undergraduate enrollments, however, such increases might not be sustainable because the pool of future women and minority faculty members is currently decreasing.

These statistics suggest that efforts to expand the reach of engineering education to the entire spectrum of American society have not succeeded. In spite of the growing importance of technology-related activities to American life in the 21st century, the number of U.S. students pursuing studies and work in technical fields is not increasing proportionally, particularly at the graduate level. For the United States to retain a position of global leadership in these fields, these trends must be reversed.

LESSONS LEARNED

In formulating responses to the challenges described here, engineering educators have taken as a guiding principle the need to attract better-prepared students into engineering programs and to provide them with an education that increasingly helps them meet their personal and professional goals.

The Need to Partner with K-12

The failure to prepare K-12 students with the knowledge they need to make an informed choice about pursuing a career in a scientific or technical area requires significantly increased cooperation between science and engineering professionals and K-12 teachers and students. We need to engage vigorously and collectively to help teachers develop new curricula and to help students understand the ways in which careers in science and engineering help society.

The Need to Reform Engineering Education

Recent changes in the practice of engineering education span the content of the curriculum, the organizational and operational principles of engineering education programs, and the opportunities for learning available in the field. This reform in engineering education has been dramatic—perhaps matched only by the development of science-based engineering education in the 1950s—and continues to occur not only in higher education but also in the K-12 arena. Codified in the Accreditation Board for Engineering and Technology (ABET) Engineering Criteria 2000, new approaches to engineering accreditation require engineering programs to incorporate critical professional skills and content into their curricula and to strive for adaptability and accountability to their constituencies in their operations and principles. In line with this trend, engineering educators have significantly revised the ways in which they assess the effectiveness of their own programs. Previously, engineering education assessment consisted largely in monitoring schools' adherence to a fairly uniform curriculum. Reform in engineering education assessment now holds schools to a standard of continuous self-improvement, encouraging schools to develop rigorous practices for defining educational missions and demonstrating results that show fulfillment of these missions.

In addition to the fundamental science and engineering content, increasingly important elements in the engineering curriculum are effective communications, working in teams, and organizational management. Recognizing that new technologies drive so much economic growth, more and more engineering educators are teaching entrepreneurship to students, many of whom will provide the technical know-how for new companies and innovative products to come. And in an effort to stem the tide of attrition among engineering students, colleges increasingly provide substantive, hands-on design and engineering content in freshman courses emphasizing the creative aspects of engineering. This marks a change from the traditional engineering curriculum that puts students through rigorous training in mathematics and science before providing a context for the engineering process.

Engineering programs are evolving to make available opportunities to pursue diverse areas of study that match the rapid pace of discovery and innovation in science and engineering, many of which are interdisciplinary. Advances in understanding and manipulating the mechanics of molecular and atomic activity have created new realms for engineering education and research. Significant new programs in bioengineering and nanotechnology have been initiated at many schools, drawing rapidly growing numbers of students.

RECOMMENDATIONS

Many engineering educators have devoted significant effort to changing the way we recruit and support our students so that as many students as possible from as many different American neighborhoods as possible have a chance to pursue a scientific or engineering career. Some general recommendations, based on this experience, follow.

K-12 Engineering Education

Starting at least in middle school, and preferably earlier, schoolchildren need exposure to engineering concepts and applications. Existing pre-college mathematics and science curricula can, in most cases, accommodate content related to engineering without departing from standards-driven educational imperatives. The significant number of highly successful engineering education outreach programs to K-12 classrooms across the country show that this is possible. Pre-college engineering education offers a vehicle for applying mathematics and science to students' real-world experiences, for developing a sense of the creative aspects of engineering, and for showing how working in teams contributes to achieving goals. Equipped with both a sense of how mathematics and science relates to their lives and an understanding of the creative aspects of engineering, high school graduates will be better able to make informed choices about studying engineering and other technical fields.

Reducing Attrition in Higher Education

Attrition among students who start out in engineering education programs results from various factors. One force behind the high attrition rates in the study of engineering is the lack of preparation in technical fields that high school graduates have when entering college. Students enter engineering programs without either sufficient preparation in math and science or a comprehensive grasp of what a career in engineering entails. As a result, they face stark academic challenges in their first year of college, which they must bear without a clear sense of how their studies relate to their future profession.

The task of attracting and retaining a diverse student body is influenced by the climate that students encounter in engineering programs. For women and minorities, the presence of role models and mentors on the faculty often increases these students' abilities to imagine themselves continuing and succeeding in the field. In addition, active peer support networks provide a community of fellow students with whom they can share their trials and successes. Increased effort is needed to create environments that combine intellectual stimulation with opportunities for social and personal growth to help the broadest range of students become successful in and committed to engineering.

Engineering education needs to accelerate the pace of reform and renewal and to consider both undergraduate and graduate programs from a holistic view. Further efforts are needed to integrate the important interdisciplinary elements of science and engineering and, equally important, the context of the practice and role of engineering in a technology-driven society in the curriculum. These measures will help reduce currently high attrition rates and make the educational experience more rewarding and efficient for students and professors alike.

Government's Role

Government at the local, state, and federal levels can help in developing the science and engineering workforce needed for the future. Government support is vital to

- encourage all high school graduates to take four years of mathematics and science;
- provide opportunities and support for in-service teacher professional development in K-12 science, technology, engineering, and mathematics and for enhancements to science, technology, engineering, and mathematics content in teacher-training programs;
- support partnerships between K-12 and higher education;
- provide graduate student support in science and engineering; and
- provide support for faculty starting their careers in science and engineering.

CONCLUSION

A final suggestion pertains more generally to how we frame studying and working in engineering, science, and technology fields within a broader social context. Aligning these fields with the services they render to society as a whole will do much to attract the best students for the best reasons—the chance to engineer, if you will, a world free from pain through bioengineering, a world free from fear through technology-supported counter-terrorism measures, and a world free from environmental degradation through appropriate uses of our natural resources and the development of renewable energy supplies. Such a message that combines the promise of personal rewards with the opportunity to make meaningful contributions to the world we all share would provide a powerful foundation for the work we are contemplating here today.

Strengthening Pre-College Science, Math, Engineering, and Technology Education: The Technological Literacy and Workforce Imperative

Susan Skemp, President
American Society of Mechanical Engineers International (ASME)

INTRODUCTION

Few issues evoke more passionate conversation than the education of children. While there has been much attention and debate over how to address school violence, drugs, and vouchers, there has been a tremendous lack of understanding and appreciation by many policymakers about the importance of strengthening scientific, mathematical, engineering, and technological (SMET) concepts and skills in the pre-college (K-12) education curriculum. As the economy becomes increasingly more global and technologically complex, it is essential that K-12 SMET education be strengthened to prepare today's students to be tomorrow's productive workers and citizens.

In addition to creating a technologically literate citizenry, there is an urgent need to develop a technologically capable workforce that can compete in the global economy. Employers are increasingly concerned about the lack of technically skilled workers. Much more emphasis must be placed on pre-college SMET education if this skill deficit is to be overcome.

Following a survey of its members, the American Society of Mechanical Engineers (ASME International), a professional society of more than 125,000 members, has included K-12 science, math, engineering, and technology education among its priorities for action by public policy makers. The Society's Board on Pre-College Education (BPC) has developed a variety of activities and resources for its members, educators, and students interested in K-12 SMET studies (visit www.asme.org/educate/k12).

RECOMMENDATIONS

Parents, educators, governments at all levels, and the private sector have important roles in ensuring that future generations will possess the skills and critical competencies necessary to be successful in a highly competitive, global, and technologically sophisticated economy. Together, these stakeholders must work cooperatively to ensure that children receive the science, mathematics, engineering, and technology training essential for future success.

ASME International offers the following recommendations for improving K-12 SMET educational performance:

- Increase federally funded research focused on SMET teaching and learning to cultivate the most effective teaching methods.
- Recruit, train, and retain qualified SMET teachers to meet demand.
- Foster partnerships among educational institutions, industry, and nonprofit organizations.
- Encourage the adoption of curriculum standards that cultivate high student performance; the development of curricula that foster creativity, experiential problem solving, and critical thinking; and the development of assessments aligned with these standards and curricula.
- Encourage women and minorities to pursue SMET coursework and careers.

Increase federally funded research focused on SMET teaching and learning to cultivate the most effective teaching methods. Policymakers should dedicate significant funds for education research, with an emphasis on how to improve teaching and learning of K-12 SMET concepts and critical thinking skills. New research must be supported and the findings applied to the development of curricula, materials, and standards. Research should focus on "how" (inquiry-based versus memorization) and "when" (at developmentally appropriate stages) students learn rather than on "what" students should learn in the areas of science, math, engineering, and technology. A long-term commitment to the application of these research results is necessary to bring about real systemic changes.

Recruit, train, and retain qualified SMET teachers to meet demand. Experts agree that one key to improving student performance is the recruitment, training, and retention of qualified teachers. Recent studies suggest that, in the United States alone, 2.2 million new teachers will be needed in the next decade; yet statistics indicate that U.S. colleges of education will not produce nearly enough graduates with degrees in education to meet the expected demand. Furthermore, graduates with degrees in science, mathematics, or engineering are unlikely to pursue teaching careers. The lure of higher salaries in the private sector is further depleting the supply of qualified K-12 science and mathematics teachers, while the pursuit of reduced class sizes and other demographic factors increase the demand for more qualified teachers.

A related concern is the number of teachers who are currently teaching out of their respective fields of expertise. In 1998, 28 percent of seventh- and eighth-grade math teachers in the United States were not certified to teach that subject, and 27 percent of science teachers at those grade levels were not certified to teach science.[1] Policy makers should enhance the recruitment, training, and retention of qualified SMET teachers by creating programs that

- improve in-service professional development focusing on SMET curricula;
- facilitate alternative certification and transition-to-teaching programs for engineers and other technical professionals;
- institute mentoring programs for SMET personnel in schools;
- implement what is already known regarding how students learn in teacher professional development programs;
- attract SMET teachers via scholarships, student loan forgiveness, bonuses, and tax incentives;
- allow for differential pay scales to help attract and retain qualified SMET educators; and,
- include/increase SMET coursework in pre-service/university teacher training.

Foster partnerships among educational institutions, industry, and nonprofit organizations. ASME International and other organizations currently partner with nonprofit organizations and educational entities (e.g., FIRST Robotics Competition, the Junior Engineering Technical Society [JETS], and the Girl Scouts and Boy Scouts) to further K-12 SMET learning. Policymakers should support the development of partnerships among educational institutions, industry, and nonprofit organizations that

- foster adopt-a-school programs;
- create incentives for SMET professionals to work with teachers and students;
- promote relevant corporate summer externships for teachers in SMET positions;

---

[1] 1999 State Indicators of Science and Mathematics Education published by the Council of State School Officers.

- develop recognition awards for private sector SMET involvement;
- produce, evaluate, and disseminate best practices in SMET programs, on-line curricula, and funding opportunities to educators via a well-publicized, centralized Web site;
- create and fund the publication and dissemination of materials for public outreach and parental education on the importance of a quality K-12 SMET education; and
- address school infrastructure needs for SMET education, including the implementation of current technology and provision of material resources.

Encourage the adoption of curriculum standards that cultivate high student performance; the development of curricula that foster creativity, experiential problem solving, and critical thinking; and the development of assessments aligned with these standards and curricula. Experience has shown that lack of high standards for student performance results in poor mastery of SMET subject matter by many students. Development of effective SMET curriculum and assessment tools must be based on high standards of achievement. These standards should extend well beyond requiring knowledge of fundamental SMET facts, processes, and techniques. They should support curricula that cultivate creative, critical thinking skills and encourage interdisciplinary approaches to issues and problems. Policymakers and other stakeholders should

- promote and endorse private sector standard-setting projects;
- support the development of hands-on, open-ended problem-solving curricula and modules of engineering problems, grouped by discipline and level of difficulty, for the K-12 classroom;
- pursue the development of better assessment mechanisms aligned with state and local standards;
- advocate the inclusion of both curriculum and assessment standards in SMET by boards of education, where they are not currently adopted; and
- resist the tendency to "push back" standards when assessment results are less than satisfactory.

Encourage women and minorities to pursue SMET coursework and careers. Remaining competitive in the global economy will require the cultivation of technological literacy, talent, and expertise across all sectors of society. Efforts should be made to attract greater participation of women and minorities into SMET fields of study and careers. Minorities and women are significantly underrepresented in the SMET workforce. Policymakers should

- provide incentives and mentoring for women and minorities to pursue K-12 SMET teaching careers;
- foster outreach and SMET career materials to K-12 guidance counselors, teachers, and parents;
- support SMET magnet schools in school districts with large minority enrollments; and
- foster public-private partnerships to ensure those schools serving large minority enrollments have computer lab and other technologies to support the delivery of high-quality SMET education.

The American Society of Mechanical Engineers is a nonprofit technical and educational organization with 125,000 members worldwide. The Society's members work in all sectors of the economy, including industry, education, and government.

A National Strategy to Face Vulnerability in Science Engineering and Technology

John Yochelson, President
Building Engineering and Science Talent (BEST)

BACKGROUND

Building Engineering and Science Talent (BEST) is a public-private partnership incorporated a week before the attacks on the Pentagon and the World Trade Center. The establishment of such a partnership had been proposed a year earlier in *Land of Plenty*, the report of the Congressional Commission on the Advancement of Women and Minorities in Science, Engineering, and Technology Development. BEST's three-year mission is to develop and execute a national action plan to increase the participation of the "underrepresented majority"—women, minorities, and persons with disabilities—in technical fields. Underrepresented groups constitute two thirds of the U.S. workforce, but hold only about one-fourth of the jobs in science, engineering, and technology.

DEFINING THE CHALLENGE

The United States should be moving aggressively to meet its current and projected needs for scientific and technical talent, with special focus on the changing face of America. The nation is not doing so for several reasons:

- Public attention has scarcely begun to focus on the forces that are reshaping the supply side of the equation—the emergence of women as the new majority in higher education and the pattern of population growth that is transforming America into a majority of minorities.
- The globalization of technical talent has created difficult trade-offs between the nation's short-term needs and its long-term stake in home-

grown scientists and engineers. Whereas human capital still takes two decades or more to develop, U.S. access to international talent has become almost immediate.

• Many of the barriers that limit the participation of under-represented groups in science, engineering, and technology persist. It will take a concerted national effort to remove barriers that are formal and informal, institutional and attitudinal, stark and subtle.

The challenge of building a stronger, more diverse science and engineering workforce is generational in time horizon and comprehensive in scope. No sector of the economy—industry, government, or academe—can meet the challenge on its own. Decisive action is required now to put the nation on a trajectory that will serve long-term U.S. national interests.

PRIORITIES FOR ACTION

1. Fill the Knowledge Gap

The nation needs to know what is really working in elementary and high school mathematics, freshman physics and chemistry, graduate schools, and corporate R&D teams to develop—and draw upon—the talent of underrepresented groups. The same wheels are being reinvented and the same mistakes made on a daily basis in every part of the country. Authoritative, readily accessible information on best-in-class and exceptionally promising programs, lessons from success and failure, and insights into scaling up would be of great value to employers, educators, parents, and students as well as policymakers at the national, state, and local levels. BEST has organized blue ribbon panels of nationally recognized experts in pre-K through 12, higher education, and workforce development to help fill this knowledge gap.

2. Engage Communities

The place to start translating knowledge into action is in communities across the country. Here the interests of industry, government, education, and the nonprofit sector intersect. Civic leaders who know what works are in a position to make concrete decisions to expand capacity to develop and retain the talent of underrepresented groups. A pilot group of communities willing to follow through on commitments to adopt best practices could set a powerful leadership example for others.

3. Develop a Galvanizing National Agenda

There is no substitute for national leadership to generate the will and the resources needed to make serious headway over the next decade. As is the case with the war on terrorism, there is no quick fix for the challenge of underrepresentation. Equally, there is a parallel need for a cohesive national strategy based on a compelling vision, clear objectives, and actionable priorities. The vision that should inform such a strategy is one of affirmative opportunity to develop the scientific and technical talents of every child in America. The objective that makes sense is to create a scientific and technical workforce that reflects the emerging demographics.

PRIORITIES FOR THE FEDERAL GOVERNMENT

Congress and the executive branch must lead on the issue of underrepresentation. This will involve giving voice to the national need—and backing that voice with direction and resources. Four priorities stand out:

1. Maximize the Value of Current Programs
The National Science Foundation, Department of Education, Department of Defense, Department of Energy, NASA, and other agencies have longstanding records of commitment to underrepresented groups. But federal resources are scattered and would have greater impact if they were more closely aligned. An interagency initiative to ensure that such alignment would enhance both the effectiveness and the credibility of federal investment. Other national programs, such as the National Teachers Corps, which recruits up to 75,000 qualified teachers annually to serve in high-need schools, should be expanded and strengthened with such measures as including subsidies for the acquisition of teaching credentials.

2. Consider a Bold Federal Initiative
While such programs are important, it may be even more worthwhile to consider a bold initiative similar to the National Defense Education Act of 1958, when Congress found "that an educational emergency exists and requires action by the federal government."

3. Leverage Federal Dollars
Federal investments to develop a stronger, more diverse talent pool should not stand alone but should be matched by states and local communities. The 25 states in which minorities make up at least 25 percent of the pre-K through 12 student population deserve priority attention.

4. Increase Investment
Congress and the executive branch cannot just re-divide the pie, but must allocate fresh resources to expand educational opportunities in mathematics and science for underrepresented groups. Important new initiatives, such as NSF's five-year $1 billion Mathematics and Science Partnerships, should represent net increases in investment. Programs that have a track record of proven value should be expanded. New investments that promise to make a real difference, such as Pell-like financial aid grants for underrepresented students in science and engineering majors, deserve serious consideration.

PRIORITIES FOR EDUCATION

Research universities have a special leadership responsibility. Not only are they strategically positioned between pre-K through 12 and the workplace, but they will educate the successor generation of American scientists and engineers. The list of "must-do's" for research universities should include:

1. Strengthen the University Presence in Pre-K through 12 Mathematics and Science Education

The crown jewels of the nation's educational institutions must engage far more intensively in the feeder system. One model that is producing results entails adopting students from low-income school districts from seventh through twelfth grade. These students receive advanced instruction in algebra, chemistry, physics, and trigonometry, as well as mentoring and college financial planning seminars for students and their parents. Such models should be shared among research universities, adapted as needed, and scaled nationwide. At the same time, universities should develop alternatives to the traditional admissions process to ensure that the abilities of prospective students from underrepresented groups are fairly and accurately assessed.

2. Nurture the Undergraduate and Graduate Education of Underrepresented Groups

Slowing the attrition of women, African-Americans, Hispanics, Native Americans, and students with disabilities will have the greatest immediate impact on the science and engineering talent pool. The causes of such attrition are understood and models exist for mitigating such attrition. The problem must be addressed by the presidents, deans, department chairs, and tenured faculty who have the authority to change the learning environment.

3. Expand Faculty Diversity

One of the greatest barriers to increasing the production of underrepresented groups is the absence of role models—both in teaching and in research. Leaders of the nation's research institutions must commit jointly to transform the composition of their junior and tenured faculties.

PRIORITIES FOR INDUSTRY

Internationally competitive companies are the U.S. economy's greatest assets, but many also face high-stakes choices between going global or strengthening both their R&D and production bases at home. The commitment of these companies to develop and utilize more homegrown science and engineering talent is indispensable. Their agendas should include:

1. Strengthen the Corporate Presence in Pre-K through 12 Mathematics and Science Education

Although some of the nation's most prominent corporate leaders have set leadership examples, industry's commitment must become a norm across the board. The professional development of mathematics and science teachers in middle school and high school is a logical focal point. In addition, discipline-based teacher models that enable scientists and engineers to transition from industry into teaching have great potential value.

2. Embed Diversity in R&D Partnerships with Universities

Companies that invest in university-based research should make clear that increased diversity would enhance the value of collaboration, and that diversity is a criterion that routinely will affect the selection of future partners. Statements by the nation's leading industry groups underscoring this point would send a powerful message.

3. Create a Culture of Inclusiveness in the Workplace

Although the business case for diversity is widely accepted, an energetic recruiting policy falls far short of what is needed to enable scientists and engineers from underrepresented groups to contribute to the full measure of their abilities. Attention at the highest executive levels is a necessity in companies large and small.

PRIORITIES FOR NONPROFIT ORGANIZATIONS

Foundations, professional societies, and the institutional advocates of underrepresented groups have an important role to play at the national level. Aligning their efforts is a challenge all its own, but it is essential that leaders of these varied organizations work together to advance common interests. Their collaboration should focus on two main priorities:

1. Project a More Positive Public Image of Science, Engineering, and Technology

Making technical careers more attractive to all Americans, especially the underrepresented, is a prerequisite of meaningful long-term progress. A coalition of foundations, professional societies, and other allied groups could bring powerful assets to bear in any such undertaking—financial resources and national outreach to millions of concerned individuals.

2. Mobilize at the Grass Roots

More professional societies of scientists and engineers should put diversity front and center on their agendas, taking active roles in helping university departments reduce attrition and prepare future faculty. Correspondingly, foundations could produce a national multiplier by making mathematics and science more prominent in their focus on school reform. When the critical nature of the nation's need for adequate science and engineering capability is understood fully and when the national will is engaged, the United States can and will gather the resources to rebuild that workforce.

Position Paper on the
U.S. Science and Engineering Workforce

Prepared by
L. *Dennis Smith,* President, University of Nebraska, Forum
Immediate Past Chairman
Roberts T. Jones, Forum Executive Committee
Warren J. Baker, President, California Polytechnic State University

Presented by
Constantine Papadakis, President, Drexel University
Business-Higher Education Forum (BHEF)

The Business-Higher Education Forum (BHEF) was founded in 1978 to address the interdependence of American businesses, colleges and universities, and museums. It has increased communication among the sectors, analyzed issues of mutual concern, and deliberated on courses of action that will effect change on these topics. Within the last five years, the majority of its initiatives have focused on critical issues related to a high-performance U.S. workforce, although none of these specifically address supply and demand workforce issues of future science and engineers. In preparing reports on these issues, the Forum was briefed by experts in the areas of interest; reviewed relevant research and reports; compiled data from a variety of sources; and conducted interviews and meetings with a broad range of participants from the K-12, higher education, military, and business sectors.

Many reports, including those of the BHEF, have articulated and documented all aspects of the workforce crisis that America is now facing. This paper does not attempt, even in a summary fashion, to capture the depth and breadth of the problem. Instead, this paper attempts to synthesize the findings and actionable recommendations of the BHEF on the workforce-related issues it has targeted and studied. BHEF's recommendations are not aimed primarily toward federal policymakers but are largely directed toward education practitioners and business partners. Issues addressed by BHEF include:

1. The preparation of college graduates for today's workplace—the role of business and higher education

2. The development of all of America's talent—promoting diversity in the classroom and workplace

3. The improvement of America's schools—sharing the responsibility

Current issues now under study include:

4. The use of technology in preparing students and workers for high-performing jobs—making learning more effective and accessible

5. The challenge of improving mathematics and science education—developing a plan to increase participation and achievement

THE PREPARATION OF COLLEGE GRADUATES FOR TODAY'S WORKPLACE

Spanning the Chasm: A Blueprint for Action, Business-Higher Education Forum, 1999.

Serious gaps now exist between the skills possessed by college graduates and those required by today's high-performance jobs. The majority of students are severely lacking in flexible skills and attributes, such as leadership, teamwork, problem solving, time management, self-management, adaptability, analytical thinking, global consciousness, and basic communications including listening, speaking, reading, and writing. *Spanning the Chasm* calls for a strong business-higher education collaborative focused on strategies to arm graduates with these skills to ensure their successful transition from the campus to the workplace.

The report offers six core recommendations that address two main questions. The first asks:

What can be done to ensure that students acquire the skills and attributes necessary to succeed in today's high-performance workplace?

In addition to providing pertinent data, the core curriculum needs to help students develop flexible and cross-functional skill sets—leadership, teamwork, problem solving, time management, communication, and analytical thinking.

• Activities and projects that require teamwork can help students value diversity and deal with ambiguity.

• Essays and open-ended questions that test for practical applications of theories should replace memorization exams.

• Faculty should utilize problem-solving teaching opportunities in addition to theoretical discussion. Professional development opportunities should be provided to develop strategies and tools focused on teaching workplace skills.

The core curriculum must address student acquisition or reinforcement of personal traits—ethics, adaptability, self-management, global consciousness, and a passion for lifelong learning.

• Foreign language, which promotes cultural understanding and global consciousness, should be required.
• Methods for acquiring the personal traits required for today's workplace should be coordinated between K-12 and colleges and universities.
• Methods of education must be revised to ensure that workers can think for themselves, make on-the-spot decisions, and think on an international scale.

The second question asks:

What can higher education and/or industry do to help students develop these skills and attributes?

Developing a collaborative process for restructuring curricula and teaching methods must become a critical priority for business and higher education.

• Faculty recognition of the need for updating the curricula is a vital step in initiating required innovations.
• Distance learning technologies and flexible class schedules offer the universities the means to reach older, working students.
• Corporate participation on university advisory boards provides for the communication link that is needed to keep curricula current.

Both the corporate and academic sectors must provide more opportunities for students to apply theoretical concepts to real learning experiences.

• Co-op courses, internships, and other hands-on work opportunities can provide students with optimal applied-learning experiences.
• Corporate and alumni mentoring and executive role modeling via video and satellite can help reach a greater number of students.
• More consistent use of case studies and examples will help students understand the practical applications of abstract concepts.

University career service advisers need to become more visible on campus and to build linkages to corporate recruiters.

• All students need to participate in job fairs, workshops, and career planning sessions throughout their college career. Faculty should encourage student participation.

• Surveys of alumni, current students, and corporate leaders need to be conducted to determine "what works and what doesn't."

• Corporate recruiters can assist career service advisers in conducting workshops on employment skills and job-search skills.

The academic-corporate dialogue should include faculty and focus on practical, action-oriented items.

• Faculty involvement in corporate programs generates awareness of skill requirements and corporate expectations.

• Clear articulation of skill requirements by employers enhances the ability of the faculty to develop appropriate curricula and teaching methods.

• Rewards and incentives need to be devised to encourage more corporate-academic interactions, externships, and professional development activities.

• A greater corporate presence on campus is necessary to help both students and faculty keep current with workplace issues and priorities.

THE DEVELOPMENT OF ALL OF AMERICA'S TALENT

Investing in People, Business-Higher Education Forum, 2002

The BHEF issued this report with three key purposes:

1. To review and summarize research evidence and other arguments that support the value of racial, ethnic, and cultural diversity in business and higher education

2. To call attention to the many programs and strategies—including internships, mentoring programs, and sophisticated academic admissions systems—that foster diversity and can serve as models for companies and universities seeking effective, legal tools for achieving racial and ethnic diversity

3. To offer recommendations for developing all of America's talent that business and academe can implement, separately or jointly.

The BHEF calls on its colleagues in business and academia, on policymakers, and on the American public to join them in implementing the following to ensure diversity in the classroom and in the workplace:

1. Support and strengthen existing outreach programs that focus on the value of attending college, ways to prepare students and assist them in applying for and attending college, and the importance of lifelong learning. Create programs where they do not exist.

2. Provide the resources to ensure that teachers are prepared to work effectively with racially and ethnically diverse students.

3. Review current strategies and policies designed to foster diversity and ensure that they are meeting their goals, and publicize the results of these reviews in the higher education and business communities.

4. Advocate that colleges and universities take the whole person into account when making admissions decisions; that is, consider all relevant qualities—not just grades and test scores—in assessing each applicant.

5. Encourage corporate foundations to provide support for diversity initiatives, and to share the programs and their results with professional peers.

6. As part of the business employee recruitment process, emphasize to campuses the importance of being able to recruit personnel from a diverse student body.

7. Urge national policymakers to increase the amount of the Pell Grant to its congressionally authorized annual maximum of $5,800 per student.

8. Strengthen learning outcomes, through continuous assessment and application of promising practices in the nation's elementary and secondary schools.

9. Encourage university governing boards and state policymakers to give priority to increasing the amount of need-based aid, even in the face of competing legislative agendas and state university budget cuts.

10. Create state and/or local coalitions between education and business leaders to promote discussion and joint action to achieve diversity and tolerance on campus and in business.

11. Provide awareness, in all appropriate forums, of the broad range of successful practices that open opportunity to, and strengthen the quality of, education.

Investing in People: Developing All of America's Talent on Campus and in the Workplace is available in PDF at http://www.acenet.edu/bookstore/pdf/investing_in_people.pdf

THE IMPROVEMENT OF AMERICA'S SCHOOLS

Sharing Responsibility—How Leaders in Business and Higher Education Can Improve America's Schools, Business Higher Education Forum, 2002

A decade of work by K-16 educators, combined with the action of policymakers and the insistent voices of business and civic leaders, has produced a standards-based reform initiative for K-12 education that is now at the core of educational improvement efforts nationwide. Yet much needs to be done to ensure that all students achieve at higher levels and that all students are prepared to assume positions in today's high performance workforce.

In *Sharing Responsibility* the BHEF proposes to strengthen the best education improvement work now under way through a new generation of focused, strategic, and sustained partnerships that elicit best efforts from leaders in business, higher education, and K-12 schools. It acknowledges the work of the many existing education partnerships but calls for more ambitious collaborations of the three sectors. These tripartite partnerships produce four powerful benefits: the generation of a comprehensive, coherent strategy; the achievement of critical mass in reform efforts; the coordination of projects to leverage resources; and the acceptance of joint responsibility for implementing reform efforts across the education system.

The BHEF recommends that leaders in the three sectors use the following best practices derived from its study of education collaborations throughout the nation.

1. Involve as many different parties as possible. Make certain that representatives from public schools, colleges and universities, and business are present. Seek involvement by elected officials, community organizations, and unions, where possible.

2. Involve the highest level of leadership: company executives, superintendents and presidents of schools, and chancellors of colleges and universities.

3. Establish ongoing, formal collaborative structures with a defined mission and clear goals and agendas. Meet regularly.

4. Focus on student achievement.

5. Develop a long-term focus and commit to a multiyear effort.

6. Develop a collaborative plan focused on systemic, coherent reform efforts.

7. Concentrate on the most important issues: the system-changing improvements that will result in higher student achievement. Be willing to tackle important issues even if they are difficult and may produce conflict.

8. Be results-oriented and establish methods to evaluate results. Hold the collaborators accountable for achieving those results, just as schools and students are being held accountable.

9. Dedicate staff and money to the collaboration.

10. Remain above politics. Insist that the organization's strategic plan and recommendations avoid partisan or special-interest advantage.

Sharing Responsibility calls for the increased involvement of higher education in K-12 education reform efforts. It recommends that

1. colleges and universities should focus on improving teacher education programs;
2. college and university leaders should step up their leadership on K-16 education reform issues;
3. higher education should link admissions and other practices to K-12 standards and assessments;
4. presidents and chancellors should devote a senior staff member to K-16 improvement activities; and
5. presidents and chancellors should initiate a high-level community or state education collaboration if none exists.

Sharing Responsibility can be downloaded from: http://www.acenet.edu/bookstore/pdf/sharing_responsibility.pdf

THE USE OF TECHNOLOGY IN PREPARING STUDENTS AND WORKERS FOR THE HIGH-PERFORMANCE WORKPLACE

In 1999, when the BHEF wrote *Spanning the Chasm: A Blueprint for Action,* it was very concerned about how to better prepare college graduates for the jobs of the future. Now, three years later, the BHEF notes a heightened sense of urgency in addressing the "skills deficit." Educators, administrators, business and government leaders are now part of an effort to promote learning transformation in ways that are more responsive to the individual learner and more effective in achieving the desired educational outcomes. However, the BHEF realizes that identifying learning solutions that help students develop the cross-functional, flexible skills in leadership, teamwork, communications, and other key attributes to success isn't enough.

The BHEF is nearing completion of a paper that will offer suggestions on how to make learning solutions widely available. It will outline the necessary investments in software and systems, training and support, and other investments in people and institutions to ensure that learning for the workplace of today and the future is a reality across the spectrum.

The core recommendations of the paper will build on the policy recommendations on the use of information technology in higher education that have been proposed by other groups, including the American Council on Education, the Career College Association, the Digital Promise, Educause, the National Association of State Universities and Land Grant Colleges, The Pew Learning and Technology Program, and the Web-based

Education Commission. The BHEF will identify three overarching goals along with specific action items for colleges and universities, the business community, government officials, and policymakers for implementing and sustaining learning transformation.

Goal I will address the need for the creation of a national vision for learning transformation. The BHEF will call on higher education leaders to take the lead in developing this national vision and for issuing a call to action for higher education to achieve greater opportunities to promote lifelong learning. It will encourage business leaders, government officials, and the military establishment to continue to articulate their needs and to work in partnership with higher education. And it will call on policymakers and government officials to develop and support policies that promote learning transformation using technology.

Goal II will focus on the needs to ground learning transformation in the collaborative research of academia, government, and the private sector. To support this goal and to ensure the dissemination and implementation of best practices, recommendations for action will include the establishment of state and regional centers for learning transformation, learning and networking transformation grants, and an interagency working group on learning transformation.

Goal III will highlight the need for significant investment in, and coordination of, networking resources to support the infrastructure necessary to deliver learning transformation. Recommendations for action will include a national advisory commission on information technology (IT) in higher education, policies to promote the development and sharing of content across institutions and federal and state governments, and policies to promote delivery and access across campuses and to a broader universe of students through partnerships with business and government.

The paper is scheduled to be released in 2003.

THE CHALLENGE OF IMPROVING
MATHEMATICS AND SCIENCE EDUCATION

In response to the well-documented need for improved mathematics and science achievement by all of America's students, the BHEF has undertaken a Mathematics and Science Education initiative. The goal of the initiative is to increase substantially the number of students enrolled in core mathematics and science courses, in every grade from K-16, and to dramatically increase the achievement levels of these students in each of these programs. The BHEF seeks collaboration with a broad array of constituencies—parents, students, K-12 educators and administrators, businesses, two- and four-year college and university faculty, school boards, K-16 councils, professional associations, government agencies, corporate and private foundations, and policymakers—to develop and implement a systemic, National Blueprint for Mathematics and Science Education. The Blueprint, a comprehensive and coordinated plan to be used by state and local jurisdictions, will outline necessary steps to change the learning culture, expectations, investments, and outcome of mathematics and science education from early grades through university. It will address all elements of the educational system and will include strategies to sustain educational change efforts over the long term.

In its recent discussions on mathematics and science education, BHEF has identified the value of surveying programs and research carried out by state education offices, K-12 systems, education reform projects, state cooperative networks, universities, corporations, government agencies, and professional associations. It would identify programs, policies, and tools that meet the principles of best practice for increasing the mathematics and science achievement of all students, and it would outline a comprehensive plan for the coordinated integration of these programs and policies nationwide. Programs such as the Louis Stokes Alliance for Minority Participation Program (AMP) and the Kids Involved Doing Science (KIDS) Program, both of which have produced measurable results in increased student achievement, are examples of the programs that could be built upon and expanded. The policy work of interstate collaboratives such as the Midwest Higher Education Consortium, a compact of 10 states that promotes cooperation and resource sharing in higher education, and the Council of Chief State School Officers' state collaboratives on assessment, accountability, reporting, and student standards, could be shared nationally as models for how states and districts can come to consensus on major educational issues. Mentoring programs, such as the undergraduate research experience in the AMP program, and teacher-in-the-workplace programs, such as the National Science Foundation's (NSF) Research Experience for Teachers Program could serve as program examples for national implementation.

The BHEF would revisit federal programs, such as NSF's Summer Institutes for Teachers, as a model to address teacher content and pedagogy issues. It would strongly support the recommendations in the report *Before It's Too Late*, the work of the Glenn Commission, that addresses all aspects of the teaching of mathematics and science. It would investigate how best to build on and expand the NSF's Mathematics and Science Partnership Program, which supports partnerships of local school districts with science, mathematics, engineering, and education faculties of colleges and universities, state governments, professional organizations, and nonprofit groups.

In its discussions of how to finance the implementation of the Blueprint, the BHEF has considered strategies that will catalyze corporate and foundation giving to supplement federal education dollars. One strategy that has been deliberated is to use the corporate and higher education voices of the BHEF to motivate the *Fortune* 1000 companies to provide up to $1,000,000 each, matched to federal contributions, to support the implementation of the Blueprint at the state and local levels.

Using the survey outcomes, research results, and collaboration with federal, state, and local education agencies, the BHEF would develop a "straw man" paper, with K-16 action plans, which would be discussed and amended in a series of five local meetings around the country. They would be hosted by BHEF members and would provide opportunity for input by educators, policymakers, and business people. The BHEF would subsequently engage the broader community to create a critical mass of support for this call to action.

Position Statement

Gen. Spence (Sam) M. Armstrong, NASA Headquarters
Coalition of the Concerned for the Vitality of the
Science and Engineering Workforce

As a result of the October 2001 Government-University-Industry Research Roundtable (GUIRR) session on S&E workforce issues there was a consensus among many of the attendees that some further work needed to be done prior to the next (GUIRR) session in the spring. I took the initiative to contact some of the individuals who had expressed an interest in working the issue. Representatives from the following organizations agreed to participate in what we later termed "The Coalition of the Concerned about the Future of the U.S. S&E Workforce": Department of Defense (DOD), United States Department of Agriculture (USDA), National Science Foundation (NSF), National Institutes of Health (NIH), Department of Transportation (DOT), Department of Energy (DOE), National Institute of Standards and Technology (NIST), NASA, Boeing, QUALCOMM, and Massachusetts Institute of Technology (MIT). The GUIRR hosted a luncheon for the Coalition in January where the initial planning occurred.

It was decided that the Coalition needed to sharpen its focus on what might be done so as to get some action going. The consensus of the Coalition was that the most immediate impact would be to somehow decrease the dropout rate of undergraduate science and engineering majors. Each of the federal participants was asked to develop a two-page summary of two of their programs that they thought was effective in decreasing the dropout rate. Interestingly enough, the agencies realized that they were not always aware of the efforts of other agencies, so this initial task shed some light on the issue. A summary of the Coalition's activities was presented at the March 2002 GUIRR session.

Other organizations were discovered to have similar interests, and they were invited to participate in the Coalition. They were Office of Science and Technology Policy, Office of Personnel Management, Office of Management and Budget (OMB), Project Kaleidoscope, BEST, The Sloan Foundation, The National Bureau of Economic Research, and Space Day Foundation. In subsequent luncheons (4) and telecoms (2), other suggestions surfaced. One was that internships had been proven to decrease the dropout rate of undergraduates. They gave the undergraduates an opportunity to do some "hands on" work. Plus, working with a scientist or an engineer provided a mentoring environment.

Some research was undertaken to determine how readily available these internship opportunities were to undergraduates. Some success was achieved using Google and Yahoo!, but it was recognized that some agency opportunities were not reachable via these major search engines. This research was done by a NASA summer intern who compiled a four-page list of URLs that contained internship opportunities and that were deemed to be only a partial inventory. Several members of the Coalition and GUIRR visited the Employment Services Division of OPM to see if they could be of assistance.

The visit resulted in a presentation at the September luncheon by OPM on the posting capabilities that they had. Their USA.JOBS site that automatically listed every federal job posting was heavily accessed. By comparison, the site where they posted student opportunities such as internship was very lightly accessed. This difference was explained by the fact that agencies were responsible for submitting these opportunities and they were not keeping their listings current. OPM was asked by the Coalition to take a more active part by eventually creating a Web portal that listed *every* opportunity, not just the federal ones.

The Coalition is in recess until the results of the Summit are known. The role of the Coalition from that point forward will then be determined. It could conceivably be greatly enlarged by the inclusion of Summit participants. It could also take on a more intense set of activities, again depending on the Summit output.

I have concluded that there are many great initiatives across the country that are important in working on the S&E issues. BEST calls them "Exemplars." However, the fact is that we are still experiencing a decline in the production of U.S. citizens in the physical sciences and engineering despite these noble efforts. Given this situation, how do we make a more significant impact across the country? My recommendation is that we do a systems engineering analysis of the S&E education function at all levels. This will be difficult because there are so many subsystems involved. For instance, there is a motivational subsystem and an economic cycle subsystem, and it will not be easy to determine how these subsystems might affect the others within the overall system.

With a systems engineering analysis completed a model can be constructed. It is unlikely that the model can have the fidelity associated with the systems engineering of the International Space Station, for example, but the premise is that an analysis based upon qualitative judgments is better than no analysis at all. All of the initiatives, surely including the "Exemplars," would be fed into the model. The metrics developed with the model will identify the overall impact of each initiative on the subsystems and the overall system, which should provide decision makers at all levels with an understanding of where more effort will have an impact.

Building a Pipeline for American Scientists and Engineers

Amy Kaslow, Senior Fellow
Council on Competitiveness

The Council on Competitiveness draws its membership from an unusual mix of leaders from business, academia, and labor. While that can mean many disparate views, our members firmly agree upon the need to compete. And what puts the United States on the leading edge of global competition is our economy's most important asset: human capital.

From the factory floor to the nation's most sophisticated laboratories, it is the *workers* who are engaging in just-in-time training to apply their newly gained knowledge to ever-changing workplace demands. It's the *talented people* who are improving on, creating, and deploying new ideas and technologies that keep the economy strong. Critical to U.S. competitiveness, of course, is our development of an American science and engineering workforce. We recognize that this development commands the learning opportunities that spark creativity and help people to develop the skills to take on new challenges. If we fail to provide those opportunities, we will never cultivate a dynamic corps of homegrown scientists and engineers. Why the emphasis on an indigenous workforce? Because it is expensive and shortsighted to rely so heavily on imported skills.

One of the striking findings from the Council's most recent Competitiveness Index (see www.compete.org) is that the number of innovator countries is fast growing and they are becoming strong contenders for the very scientists and engineers American firms have been able to lure. Evidence of global competitiveness in the production of technically trained workers can be seen in Figures 1-6. Where the research is weak, and greatly needed, is in determining (1) precisely where the talent pool for innovator countries is drawn from, and (2) the rates at which foreign sci-

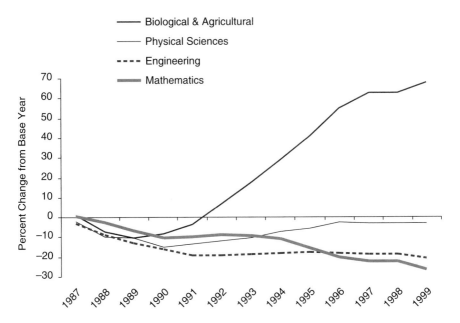

FIGURE 1 Growth in U.S. S&E degrees, indexed to 1986.

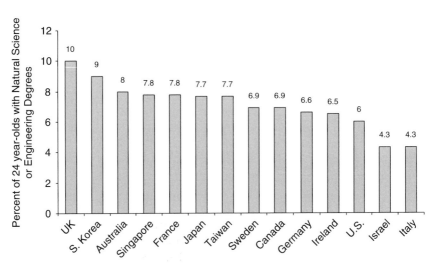

FIGURE 2 Ratio of Natural Science and Engineering degrees to the 24-year-old population, 1999 or latest year available.

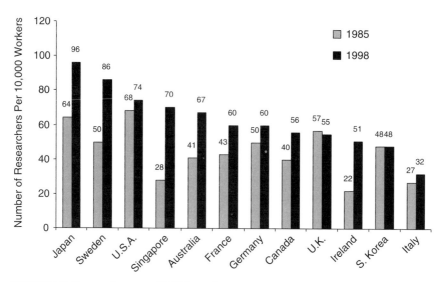

FIGURE 3 Researchers per 10,000 workers.

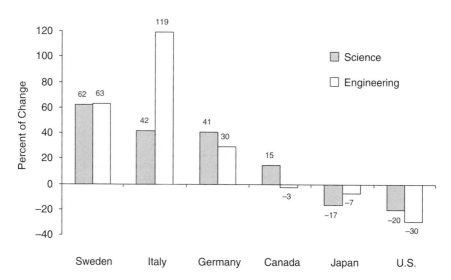

FIGURE 4 Change in S&E degrees as a percent of first university degrees.

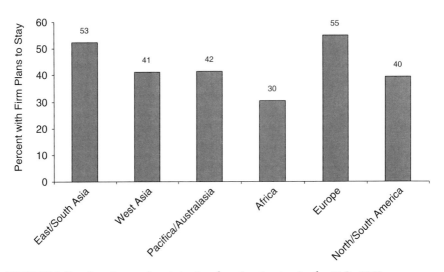

FIGURE 5 Foreign doctoral recipients who plan to stay in the U.S., 1999.

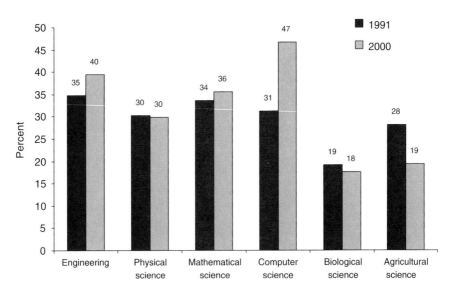

FIGURE 6 Percent of master's & doctorate degrees in S&E earned by foreign citizens by field, 1991 and 2000.

entists and engineers are repatriating. We see anecdotal evidence in many middle-income countries where one of the principal exports is human capital, and where a stronger economy and more robust innovation are attracting more of this "export talent" back home. This is a concern, of course, because American companies will quickly follow in their wake.

Another area we plan to look at more closely is the troubling *trend* of American companies producing their intellectual property overseas. It's an economic necessity if our firms forage for workers abroad, if they set up operations overseas to meet local demand; it's a national economic loss if our firms move their creative capacities out of our country.

This, by the way, is where real public-private partnerships make all the difference in keeping that innovation stateside. Historical successes like Research Triangle demonstrate the economic power generated by university, business, and government partnerships. We've documented and continue to support that nexus on the local, even grassroots, level. We know that innovation—from workforce preparedness to research and development—is best accomplished community by community (see *Winning the Skills Race*, a Council on Competitiveness report generated in 1998 after more than a year of field work, task force assessments, and national meetings to document best practices in bridging the skills and income gaps among U.S. workers).

The past years' liberalizations of visa restrictions to accommodate employers' urgent needs have been acts of triage, not strategic planning. They are a reflection of how short-term the United States has become in its approach toward a problem with profound, and long-term consequences. The Council knows that the hardest choice is to make a generational investment in preparing, and to engage all of the players with a stake in the success of, a vibrant population of homegrown scientists and engineers. Because without that effort, American companies will continue to go offshore for their talent, or worse, set up shop abroad and never look back.

The Council strongly argues for building our own American capacity, but we are *not* suggesting that the United States operate in a vacuum. As the Council's university vice chairman and Massachusetts Institute of Technology (MIT) president Charles Vest wrote persuasively in a recent *Wall Street Journal* op-ed, science is a collective endeavor; it is a global enterprise of independent and interactive verification of discoveries made around the world. Knowledge is honed through global dialogue. Dr. Vest points to European and Asian universities, which together produce more Ph.D. degrees in science and engineering than U.S. universities. Knowledge creation, and the leadership that flows from it, thrives in openness. Indeed, Vest warns, they suffer in isolation. Yet if we are to forge these global ties, we must do so from a strong national base. To do otherwise is to lose our leadership in innovation.

The Council supports policy initiatives to sharpen the competitive edge of American workers in the critical fields of science, engineering, and math.

- We want to see a far greater diversity of the workforce. We want to see women and minorities, the fastest-growing segments of the workforce, transform from being underrepresented in technical occupations to being the dominant new entrants into the S&E marketplace.
- We support financial incentives for universities to train scientists and engineers. It's an expensive education, and cost prohibitive to many, especially for the fastest-growing subsets of the workforce—women and minorities.
- We want to see graduate students choose their preferred specializations based on market factors and career opportunities, rather than gravitate to fields where funding just happens to be available.

We also know that K-12 issues are embedded in all of the workforce policy debates. Although K-12 education is a national priority, the science and math component merits special attention for several reasons. First, the demand for technical literacy and independent problem solving in the workplace puts a *premium* on math and science education in schools—and not just for students pursuing science and engineering careers. Second, our democracy requires a population that can understand the scientific and technical underpinnings of contentious political issues: cloning, global warming, energy efficiency, missile defense, and stem cell research, to name a few. But finally, and most compelling, is the reality that math and science command special attention because even our *best* students are *underperforming* compared with the rest of the world. The deficiencies represented in our education achievement—that science and math weakness cuts across all schools, that relatively strong-performing fourth graders lose a lot of steam by their senior year in high school, that U.S. twelfth graders score far lower in math and science than their peers in other countries—these deficiencies are well documented.

In addition, the Council supports a number of policy recommendations to enhance math and science teaching and learning, including important curriculum changes, more rigorous graduation requirements, higher teacher pay, more professional development opportunities, and ways to strengthen the scholastic connection between K-12 and beyond.

The Council has done a great deal of cross-country fieldwork to determine the most practical, the most cost-efficient, and the most effective local initiatives to build and broaden the talent pool. We have broken ground in documenting how local coalitions made up of learning institutions, businesses, workers' advocates, and governments are bridging the skills and income gaps among U.S. workers. Skills shortages, we quickly learned, know no borders. They transcend demographics, geography, income levels, and every other divider in American society. We have done a great deal with clusters, with Council Executive Committee member and Harvard professor Michael Porter. And now we are embarking on ways to develop innovation models of so-called underachieving areas around the country. At present, our focus is on midsized cities such as Akron and Albuquerque where public-private partnerships go a long way toward affecting change.

The Council has acted on its commitment to a world-class workforce by initiating programs like Building Engineering and Science Talent (BEST), which encourages diversity in the S&E pipelines, and Getsmarter.org, which strives for excellence in math and science education in America's primary and secondary schools. As the economy becomes more knowledge based, there is a surge in demand for more knowledge workers. To boost the growth prospects of the science and engineering workforce, the Council launched BEST in 2001. It's a public-private partnership designed to identify the best strategies for generating a more diverse science, engineering, and technical workforce and to bring these best practices to communities around the country.

One of the more immediate and practical ways we've approached the K-12 priority is through Getsmarter.org, which is a recent spin-off of the National Association of Manufacturers. The Council created the interactive Web site to increase students' interest and literacy in science, mathematics, and technology. A complementary goal is to provide a useful resource for parents and teachers. The site offers free, no-risk K-12 self-assessment for students to instantly compare their performance in science and mathematics with that of students around the world. They can also use the entertaining Web portal to gain access to hints, tutorials, and links to the best Web sites on improving math and science skills. Inspired new additions to Getsmarter.org include Math and Science Television (MSTV), a feature that shows high schoolers how relevant math and science are to their daily lives.

Finally, the Council this year launched a multiyear initiative called Competitiveness and Security to determine the economic implications of sudden (and what experts expect will be sustained) investments to make our society safe. Along with panels of experts, we are examining the roles of both the public and the private sectors in virtually every sector of the economy—from critical infrastructure to financial services to food safety. The nation's leading economists will help us to examine the links between those investments and productivity. And of course, the Council is looking closely at the impact of security issues on our *workforce*. These include the increased pressure put on our incumbent workers to embed security in

their daily routine, as well as pressures on the composition and movement of the science and engineering workforce that have surfaced in the
current concerns about protecting our country and keeping our universities open.

The Council on Competitiveness is working on many policy and practical fronts to make certain the United States has an adequate pipeline of
American scientists and engineers. As we continue to help build it, we are
intent on cultivating partnerships.

Position Paper on the U.S. Science and Engineering Workforce

Eleanor L. Babco, Executive Director
Commission on Professionals in Science and Technology (CPST)

INTRODUCTION

The Commission on Professionals in Science and Technology (CPST) was founded by eight scientific societies[1] in 1953 as the Scientific Manpower Commission. The founding members were concerned by the lack of institutional focus on issues of scientific "manpower" supply and demand, particularly as related to utilization and apportionment of scientists and engineers between military and other needs.

Specifically, the Commission was charged with

- collecting, analyzing, and disseminating reliable information about the human resources of the United States in the fields of science and technology;
- promoting the best possible programs of education and training for potential scientists, engineers, and technicians; and
- developing policies for utilization of scientific and technological human resources by educational institutions, industry, and government for optimum benefit to the nation.

---

[1]American Association for the Advancement of Science, American Chemical Society, American Geological Institute, American Institute of Biological Sciences, American Institute of Physics, American Psychological Association, Policy Committee for Mathematics (later renamed the Conference Board of the Mathematical Sciences), and the Federation of American Societies for Experimental Biology.

Although there were three charges, there was only one goal—to work together to build and maintain a strong U.S. science and engineering (S&E) workforce. Throughout its existence, CPST focused on different aspects of this charge. In the 1960s, the Commission was primarily involved in the utilization phase—how do we best utilize the scientific and engineering talent for optimum benefit to the nation, both in the military and in the civilian workplace? Do we allow those preparing for careers in science and engineering to continue on that path? Do we provide for those scientists and engineers already employed in industry, academe, or government to continue their work? Or is there a greater current need—i.e., protecting and serving our nation—and is there more than one way to protect and serve our nation?

Since the 1970s, the Commission, continuing its mission to assure an adequate U.S. science and engineering workforce, began its efforts to make the S&E workforce more inclusive. It began to urge that collection of human resources data be broken out by gender and race/ethnicity. In 1975, it published its first compendium of data of scientific and engineering "manpower," data broken out by gender, race/ethnicity and citizenship—well before the Congress mandated that the National Science Foundation provide such information in a biennial report. The CPST publication[2] is now in its 14th biennial edition. Our concerns about the gender/race/ethnicity/citizenship issues have only intensified since the 1970s, for how can we gauge our progress as a nation toward having an inclusive U.S. science and engineering workforce if we have insufficient data to do so?

FINDINGS

Today, the U.S. is leading the global S&E enterprise, but challenges are coming from many directions, just as the demand for technically trained workers is expected to grow dramatically from 2000 to 2010. For example, the number of job openings for computer specialists is projected to grow by nearly 69 percent to about 4.9 million jobs. Job openings for physical scientists, life scientists, and engineers are also expected to show substantial growth of 44 percent, 18 percent, and 9 percent, respectively.[3] Accompanying this increased demand are changes in the composition:

• Traditionally, in the U.S., the majority of the S&E workforce has been white, non-Hispanic men, but that is changing. The proportion of

---

[2]Commission on Professionals in Science and Technology, *Professional Women and Minorities—A Complete Human Resources Data Compendium,* July 2002.

[3]Daniel Hecker, "Occupational Employment Projections to 2010," Monthly Labor Review, November 2001, pp. 65-66.

U.S. white non-Hispanic men earning degrees in S&E declined at every level in the decade of the 1990s—at the baccalaureate level, from 79 to 70 percent; at the master's level, from 61 to 52 percent; and at the doctorate, from 56 to 52 percent.[4] These declines are, of course, impacting their proportion of the S&E workforce, with the proportion of white, non-Hispanic males in the S&E workforce dropping two percentage points from 1993 to 1999.

• While some progress has been shown in increasing the proportion of S&E degrees earned by underrepresented minorities (African-American, Hispanic, and Native American), much more needs to be done. During the decade of the 1990s, underrepresented minorities increased their proportion of S&E degrees from 10 to 16 percent at the bachelor's level, from 6 to 9 percent at the master's level, and from 4 to 6 percent at the doctoral level.[5] But, despite these gains, their representation in the S&E workforce continues to be small.

• Women have increased their proportion of the degrees earned in S&E at every level so that, by 2000, they earned over 50 percent of the bachelor's, 43 percent of the master's, and 36 percent of the doctorates.[6] Can this kind of dramatic growth be expected to continue when there are signs of plateaus being reached in some fields such as engineering? While the absolute number of women enrolled in undergraduate engineering programs continues to increase, their proportion of the total has been declining since 1999.

• Non-U.S. citizens have become a growing part of the S&E workforce, particularly at the doctoral level, and in some high-demand fields such as computer science. As a national policy, however, dependence on foreign talent has many drawbacks, especially if the dependence is long term and large scale.

The nation's scientific and engineering workforce is critical. As the country faces the challenges of globalization, technology, equity, and economic uncertainties, it will be the scientists and engineers who determine the nation's ability to provide for its citizens, compete effectively in the global marketplace, and continue to improve the quality of life. But to build and maintain such an S&E workforce requires the efforts of many and attention to all points along the educational and career path.

---

[4]Susan T. Hill, *Science and Engineering Degrees by Race/Ethnicity of Recipients: 1991-2000,* August 2000, p. 13.

[5]Ibid, p. 13

[6]Susan T. Hill, *Science and Engineering Degrees, 1966-2000,* July 200, p. 15

In addition, it is important to understand the processes and mechanisms that produce the changing supply and demand in the scientific workforce. Without that, we have little understanding of the differential outcomes for different groups participating in this workforce.

ACTION STEPS

Since its incorporation, the Commission has worked toward the recruitment, retention, and utilization of all students and practitioners in science and engineering. It specifically urges that all the stakeholders—educational institutions at all levels, businesses, government agencies, professional societies, policymakers, and individuals—work together to effect systemic changes that would accomplish the following:

• Provide a pre-college education (K-12) for all of its citizens, regardless of gender, race/ethnicity, and disability that allows this talent to pursue careers in science and technology occupations. Students should be exposed to rigorous math and science courses in seventh through twelfth grade from experienced, certified teachers. Many students currently are afforded this opportunity, but as a nation, we must make certain all students are.

• Provide sufficient financial support so that any qualified student can pursue S&E studies at both undergraduate and graduate levels.

• Encourage further research on how to identify, attract, mentor, and retain talent in all the S&E disciplines.

• Make universities and colleges bear the responsibility for carrying out national goals to increase the participation of students from underrepresented groups. Since they are the major recipients of federally funded research and as such generate knowledge and bear the responsibility for training the next generation of researchers, they should also take on the additional responsibility, and be rewarded if they do so. These institutions must be encouraged to track student outcomes to measure their success.

• Reexamine the large-scale importation of foreign-born talent to fill our S&E needs. Dependence on imported talent makes our economy vulnerable to shifts in political, economic, and military events in other countries. We must concentrate more resources to developing the domestic S&E workforce and lessening our dependence on imported labor.

• Continue the robust support to the National Science Foundation for collection of data to provide indicators of participation in science and engineering by gender, race/ethnicity, and disability status so that our progress toward an inclusive S&E workforce can be measured.

CONCLUSION

Why do barriers of prejudice and custom continue to impede the preparation and progress of some of our citizens in science and engineering? This question has been asked numerous times over CPST's history. Will it be asked a decade hence? Betty M. Vetter, the former executive director of the Commission, in addressing how to change the barriers, noted, "If employers wanted them changed, if the government wanted them changed, if academic administrators or faculties wanted them changed," no matter how entrenched the patterns,[7] the barriers would be changed. Working together, all the stakeholders can make things change.

---

[7]Vetter, Betty M. *The Equity Equation: Fostering the Advancement of Women in the Sciences, Mathematics, and Engineering,* pp. 29-55. (1996): Jossey-Bass Inc., San Francisco, CA.

Increasing the Supply of Underrepresented Persons of Color in Science and Engineering Occupations

Kurt Landgraf,[1] President
Educational Testing Service (ETS)

FINDINGS

The United States is expected to face a growing demand for technically trained workers over the next 20 years as the baby boomers retire. From 2000 to 2010, for example, the number of job openings for computer specialists is expected to grow by a remarkable 69 percent, to about 4.9 million jobs. Employment growth for physical scientists (+18 percent), engineers (+9 percent), and mathematical scientists (+6 percent) is also expected to be substantial.[2]

At the same time, the supply of young persons who have the technical education and training to fill these job openings appears to be shrinking—or, at least, the pool is not growing quickly enough to fill the projected demand. From 1987-88 to 1997-98, the percentage of bachelor's degrees awarded in engineering (–14 percent), computer science (–22 percent), and mathematics (–26 percent) dropped substantially, while over the same period the percentage of degrees awarded in physical science and science technology rose by 9 percent.[3]

---

[1]The author wishes to thank Paul Barton and Tony Carnevale of Educational Testing Service for their contributions to this paper.

[2]Daniel Hecker, "Employment Outlook: 2000-10," Monthly Labor Review, November 2001, pp. 65-66.

[3]National Center for Education Statistics, *Digest of Education Statistics*, 2000.

UNDERREPRESENTATION OF PERSONS OF COLOR

The training of future scientists and engineers who are Black or Hispanic is a matter of particular concern because these groups have historically been underrepresented in these fields and because they are a large and growing proportion of our nation's population. As Educational Testing Service (ETS) policy analyst Paul Barton has observed, "When we look at where we are going to get more scientists and engineers from our population growth, we run into the stark fact that the minorities are the majority. . . . There is thus no clear demarcation between a discussion of the needs in the science and engineering arena in general, and a discussion of the needs of increasing 'minority' representation in specific."[4]

In recent years, some progress has been made in raising the proportion of higher-education degrees conferred to Black, Hispanic, and Native American students—in particular, bachelor's degrees in science and engineering. Nonetheless, underrepresentation continues to be a serious problem (see Table 1). In 2001, about 3 in 10 individuals in their 20s in the U.S. were Black non-Hispanic, Hispanic, or American Indian/Alaskan Native. However, only 15 percent (or fewer than 2 in 10) of the bachelor's degree recipients in this country were members of these racial/ethnic groups, and even lower proportions of master's (8 percent, or fewer than 1 in 10) and doctorate degree recipients (6 percent) were of these groups.[5]

TABLE 1 Science and Engineering Degrees Awarded to Underrepresented Persons of Color as a Percent of Total Degrees in Those Fields, 1990 and 1998.

	Bachelor's Degrees		Master's Degrees		Doctorate Degrees	
	1990	1998	1990	1998	1990	1998
All Underrepresented Groups of Color	9.7	14.7	5.0	8.2	3.9	5.5
Black Non-Hispanic	5.3	7.6	2.6	4.3	1.6	2.4
Hispanic	4.0	6.5	2.2	3.5	2.0	2.8
American Indian/Alaskan Native	0.4	0.6	0.3	0.4	0.2	0.4

Source: Susan T. Hill, National Science Foundation, 2001; cited in Paul Barton, *Meeting the Need for Scientists, Engineers, and an Educated Citizenry in a Technological Society,* ETS Policy Information Report, May 2002

---

[4]Paul Barton, *Meeting the Need for Scientists, Engineers, and an Educated Citizenry in a Technological Society.* ETS Policy Information Report, May 2002, p. 18.

[5]Susan T. Hill, *Science and Engineering Degrees by Race/Ethnicity of Recipients: 1990-1998,* National Science Foundation, June 2001.

PREPARATION DURING THE K-12 YEARS

K-12 education is obviously an important factor in determining whether students pursue (and attain) science and engineering degrees and subsequent career opportunities. While progress appears to have been made over time, students of color in grades K-12 continue to perform less well than other student groups, on average, in mathematics and science as well as in other subject areas.

Further, students of color are less likely to reach the highest levels of achievement. For example, in the 2000 National Assessment of Educational Progress, only 4 percent of Hispanic twelfth graders and 3 percent of Black twelfth graders reached the "proficient" level of mathematics achievement, compared with 20 percent of white students and 34 percent of Asian/Pacific Islander students.[6] These performance disparities do not suddenly appear in high school; in fact, researchers have found that racial/ethnic differences in cognitive development and performance are evident even at the time children enter kindergarten.[7]

Part of the problem is that students of color are disproportionately likely to attend "disadvantaged schools where overall academic and supporting environments are less conducive to learning."[8] As a result, they continue to be substantially underrepresented in advanced high school courses in mathematics and science, as well as in other areas of study. For example, only about 3 to 4 percent of Black and Hispanic students take advanced placement (AP) calculus in high school, compared with about twice as many white students (7.5 percent) and more than three times as many Asian/Pacific Islander students (13.4 percent) (see Table 2).

This is a matter of particular concern because research has shown that the intensity of a student's high school curriculum is the best predictor of persistence to college degree; in fact, it is a better predictor than test scores, GPA, or class rank.[9]

---

[6]Paul Barton, *Meeting the Need*, p. 16.

[7]Rich Coley, *An Uneven Start: Indicators of Inequality in School Readiness, Policy Information Report*, Educational Testing Service, March 2002; Jerry West, Kristin Denton, and Elvira Geronimo-Hausken, America's Kindergartners, National Center for Education Statistics, 2000, cited in Barton, p. 19.

[8]Samuel S. Peng, DeeAnn Wright, and Susan T. Hill, *Understanding Racial-Ethnic Differences in Secondary School Science and Mathematics Achievement*, U.S. Department of Education, National Center for Education Statistics, cited in Barton, p. 22.

[9]Clifford Adelman, *Answers in the Tool Box: Academic Intensity, Attendance Patterns, and Bachelor's Degree Attainment*, U.S. Department of Education, June 1999, cited in Barton, p. 24.

TABLE 2 Percentage of Public High School Graduates Taking Selected Mathematics and Science Courses in High School, by Race/Ethnicity, 1998

Courses (Carnegie units)	Total	White	Black	Hispanic	Asian/ Pacif Isl
Mathematics					
Calculus	11.0	12.1	6.6	6.2	18.4
AP Calculus	7.3	7.5	3.4	3.7	13.4
Science					
AP/honors biology	16.2	16.7	15.4	12.6	22.2
AP/honors chemistry	4.7	4.8	3.5	4.0	10.9
AP/honors physics	3.0	3.0	2.1	2.1	7.6

Source: Digest of Education Statistics, 2001, Ch. 2, table 142; http://nces.ed.gov/pubs2002/digest2001/tables/dt142.asp

PERSISTENCE IN SCIENCE AND ENGINEERING DEGREE PROGRAMS

The number of students of color who succeed in advanced high school math and science curricula is disproportionately small to begin with, and many of those who do excel in these courses in high school end up deciding not to pursue science, engineering, or mathematics degrees in college. Further, those who initially plan to do so often change their minds, opting for other majors instead.

In fact, while 10 percent of Black undergraduate students stated that their intended major was in the natural sciences, only 6 percent actually received a degree in that area. Similarly, while 12 percent of Hispanic undergraduates initially identified engineering as their intended major, only 6 percent went on to attain an engineering degree.[10]

Part of the reason for this attrition may be that students who pursue math, science, and engineering majors in college have to endure more difficult requirements and grading standards than other students do. The college grades of students who passed AP calculus in high school, for example, vary tremendously by subject area—about 85 percent received an A or B for their English courses, versus about 55 percent for their mathematics courses.[11]

---

[10]Tony Carnevale, Educational Testing Service, personal communication.

[11]Tony Carnevale, analysis based on Rick Morgan and Len Ramist, *Advanced Placement Students in College: An Investigation of Course Grades at 21 Colleges,* ETS Report No. SR-98-13, February 1998.

However, academic pressure and grading practices are not the only explanations for the defection of students of color from advanced degree programs in science and engineering. When students of color who drop out of Ph.D. programs are asked why they left, their reasons tend to have less to do with the difficulty of the work and more to do with the culture of the institution or program; 13 percent cited personal reasons for leaving.[12]

RECOMMENDATIONS

Start early, start fairly. Expanded (and improved) early childhood development and education programs can help to even the academic playing field for underrepresented students of color. By preparing all children for school success from the earliest years of their lives, we can help to reduce inequalities in achievement in the K-12 period as well as expand the supply of high school graduates who are prepared to pursue higher education—and ultimately, careers—in science and engineering.

Strengthen K-12 math and science education. Strengthening the teaching of math and science in grades K-12 will be necessary to increase the number of students who reach the highest levels of achievement and to reduce racial/ethnic disparities in performance that currently exist. Improving K-12 science and math education will not only mean increasing the number of teachers, it will also mean changing how teachers are prepared for science and math teaching, as well as making the teaching profession more attractive by improving the working environment.[13]

High schools must ensure that they offer rigorous math and science courses—and that they encourage and support students of color to take them. As research has shown, the intensity of the high school curriculum is an important predictor of whether a student of color succeeds in a college science or engineering degree program. Success and persistence in higher education depend on a strong foundation in high school math and science.

Some have recommended the creation of a pre-engineering course of study from middle school through high school. Such a program would include a comprehensive high school curriculum offering college-level certification and course credits, a middle school technology curriculum, extensive training for teachers and school counselors, and access to affordable equipment.[14]

---

[12]Adapted from Barbara Lovitts, *Leaving the Ivory Tower*, 2001.

[13]*Before It's Too Late: A Report to the Nation from the National Commission on Mathematics and Science Teaching for the 21st Century*, September 2000.

[14]For example, the High Schools That Work project, cited in Barton, p. 20.

The need for counseling deserves special comment. Even those students who achieve well enough in high school to be qualified to enter a college degree program in science, math, or engineering require counseling and support to ensure that they do go to college and succeed there. This is particularly true for students from underresourced backgrounds, students of color among them—because many of these young people lack the kind of support at home and from relatives that is more readily available to students from advantaged families. Beyond increasing the availability of school guidance services and improving the ratio of counselors to students, there is a need for involvement and support from volunteers and staff from concerned corporations.

Promote persistence in undergraduate degree programs. Many students who enter college, including but not limited to those from ethnic groups that are underrepresented in college, fail to stay and complete the degree. Given the projected future shortage of scientists and engineers, it will be extremely important to take steps to ensure that all students, and high-ability students of color in particular, persist to graduation.

Although research has shown that ethnicity per se is a poor predictor of persistence (in fact, the persistence rate among high-ability students of color is particularly high), there is still room for improvement. Exploring why some students persist and others do not helps to uncover areas in need of intervention.

An ETS study has shown that one important characteristic of "persisters" is that they find the study of math, science, or engineering at the college level to be enjoyable, interesting, and rewarding, and they have a personal commitment to these fields as a career. Further, students are more likely to persist if they have been involved in recruitment or enrichment programs for students of color; and if a scientist or engineer through a summer job or part-time work has influenced them.[15]

These findings indicate the need for programs that give promising students of color opportunities for summer work in science and engineering, as well as programs that focus on improving the climate of undergraduate schools for persons of color.

Train more scientists for industry. As the baby boomers retire over the next 20 years, the United States will face a substantial shortage of workers who are trained in science, engineering, and mathematics, especially for technical or R&D occupations in private industry. Higher-education degree programs in science, engineering, and mathematics must respond to this demand. At present, colleges and universities are producing an oversupply of science, engineering, and mathematician research assistants and Ph.D.'s with limited academic job prospects. The real need is for individuals who are professionally trained in science, engineering, and mathematics and equipped to work in technical industries and occupations outside of academia.

CONCLUSIONS

As the research summarized here shows, our nation's failure to draw scientists and engineers from its entire population—to increase the representation of persons of color—is a significant and growing problem, given demographic trends and the rising demand for scientists and engineers. Fortunately, there is no shortage of information about ways to address this problem. The challenge is to use the available research wisely to design programs and interventions that will eradicate racial/ethnic disparities in academic performance and greatly expand educational and employment opportunities for persons of color.

Clearly, it is not enough to focus efforts at the graduate education level and ignore what comes before (or after). To achieve the goals highlighted here, it will be necessary to take a comprehensive approach, starting at the earliest years of schooling and continuing through the entire educational and employment spectrum.

Position Paper on the U.S. Science and Engineering Workforce

Yolanda George, Co-Director
Global Alliance

INTRODUCTION

The Global Alliance for Diversifying the Science and Engineering Workforce is a collaborative initiative to increase the participation and promote the advancement of women in the science and engineering (S&E) workforce worldwide. The Global Alliance is an outgrowth of the 1992 international program started by the Women in Engineering Program & Advocates Network (WEPAN). The primary collaborating organizations include WEPAN; the Association for Women in Science (AWIS); and the American Association for the Advancement of Science (AAAS).

The goals of the Global Alliance are to (1) develop international collaborations with higher-education institutions, government agencies, corporations, and professional associations and (2) to facilitate the development of long-term, sustainable infrastructures in S&E for a diversified workforce. Strategies for accomplishing these goals include:

• Facilitating the participation of women scientists and engineers, as well as other underrepresented groups in S&E, in international conferences and summits on science, engineering, or gender and science and technology.

• Identifying and disseminating international best practices in the recruitment and retention of women in S&E higher-education programs, as well as in the S&E workforce

• Fostering common standards for data collection and conducting research on the S&E workforce, worldwide

• Fostering international scientific research collaborations for U.S. women scientists and engineers
• Developing S&E career and mentoring resources, including a Web site, http://www.globalalliancesmet.org.

The Global Alliance has ongoing working relationships with other organizations on gender, science, and technology issues that include the following:

• Gender Advisory Board, established in 1995 to advise the United Nations Commission on Science and Technology Development (UNCSTD)
• Gender and Science and Technology Association (GASAT), founded in 1981
• International Council for Science (ICSU), a nongovernmental organization founded in 1931
• Once and Future Action Network (OFAN), founded in 1994
• United Nations Educational, Scientific and Cultural Organization (UNESCO), University, Industry, Science Partnerships (UNISPAR), started in 1993
• World Federation of Engineering Organizations (WFEO), founded in 1968.

Activities of the Global Alliance have included coordinating the following:

• UNESCO/United Nations Development Fund for Women (UNIFEM) international delegations that were instrumental in getting language about gender, science, and technology in *Framework for Action* documents produced by the Fourth World Conference on Women (Beijing, China, 1995) and the World Conference on Science (Budapest, 1999)
• A forum and exhibition on women in engineering for the first World Engineers' Convention in Hannover, Germany, 2000.

Current projects include developing an online mentoring tool for use by women in engineering associations in Egypt, Mali, and Nigeria; a joint U.S./Sweden research project focused on recruitment and retention of women in college and engineering majors and in the workforce; and preparing for the Second World Engineers' Convention in China in 2004.

LESSONS LEARNED ON GENDER AND INTERNATIONAL S&E[1]

From national studies and world conferences with scientists and engineers, policymakers, and educational and business leaders, the following lessons have been learned about gender, science, and technology issues:

- While some progress is being made, studies continue to show that, worldwide, the S&E talents of girls and women are for the most part unrecognized, underdeveloped, or underutilized. The reason for these gender disparities are complex and are often due to family, legal, economic, cultural, social, or educational barriers.

- Both Sweden and the U.S. have been leaders for over two decades in increasing the participation of women in engineering. Each country has developed programs and policies that target this untapped pool of talent to address the worldwide shortages of engineers. Yet both the U.S. and Sweden have reached a plateau in terms of employed female engineers, 10 percent and 14 percent, respectively.

- Most professionals working in S&E are insufficiently aware of the potential of science to serve goals of society and the basic needs of people. Equally, citizens are insufficiently aware of the positive potential of S&E to meet these needs. In particular, the gender-specific nature of the needs and the differential impact of S&E on the lives of men and women are inadequately recognized by both S&E professionals and citizens.

- There is a paucity of data available, at both the national and the international level, on the participation rates of men and women in both S&E education systems and the workforce. Still there are no coordinated approaches or methods for ensuring the systematic collection of gender-disaggregated data on S&E. Of equal importance for policymakers is the availability of data on the differential impact of technical change on men's and women's lives.

- More flexible and permeable structures should be set up to facilitate the access and participation of scientists and engineers to careers in S&E. Measures aimed at attaining social equity in all S&E activities, including working conditions, should be designed, implemented, and monitored. This includes policies to ensure that all workers are able to balance family responsibilities with professional responsibilities and career development.

Recommendations from U.S. and international committees, task forces, and conferences generally agree that an integrative, multisector approach by governments, educational institutions, professional societies, businesses, and nongovernmental organizations is needed to ensure the full participation of women and girls in all aspects of S&E. Recommendations from these groups include the need to

- promote the access of girls and women to scientific education at all levels;

- improve conditions for recruitment, retention, and advancement in all S&E fields;
- launch national, regional, and global campaigns to raise awareness of the contribution of women to S&E to overcome existing gender stereotypes among families, teachers, scientists and engineers, policymakers, and the community at large;
- collect reliable education and workforce data, in an internationally standardized manner, for the generation of gender-disaggregated data, as well as data on S&E
- undertake research, supported by collection and analysis of gender-disaggregated data, documenting constraints and progress in expanding the role of women in the S&E workforce;
- document and monitor the implementation of best practices and lessons learned through impact assessment and evaluations of S&E programs; and
- ensure an appropriate representation of women in national, regional, and international S&E policy and decision-making bodies and forums.[2]

While much of the work of the Global Alliance is focused on gender, science, and technology, lessons have also been learned about international S&E collaborations and policymaking. For the most part, these lessons are summarized in the 2001 National Science Board (NSB) report on *Towards a More Effective Role for the U.S. Government in International Science and Engineering.* The NSB recognized

- *the need for more effective coordination of the U.S. government's international S&E and S&E-related activities and greater consistency in meeting its international commitment;*
- *the importance of increased international cooperation in fundamental research and education, particularly with developing countries and younger scientists and engineers; and*
- *the need to improve the use of S&E information in foreign policy deliberations and in dealing with global issues and problems.[3]*

While the NSB makes seven specific recommendations, they make the following keystone recommendation:

- *The U.S. Government should move more expeditiously to ensure the development of a more effective, coordinated framework for its international S&E research and education activities. This framework should integrate science and engineering more explicitly into deliberations on broader global issues and should support cooperative strategies that will ensure our access to worldwide talent, ideas, information, S&E infrastructure, and partnerships.*

OVERALL RECOMMENDATIONS

While many groups have defined key issues and transformative action related to gender, science, and technology, many of these efforts are isolated and are not connected to infrastructure changes and long-range planning for S&E education and research activities. Given this context, as the U.S. government implements the recommendations of the NSB in regard to the international S&E arena, attention and increased resources should be given to integrating gender, science, and technology issues into the U.S. framework for international S&E research and education activities, including:

• **Increased international research on gender, science and technology.** There is a need for more international research on gender, science, and technology to increase our basic understanding of educational interventions and the S&E workplace.

• **Support for NSF continued collection of international indicators of S&E.** These data are critical for U.S. policymaking in S&E. In addition, NSF needs to continue its leadership role in the development of common standards for international S&E data collection. Data need to be disaggregated by gender, when appropriate.

• **Reexamination of the S&E college and university curricula.** In the new context of increased globalization and international networking, colleges and universities are faced with new opportunities and challenges. They are responsible for educating a highly skilled workforce for the future and equipping their students with the skills and capabilities needed to deal with global issues in innovative ways. This new context calls for a reexamination of the S&E curricula to ensure that the teaching of science be broadened to include elements addressing the economic, social, and ethical implications of science and technology in both developed and developing countries.

• **Development of graduate programs in international S&E policy and social aspects of S&E.** Training in legal and ethical issues and regulations guiding international R&D in strategic areas such as information and communication technologies, biodiversity, and biotechnology should be developed for scientists and engineers.

• **Support for scientists, engineers, and educators to continue work on gender science and technology with the UN and as part of other world S&E conferences**. This work ensures that gender, science, and technology education and workplace issues will be integrated into international frameworks for action in S&E.

REFERENCES AND NOTES

[1]Lessons learned are selected recommendation from reports in *Girl's and Women's Education: A Conceptual Framework.* United States Agency for International Development, 1996; http://www.globalalliancesmet.org/reports.htm; *For Such a Time as This . . .* Wanda Ward, 2000 http://www.awis.org/v_fmagforsuch.html; and The Gender Advisory Board Web site, http://gab.wigsat.org/uncstd.htm, 1995.

[2]Selected recommendations are from the 1999 World Conference on Science Framework for Action, http://www.unesco.org/science/wcs/eng/framework.htm and The Gender Advisory Board, http://gab.wigsat.org/uncstd.htm, 1995.

[3]*Towards a More Effective Role for the U.S. Government in International Science and Engineering.* 2001. National Science Foundation. Arlington, VA. NSB 01-187 http://www.nsf.gov/pubsys/ods/getpub.cfm?nsb01187

IRI Initiative on Precollege Science, Math, and Technology Education in Support of the U.S. Science and Engineering Workforce

F. M. Ross Armbrecht, President, Industrial Research Institute (IRI)
James S. Clovis, Educational Outreach Committee

The Industrial Research Institute (IRI) is a nonprofit organization of 235 leading industrial companies. These companies—representing such industries as aerospace, automotive, chemical, computer, and electronics—carry out over 60 percent of the industrial research effort in the United States' manufacturing sector, employ some 500,000 scientists and engineers, and account for at least 30 percent of its gross national product. IRI's mission is to enhance the effectiveness of technological innovation in industry.

As the organization that represents the largest body of private-sector research employees in the United States, the IRI and its member companies stand to benefit from high-quality math and science education. The benefits stem from a high-quality workforce and a public that is able to make informed decisions regarding the development and use of science and technology.

The IRI realizes that K-20 science, math, and technology education are the keys to achieving a viable workforce. We have long been a supporter of precollege science and math education. In its Position Statement on U.S. Economic and Technology Policy (Section 3), the IRI recognizes the need to "[p]romote strong collaboration between universities and industry to help improve pre-college education."

Additionally, in the early 1990s, the IRI developed a position statement on pre-college education that recognized the need to "provide a solid science and mathematical foundation for young Americans. This understanding will prepare them to become citizens who can make informed choices on technical and environmental issues in an increasingly complex society. Quality education is essential for maintaining high employment levels, a high standard of living, and technological leadership." This position statement is reproduced at the end of this document.

In support of the positions just described the IRI has carried out a number of initiatives: We recognize outstanding efforts of member companies in support of pre-college math and science education; we hosted a conference in cooperation with the National Science Resources Center (NSRC) at an IRI national meeting in support of inquiry-based science education; we have spread best practices among member companies at a regional level; and, most recently, we have begun a major effort in support of programs to improve the quality and quantity of teachers of science, math, and technology at the K-12 level.

To understand the forces that influence the choice of science and engineering as careers, one can turn to both published and anecdotal information. In 1968 Spencer Klaw published *The New Brahmins, Scientific Life in America*. Most of the book talks about what it's like to be a scientist. In the first chapter, however, he describes those who actually become scientists and, presumably, engineers. His comments have stayed with me these past 34 years because they described my personal situation to a "T." He based his comments on such publications as *The Professional Scientist*, released in 1962 and *Graduate Education in the United States*, released in 1960. He states, "Americans who go to graduate school and become scientists tend to differ in one sociologically significant respect from those who become doctors or business executives or corporation lawyers. As a rule they come from poorer families." A 1960 survey indicated that something over half of the members of the American Chemical Society (including more than half of those with Ph.D.'s) had fathers who were manual or subprofessional, white-collar workers. A 1948 *Fortune* magazine article noted that "The broadest generalization that may be made is that scientists tend to come from lower income levels." In *The Origins of American Scientists*, published in 1952, the authors pointed out that in the late 1920s and early '30s colleges like Kalamazoo, Hope, and DePauw were turning out many more scientists, in proportion to their size, than Harvard and Yale. They argued that one reason for this was that many of these students were from farms or small towns and "almost literally had a choice between the test tube and the plow." One of the reasons for the choice of the science career, Klaw argued, was that one could aspire to an advanced degree in science without worrying about the funding since graduate schools covered the needs with teaching assistantships and scholarships.

More recent studies of the origins of American scientists and engineers are hard to come by. The NSF does publish data on ethnic background of scientists in its SESTAT data base (see www.nsf.gov/sbe/srs/). These data show, not surprisingly, that people of Asian origin make up a greater percentage of the science community than of the overall workforce and that the reverse is true for African-Americans. The latest reference on social origins I could find was an article by Kenneth Hardy, "Social Origins of American Scientists and Scholars," *Science* (August 9, 1974), pp. 497-506. Hardy has studied correlations of students obtaining Ph.D.'s with their geographic, religious, and college origins. The studies are interesting, but the data don't go past 1961.

The descriptions given by Klaw suited me perfectly. I spent my early summers working on our family farm and longing for other pursuits. My parents, while educated, were of very modest means. My eight years of education from college through postdoctoral studies probably cost my parents about $1,500. As I noted earlier, Klaw's observations have stuck with me for years and during this time, I've made many personal observations about what causes one to choose science and engineering as a career. I've done this while spending considerable time involved in K-12 education in the public and private sector.

Before I discuss these observations, I would make the recommendation that if one wants to develop policy and action, more up-to-date demographic studies on scientists and engineers are what is needed and not personal observations by former managers of industrial research such as myself. Nevertheless, I would argue that two very important factors in determining one's career directions are socioeconomic background and the peer environment. For students with the requisite aptitude, science and engineering are paths of upward mobility for those with modest means. Moreover, they are fields where meritocracy rules, and thus groups who are discriminated against or who perceive discrimination see their opportunities as greater. This was true in the early and mid-20th century and I would argue is true today.

A second observation, consistent with what Klaw reported, is that youth from more affluent families and also from private schools tend to pursue fields other than science and engineering. There are a variety of reasons for this. In no particular order, their parents can afford to pay for education in fields where scholarships are less available; they are exposed to successful doctors, lawyers, and business people in their daily environment; their high schools expose them to many more choices and also involve them in current social and political issues that cause them to be interested in nontechnical areas. Finally, the required courses in science and math are, by nature, hard work. Bright young students in our better high schools are inundated with opportunities and choices in their daily academic and social life. They have to make choices about where they spend their time. It is only natural that many will do what is necessary to get their science and math grades but not spend the time to really master these subjects.

What the preceding implies to me is that teachers will have to be more creative to interest their students in science and math in competition with other subjects. Certainly, hands-on/active learning curricula are a positive step. I would encourage the listeners/readers to read the works of Sheila Tobias, such as, *They're Not Dumb, They're Different* and *Succeed with Math,* to hear recommendations as to how to attract students who won't respond to the classical teaching approach for science and math.

This leads me to how the IRI is approaching the pipeline issue. First, the IRI recognizes that continuous improvement of math, science, and technology education at all grade levels from K-20 and beyond is needed. Moreover, this is recognized as a total systems issue involving curriculum, assessment, professional development, resources, and community involvement. The foundation for the system needs to be a total commitment to success at all levels of society. The IRI is committed to do its part to achieve this goal.

Because the IRI works through its member representatives and emeriti like me, we have to have very targeted initiatives if we are to make any impact at all. We have taken the position, approved by the IRI Board of Directors, that an emphasis on teacher education is the best place for us to place our primary efforts. The Glenn Commission Report, *Before It's Too Late,* makes the point that "evidence of the positive effect of better teaching is unequivocal; indeed the most consistent and powerful predictors of student achievement in mathematics and science are full teaching certification and a college major in the field being taught." We believe that this is where the IRI, working through its member companies, can make its greatest impact.

There are two initiatives that the IRI is supporting. The first is to review proposals from organizations that are working on pre- and in-service teacher education, select the best ones, and recommend them to our member companies as worthy of support. These proposals can be viewed on our Web site at http://www.iriinc.org/webiri/Committees/pre-collegeeducation.cfm. The second initiative is the facilitation of a meeting involving a broad cross section of groups working in this area with the following goals:

- Sharing of information among groups
- Creating possible cooperation among the groups as appropriate
- Stimulating those groups who are less active to be more ambitious
- Getting feedback and advice re how the IRI can best support their efforts
- Making plans, if appropriate, for a larger stakeholder meeting, including key corporate and private foundations.

The initiatives outlined have been primarily carried out by volunteers from member companies and from our Academic Advisory Council, with support from IRI's limited staff. Because our resources are limited, we have by necessity chosen to focus exclusively on initiatives through which we can make unique contributions. Because we aren't educators, we see our role as one of facilitation and, as an "honest broker" between program purveyors and our member companies, a source of support for high-quality initiatives.

In conclusion the IRI recognizes the pressing need for improving science, math, and technology education in the U.S. in order to have a deeper and better-qualified pool of scientists and engineers for the future workforce. We will continue to work with similarly committed people and organizations, many of whom are in attendance today. We invite others to join these organizations and the IRI to improve our effectiveness through mutual sharing of experience and through closely coupled involvement with industrial partners.

K-12 EDUCATION: PRINCIPLES FOR A QUALITY SYSTEM

Background

The Industrial Research Institute unites companies engaged in industrial research. The quality of industrial research is critically dependent on a well-educated workforce, and the economic sustainability of a country is critically dependent on the literacy of its citizens. This Statement articulates IRI's position on actions that it believes are required to achieve excellence in K-12 education, with special emphasis on math and science. Many of these recommendations are in support of GOALS 2000, as set and recently reaffirmed by the president, Congress, and the nation's governors.

Pre-college education, K through 12, must provide a solid science and mathematical foundation for young Americans. This understanding will prepare them to become citizens who can make informed choices on technical and environmental issues in an increasingly complex society. Quality education is essential for maintaining high employment levels, a high standard of living, and technological leadership.

The IRI joins its voice with others who stress the need for improvement in K-12 education across the nation, and advocates that implementation of educational goals, such as those articulated in GOALS 2000, not be neglected as a result of the present public attention given to other important national priorities concerning crime, the budget, and health.

RECOMMENDATIONS

For the Education System

Teacher Assessment and Development

- Require teachers to meet content qualifications for the courses they are to teach.
- Require students graduating with teaching certification either to have completed a major or to have equivalent assessed education in the area they are to teach.
- Provide and require regular ongoing professional development opportunities for teachers based on assessment of skills.
- Foster greater recognition and respect for teachers and the teaching profession.
- Support the development of national assessment standards for teachers and adhere to them in teacher evaluations.

Facilities and Infrastructure

- Provide adequate teaching equipment and hands-on facilities.
- Use computers both as teaching tools and as ongoing hands-on tools for schoolwork.
- Support the development and use of a national computer network to link teachers with other school systems and facilitate the use of best practices and educational tools.
- Assure school facilities and an environment that are both safe and conducive to learning.

Curricula

- Recognize and utilize National Standards as the cornerstone for curriculum development, assessment, and professional development.
- Develop, support, and use integrated teaching methods for science, math, reading, writing, and social studies.
- Utilize teams for educational development of students so that topics are learned in a social and interactive context, i.e., more student-centered learning.
- Require and foster laboratory-based learning.

External Interactions

- Involve parents and caregivers in educational activities.

- Establish linkages with business to assure involvement from its perspective on a regular basis.
- Involve school boards in the improvement of the system.

For Government and Certifying Groups

Legislation

- Increase federal, state, and local funding for teacher development and in-service activities with a focus on subjects to be taught.
- Modify existing teacher certification programs to allow midcareer professionals in the sciences with some education courses to teach in schools.
- Expand federal and state funding mechanisms and opportunities that support instructional and laboratory instrumentation.
- Provide opportunities for teachers to obtain low-cost loans for personal development.
- Provide funding and incentives for underrepresented groups to become teachers and mentors.

Leadership

- Take a leadership role in developing and implementing standards-based K-12 education across the nation.
- Establish and maintain a systemwide, nationally accessible, on-line library and curricula resources clearinghouse.
- Define opportunities to use tax incentives to encourage industry and individuals to donate time, equipment, and expertise to the school system as well as hire teachers during the summer.

For the Business Community

Teacher Development and Assessment

- Provide internships for teachers to allow them access to industry interests and concerns.
- Develop options for mentoring programs between teachers and industry to ensure a steady stream of technical expertise.
- Support teacher in-service programs with funding and instructors.

Curricula

- Establish school-business partnerships as a method to allow current business information to be a standard part of the curriculum.

- Develop and implement mechanisms to allow input from business to aid in standards-based curricula development.
- Support standards-based educational reform.

Facilities and Infrastructure

- Donate money and equipment to assure state-of-the-art teaching facilities.
- Provide opportunities, time, and funding for business individuals to be in the classroom and for students to visit business locations.

Business Interaction

- Establish a network of business and professional organizations to galvanize activity in K-12 pre-college education.
- Foster and develop networking of IRI member companies to generate best practices in support of pre-college education.

ABOUT THE INDUSTRIAL RESEARCH INSTITUTE

The Industrial Research Institute is an organization of some 235 industrial and service companies working together to enhance the effectiveness of technological innovation in industry. IRI member companies invest over $70 billion annually in R&D, representing more than 60 percent of the nation's privately funded effort. These companies, spanning diverse industries, compete in the global marketplace and provide jobs for more than 10 million of America's workers. Together they generate almost $1.5 trillion in annual sales or 15 percent of the gross domestic product. IRI welcomes the opportunity to discuss its views on the recommendations in this position statement.

Effects of the Current Economic Downturn on the U.S. Science and Technology Workforce: Long Term Implications

Harris N. Miller, President
Information Technology Association of America (ITAA)

Abstract:

The current slowdown in the information technology (IT) industry due to the overall American economic downturn has resulted in decreased demand for IT workers this year. IT and non-IT companies have slowed hiring and increased dismissals in 2001 and 2002. Despite this downturn, a skills gap persists for IT workers in the U.S. Over the last five years, employers of IT workers from both IT and non-IT organizations have consistently told ITAA that there is a lack of properly skilled technology workers. ITAA original research suggests that even as demand falls for IT workers, the skills gap remains largely unchanged, presenting employers with limited pools of qualified applicants. Of deep concern is the long-term ability to maintain and train an adequate supply of technology workers with requisite math and science skills.

FINDINGS

The U.S. information technology workforce has grown less than 1 percent since the start of 2002, while the future demand forecast by IT hiring managers for new workers has dropped sharply. Data from ITAA original research show that demand for IT workers fluctuates with the strength of the economy, but that no matter how high or low the demand, hiring managers consistently identify a lack of workers with the *right skills* suitable for IT jobs. Table 1 illustrates this reported demand and gap over time.

TABLE 1 Demand for IT Workers

Year	2002	2001	2000
Total Demand	1,148,639	901,589	1,608,499
Total Gap	578,711	425,358	843,328

In May 2002, ITAA released *Bouncing Back: Jobs, Skills, and the Continuing Demand for IT Workers.* The report indicated a 5 percent drop in the size of the U.S. IT workforce between January 2001 and January 2002, with hiring managers in IT and non-IT companies indicating that, although they hired nearly 2.1 million IT workers in 2001, they dismissed over 2.6 million in the same period. Table 2 indicates the 2001 hirings and firings by IT position.

In September, 2002, ITAA released an update to the *Bouncing Back* report, finding that the overall size of the IT workforce grew by a net 85,437 positions between January and July 2002 from 9,895,916 to 9,981,353 workers. Employers added 782,466 IT workers and dismissed 697,029 IT workers during the period. While growth is low, we believe that the update indicates that the IT workforce is back on a slight growth track after the reductions of 2001.

The update also found that hiring managers have adjusted their 12-month hiring outlook considerably since earlier in 2002. Where in January 2002 these individuals indicated their intent to fill 1,148,639 IT positions over the subsequent 12 months, by July 2002, the volume of demand had dropped by 27 percent, to 834,727.

The following are among the most notable findings of the September 2002 ITAA quarterly update:

TABLE 2 IT Position Turnover by Field

Information Technology Position	Base 2001 Employment	Total 2001 Hired	Total 2001 RIF
Programming/SW Engineer	2,218,052	308,559	486,731
Tech Support	1,781,955	881,534	911,937
Other	1,433,025	48,648	181,650
Enterprise Systems	1,281,659	123,699	444,731
Database	1,042,978	122,890	79,848
Web Dev/Admin	795,893	311,392	269,368
Digital Media	789,629	157,925	214,081
Network	594,302	74,205	12,519
Tech Writing	486,920	61,640	18,123
Total	10,424,413	2,090,492	2,618,988

• *Despite the uncertain economic outlook, the worst may be over for currently employed IT workers.* The number of IT worker dismissals has dropped substantially in the last 12 months. Between January and December 2001, companies released 2.6 million IT workers or over 218,000 per month. Between July 2001 and June 2002, the monthly total dropped to 116,000. This suggests that companies may have made the cuts necessary to their IT worker rolls, and current employment levels are in tune with current economic realities;

• *IT jobs are harder to get.* Companies hired far fewer IT workers in the last 12 months. Between January and December 2001, companies hired 2,090,492 IT workers, compared to 1,564,931 workers between July 2001 and June 2002. Hiring dipped 25 percent during this tracking period;

• *IT companies are hiring fewer workers.* At the start of the year, IT companies (as opposed to companies not primarily in the IT business) accounted for almost 20 percent of all IT worker hiring. By July, that percentage had dropped to less than 5 percent. Hiring by large IT companies is off 85 percent and hiring by small IT companies is off by 79 percent. This suggests that IT companies continue to be buffeted by unfavorable economic conditions, and that IT job prospects are more favorable outside of the IT industry;

• *IT workforce growth will remain relatively flat through 2002.* If current hiring trends hold, the total U.S. IT workforce will reach just over 10 million workers by year's end, 10 percent below expectations earlier in 2002.

• *Tech support specialists remain the most often hired workers.* Of 440,282 IT workers hired in the last three months, almost one third (147,649) were in the tech support category. Web developers were the next most popular hiring category, with 93,410 added to work rosters, followed by network design/administrators with 47,463.

• *Top skills holding steady.* Top in-demand skills haven't changed much since the release of the Dice Tech Skills Profile, compiled for the ITAA from dice.com job listings data. Hard tech skills including C++, Oracle, SQL, and Java remain at the top of the list, and demand for these skills has held steady or increased slightly.

ITAA contracted with Market Decisions Corporation of Portland, Oregon, to collect the workforce statistics in *Bouncing Back*. The survey is based on telephone interviews with 300 hiring managers, selected at random at IT and non-IT companies. Results have sampling variability of ±6 percent at the 90 percent confidence level.

RECOMMENDATIONS

Since 1997, ITAA's studies have provided the nation's most comprehensive analysis of IT workforce trends. Although demand is lower for IT workers today than in the boom years of the late 1990s, there is a growing concern that this temporary dip in demand will result in fewer college enrollments in computer science courses, and fewer graduates with technical skills. Down the road, this could make our skills shortages even more acute, reminiscent of the mid to late 1990s in America. One recent report showed declines in enrollment in computer science courses and degrees by as much as 50 percent at some universities in the fall of 2002.[1]

Reduced enrollments today could result in severe shortages once enterprises start spending on IT products and services again. The gap between demand for IT workers and suitably skilled employees could quickly exceed the high of 2000, when hiring managers estimated a gap of nearly 850,000 high-tech workers.

ITAA recommends a reexamination and strengthening of the U.S. public education system through a focus on higher academic standards, more emphasis on community colleges and for-profit training institutions as viable training venues for the current and future workforce, and continued government support of lifelong learning to overcome the skills gap. ITAA also supports strong industry and government efforts to recruit and train women and minorities to arm them with the skills employers require for today's and tomorrow's IT positions. Additionally, there is an ongoing need to foster and promote partnerships among industry, education, government, and community organizations to develop initiatives that will train, recruit, and retain individuals for technology careers. All of these measures are necessary to maintain the United States' position as a global leader in IT.

---

[1]Tech's Major Decline: College Students Turning Away from Bits and Bytes, *The Washington Post*, August 27, 2002.

Trying Times for U.S. Engineers

LeEarl A. Bryant, P.E., President
The Institute of Electrical and Electronics
Engineers—United States of America (IEEE-USA)

INTRODUCTION

The Institute of Electrical and Electronics Engineers (IEEE) is a transnational professional engineering society made up of more than 360,000 electrical, electronics, and computer engineers in 147 countries. Our primary purposes are to advance the theory and practice of electrical, electronics, and computer engineering to advance the careers of electrical, electronics, and computer engineers; and to improve their ability to innovate and create wealth for the benefit of the societies in which they live.

IEEE-USA was established in 1973—during an earlier economic downturn—to promote the professional careers and technology policy interests of IEEE's 235,000 U.S. members.

NEW ECONOMY WORKFORCE UTILIZATION PRACTICES ARE PUTTING AMERICAN ENGINEERS AT RISK

One of IEEE-USA's principal concerns is that recent increases in engineering unemployment may not be a short term, cyclical phenomenon, but the result of a much more fundamental structural change in engineering utilization that could have a long-term negative impact on our nation's security and economy. We are apprehensive that current engineering workforce management practices are driven by cost savings that shorten the careers of U.S. engineers, while increasing our nation's reliance on temporary foreign workers, short-term contract employees (perma-temps), and the exportation of engineering work to lower-cost, off-shore locations. The corporate mantra seems to have become more, better, faster, cheaper; and when it comes to workers, more is always better, and cheaper is best.

These changing labor practices make engineering jobs less secure and careers more tenuous than ever. U.S. engineers—new graduates, middle-age, and older professionals—are having a harder and harder time getting and keeping jobs in an economy in which technologists are treated as a disposable commodity.

• **Increasing Unemployment:** In the past 18 months, unemployment among America's engineers and computer scientists has reached historically high levels. According to the Bureau of Labor Statistics (BLS), 68,000 engineers and 84,000 computer scientists are currently looking for work. Unemployment among electrical and electronics engineers peaked at 4.8 percent earlier this year. (See Figure 1) Even more ominous are BLS data showing that the gap between general unemployment and engineering unemployment has narrowed considerably in recent years. This gap is alarming because engineers are the innovators who turn ideas into high-value-added goods and services that increase productivity and generate wealth. Substantial numbers of unemployed engineers may be a signal that the economy has stalled. Further increases in engineering unemployment could complicate already shaky prospects for a national economic recovery.

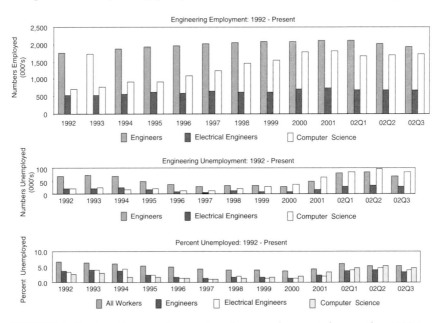

FIGURE 1 Engineering employment and unemployment figures for 1992 to present. *Source*: U.S. Department of Labor; Bureau of Labor Statistics.

• **Job Shrinkage:** More than 100,000 engineering jobs disappeared in the third quarter of 2002 (see Figure 1 for BLS Employment Statistics).

• **Flat/Declining Compensation:** Engineers are expected to work longer hours for salaries that have been flat or declining when adjusted for inflation since the 1980s (see Figures 2 and 3 for Engineering Workforce Commission [EWC] Salary Statistics).

• **Lack of Support for Training/Lifelong Learning:** To remain employed, engineers are required to keep pace with changing technologies and learn new skills but, increasingly, employers are not providing time off or financial support for this training. Engineers who are unemployed or underemployed are also required to keep pace with changes in technology with little to no financial means for doing so.

If current workforce utilization practices continue to devalue engineering careers, even more of our best students will pursue careers in other fields, further increasing our growing reliance on foreign sources of engineering talent.

THE SCIENCE AND ENGINEERING PIPELINE AND THE RISK OF UNINTENDED CONSEQUENCES

IEEE-USA is greatly concerned that policies designed to expand the workforce based on unsubstantiated claims of shortages will create a self-fulfilling prophecy as high school and college students perceive that the reality of an engineering career means periodic unemployment, career insecurity, and flat or declining compensation.

In the past, U.S. students elected science and engineering majors or decided to pursue careers in science, engineering, and technology for a number of reasons. They were attracted to the opportunity to pursue intellectually challenging work. They were drawn to technical careers by family interests (e.g., a parent or relative who was a scientist or engineer). And/or they were attracted by perceived financial rewards, expectations of job security, or related considerations. In making their choices, they also considered the relative difficulty of the curriculum, but often selected the more difficult education path in order to have the perceived benefits offered by the career choice.

U.S. students are influenced by their peers' attitudes about the scientific and technical professions. They are also influenced by their experiences at the pre-college and introductory-level courses within the discipline. They take stock of the employment opportunities and salaries available to recent graduates in these various degree fields (see Figures 2 and 3). In weighing these considerations, they choose from among a number of attractive professional alternatives, including business, law, and medicine. In today's work environment, college students often decide that

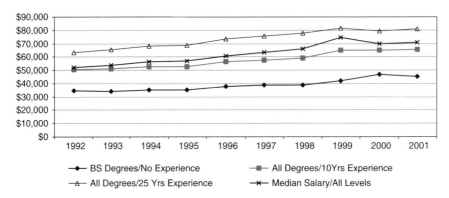

FIGURE 2 Median engineering salaries: 1991-2001 (actual). *Source*: American Association of Engineering Societies; Engineering Workforce Commission.

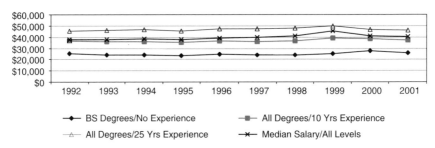

FIGURE 3 Median engineering salaries: 1991-2001 (constant). *Source*: American Association of Engineering Societies; Engineering Workforce Commission.

engineering and related degrees do not offer enough benefits to warrant the more rigorous curriculum.

Artificial manipulations of the supply-demand cycle, management practices that devalue engineering careers, and inadequately supported projections of job demand all serve to discourage students from electing careers in engineering. Initiatives designed to fill the science and engineering pipeline with significant numbers of U.S. students will ultimately fail and compound the U.S. workforce problem, if the destination that lies beyond the end of that pipeline continues to be unattractive.

GETTING BACK TO BASICS IN EDUCATION AND WORKFORCE DEVELOPMENT

What's gone wrong in recent years is due in part to what Federal Reserve chairman Alan Greenspan calls irrational exuberance and in part to an overemphasis by many businesses on short-term shareholder value.

Too many managers feel compelled to concentrate on the short term to satisfy the demands of the financial community at the expense of their real stakeholders—their customers, their employees, their communities, and their shareholders. IEEE-USA believes that the United States needs to return its focus to the long term and get back to basics in building a sustainable science and technology (S&T) workforce that attracts and retains America's best and brightest by delivering rewarding scientific and engineering careers.

Therefore, IEEE-USA recognizes that there is a need to have a well-educated, technically literate public and that we also need to educate, retain, and reward capable people at all levels, including support for

- talented, motivated engineers and computer scientists, including women, minority, handicapped, and older Americans;
- continuing education programs that address lifelong employment needs of the engineering workforce;
- qualified K-12 math, science, and technology teachers;
- adequate population of focused and diverse university students; and
- talented researchers and education-focused engineering faculty members.

Since resources are limited, the education focus must be on how to leverage available resources and target stakeholder partnerships. Key technology stakeholders include the engineering and scientific workforce, employers, educators, government agencies, professional societies, labor unions, and others with a record of success in training, retraining, and rewarding capable people. And to be successful, much of the work must be done at the local and regional levels.

THE S&T WORKFORCE, IMMIGRATION AND NONIMMIGRANT ADMISSIONS

IEEE-USA honors the immigrant scientists and engineers from Benjamin Franklin to Albert Einstein to Andy Grove who helped build this country and who continue to make important contributions to America's economy, technological competitiveness, and national security. Similarly, we understand that many foreign nationals on temporary educational and work visas bring special talents and diverse skills to classrooms and job sites throughout the nation. However, we also know that various issues including economic and employment status of the resident U.S. workforce need to be taken into consideration when immigration and temporary worker visa quotas are changed.

There are various ways to bring talented engineers and scientists to the United States and facilitate their transition to legal permanent resident status. Permanent employment-based programs include: an EB-1 program for extraordinary-ability individuals, outstanding professors and researchers, and multinational executives; an EB-2 program for professionals with advanced degrees; and an EB-3 program for baccalaureate degree professionals and certain skilled and unskilled workers.

U.S. engineering labor markets are also impacted by foreign students and professionals who are admitted on temporary educational and work-related visa programs. Among the most important are the B-1 (business visitor); E (treaty trader or investor); F (academic student); H (temporary worker); J (exchange visitor); L (intracompany transfer); O (extraordinary ability); and TN (NAFTA professional) temporary visa programs. Most have no annual admission ceilings.

Although limited in size and scope, the H-1B baccalaureate degree professional visa program is by far the most controversial. This program was originally intended to facilitate the temporary admission of limited numbers of foreign professionals with specialized skills not readily available in the United States. However, the cap on H-1B visas has been steadily increased from the original authorization of 65,000 a year to the current temporary level of 195,000 with additional exemptions for workers in research institutions. In addition to the increased authorization level, the visa duration has been extended from three years to a total of six years with renewal.

As an indication of the continual focus on temporary workers, the 21st Century Department of Justice Appropriations Authorization Act (H.R. 2215) incorporated provisions allowing out-of-status guest workers who have filed for permanent resident status to remain until a decision is made on their application. As long as an application has been in process for at least 365 days and the job for which they were recruited ends, the temporary worker is free to compete with U.S. scientists and engineers for other positions.

As a result of the various changes to H-1B visa caps, it is estimated that more than 750,000 H-1B guest workers are currently living and working in the United States. More than half of these temporary workers are in the science, engineering, and technology workforce.

IEEE-USA believes that instead of providing a short-term remedy for spot skill shortages, the H-1B visa has become widely used by employers as a reduced-cost probationary employment program for foreign professionals and students seeking work sponsorship for legal permanent resident status. These professionals and new graduates are willing to trade lower salaries and a temporary work status for the ability to enter and/or remain in our nation.

As the National Academy of Engineering noted in its 2001 report *Building a Workforce for the Information Economy*, "[T]o the extent that foreign workers compete with native U.S. workers, economic principles suggest that (a) the foreign workers may displace the domestic workers and (b) the presence of the foreign workers may hold down wages in those jobs. Wages may be depressed even if all employers paid temporary nonimmigrant workers the wages prevailing for the jobs for which these nonimmigrant workers are hired."

Or as stated by noted economist Milton Friedman (*ComputerWorld*, July 22, 2002): "There is no doubt that the (H-1B) program is a benefit to their employers, enabling them to get workers at a lower wage, and to that extent, it is a subsidy."

IEEE-USA also believes that the labor condition attestation requirements established to safeguard jobs, wages, and working conditions in the United States are weak and unenforceable; and that the H-1B program, like other "guest worker" programs, is subject to fraud and abuse.

And because H-1B workers are dependent on their employers to sponsor the much sought after legal permanent resident status, there is significant potential for improper exploitation of these workers with respect to wages, hours, and living conditions.

NATIONAL SECURITY CONSIDERATIONS

A new and increasingly important S&T workforce consideration in post-9/11 America relates to national security. Current workforce development and admission policies are increasing our dependence on foreign sources of technical expertise for maintenance of critical defense, energy, financial, intelligence, telecommunications, and transportation infrastructures. As recently reported by Congress's General Accounting Office (see GAO-02-972), at least 15,000 foreign S&T workers from "countries of concern" that are subject to security-related export licensing restrictions were able to take 15,000 U.S. jobs in 2001. These 15,000 foreign workers have access to sensitive technologies; and their countries avoid Commerce Department export license screening safeguards while transferring technology through their citizens.

The U.S. security risk is compounded by the forecasted imminent retirement of substantial numbers of scientists and engineers employed by the Departments of Defense and Energy, the National Aeronautics and Space Administration, and national laboratories. This is of some concern because the duration of the present economic downturn may serve to divert more U.S. students from engineering and scientific degrees. More importantly, disenchanted unemployed engineers are becoming more vocal and personally steering students away from engineering. While employers and government officials have ignored the concerns of engineers who feel thrown away, the younger population may be inclined to take the engineers' advice as appropriate and act accordingly.

CONCLUSIONS AND RECOMMENDATIONS

In conclusion, IEEE-USA believes that all of the organizations represented at this summit face an incredibly formidable, five-part challenge:

- How to assign responsibility for and share the cost of lifelong learning that will enhance the viability of engineering careers with continual focus on performance, productivity, and employability
- How to make professional careers in engineering more attractive to U.S. citizens and legal permanent residents at a time when more and more employers view engineering services as commodities to be purchased at the lowest possible cost, here or overseas
- How to address U.S. corporate needs for maintaining a positive worldwide competitive position while also maintaining a viable technical workforce for the security and economic vitality of the U.S.
- How to reconcile fundamental economic laws of supply and demand with the special interest pleadings of powerful political constituencies
- How to minimize the unintended consequences of targeted government interventions, like the H-1B visa program, that often distort labor market supply and demand balancing mechanisms, depress wages, and increase unemployment.

Our engineering workforce policy recommendations include the following:

Lifelong Learning

- Commit to a substantial, long-term collaborative effort to improve the access to and the quality of continuing education opportunities for employed, underemployed, unemployed, and recently displaced engineers and scientists.
- Improve the utilization of federal tax dollars and user fees (including H-1B visa fees) by funding educational scholarships and skills retraining programs offered by public and private sector entities with an established track record for meeting the current and future workforce development needs of communities in which they operate.
- Make cost-effective use of new and emerging Internet-based technologies to meet the instructional needs of individual professionals and improve the effectiveness, convenience, and affordability of conventional educational offerings.

Workforce Data Needs for the 21st Century

Better data are needed for effective education and workforce planning and policy development. Special needs include:

- Improved forecasting capabilities that can be used to more effectively assess the probable impact of changing demographic, economic, societal, technological, and national security conditions on science and engineering workforce needs
- Timely national, state, and local labor market information, including total U.S. population (supply) of engineers and computer scientists; reliable population of unemployed and underemployed engineers and computer scientists; inventory of high demand knowledge and skills requirements and identified training for satisfying skills requirements, employment and retraining opportunities, types and levels of compensation, and available financial assistance
- Better statistics on educational and employment-based visa holders, including countries of origin, educational attainment, profession or occupation, age and sex, sponsorship, and levels of compensation
- More effective means for assessing the validity and reliability of international comparisons of pre-college student achievement.

Non-Immigrant Worker (H-1B) Visa Reforms

- Reduce the current H-1B visa quota to the original levels of 65,000 by the end of FY2003; work to reduce levels below 65,000, and limit visa duration to one nonrenewable, three-year period.
- Immediately repeal the H-1B extension feature of the 21st Century Department of Justice Appropriations Authorization Act (H.R. 2215), which allows out-of-status H-1B visa holders to extend their stay beyond the statutory six-year period if their labor certification request has been pending for at least 365 days.
- Ensure that the educational qualifications of H-1B petitioners are rigorously verified as part of the visa application process, and conduct an audit of H-1B visa applications to see if there is a problem with respect to fraudulent representation of academic qualifications.
- Ensure that foreign S&T services companies are not utilizing the L visa (intracompany transfer) to circumvent the H-1B restrictions by establishment of U.S. subsidiaries designed solely for the purpose of importing temporary S&T workers.
- Strengthen essential safeguards for U.S. and foreign workers by requiring all sponsors to make domestic recruitment and retention as well as prevailing wage attestations.

• Mandate the collection and timely publication of pertinent statistics, including age, educational attainment, profession or occupation, country of origin, compensation, and sponsorship for all recipients of educational and employment visas.

• Establish a viable Immigration and Naturalization Services (INS) tracking system to ensure that out-of-status H-1B visa holders and other non-immigrant admissions do not become undocumented aliens (see General Accounting Office report GAO-03-188, November 2002).

Immigration Reform ("Green Cards, Not Guest Workers")

• Encourage employers to decrease our national dependence on temporary skilled professionals and other knowledge workers by retraining the present workforce and/or hiring holders of permanent resident visas.

Undergraduate and Graduate Education

• Increase the cost-effectiveness and relevance of technical and professional science, engineering, and technology education programs at America's accredited colleges and universities;

• Increase support for stipends and assistantships that will enable more U.S. students to pursue graduate and postgraduate education, while also decreasing use of foreign students and professionals as a means to stretch research dollars.

• Conduct a comprehensive assessment of the impact of increasing reliance by American colleges and universities on foreign students and instructional and research personnel on the quality of U.S. undergraduate and graduate education, and implications for U.S. students, including women and other underrepresented minorities.

Pre-College Education

• Continue to work together to improve the quality of instruction in math, science, communications, and problem-solving and increase technological literacy in grades K-12.

• Support funding for recently established math and science partnerships programs at levels originally authorized by Congress.

• Increase public and private support for programs with an established track record for successfully recruiting, training, retaining, and rewarding capable teachers and students, including those from groups that are underrepresented in scientific and engineering fields, such as women, minorities, handicapped, and older Americans.

The Underrepresentation of Women in Engineering and Related Sciences: Pursuing Two Complementary Paths to Parity

Carol B. Muller, Founder and CEO
MentorNet[1]

Despite some concerted attention and resources devoted to recruitment and retention of women in engineering over the last couple of decades, they are still woefully underrepresented in engineering and many related sciences. This underrepresentation is problematic from several perspectives: From the point of view of the U.S. science and engineering workforce, nearly half the potential talent for the technical workforce is missing. There is also cause for concern on the part of those seeking quality, talent, and creativity for the engineering and scientific disciplines and professions. And women themselves are missing out on opportunities to leverage learning and skills in interesting and rewarding careers, explore new fields, develop new knowledge, design new solu-

---

[1] MentorNet (www.MentorNet.net), *the e-mentoring network for women in engineering and science,* is a nonprofit organization. MentorNet's mission is to further women's progress in scientific and technical fields through a dynamic, technology-supported mentoring program and to advance women and society by developing a diversified, expanded, and talented workforce. The vision is threefold: to establish excellence in large-scale e-mentoring, to create the e-community of choice for women in engineering and science through online mentoring and networking, and to leverage that community for positive social change.

MentorNet leverages technology to build large-scale impact for women and positive social change, on a scale which has increased over its five year history. During 2001-02, more than 3,000 undergraduate and graduate women studying engineering and related sciences at more than 100 colleges and universities across the U.S., and in several other nations, were matched in structured, one-on-one, email-based mentoring relationships with male and female scientific and technical professionals working in industry and government.

tions, and benefit from the rewards of financial independence and economic equity.

DATA

When we consider why there are so few women in science and technology fields, it's important to consider a few facts. Women represent more than half the population and 46 percent of the U.S. workforce, but just 24 percent of those working in science and engineering combined and only 10 percent of the engineering workforce (NSF, 2002). Since 1980, the percentage of women receiving bachelor's degrees in engineering has slowly increased from about 10 percent to nearly 20 percent. But in some of those years, the percentage remained flat, and in recent years, even when the percentage increased, the total numbers remained the same or decreased.

Those less engaged with developing the scientific and technical workforce may be lulled into complacency. Since the social changes of the women's movement and legislation removing barriers and addressing gender equity changed the landscape for women's opportunities 30 years ago, women have made considerable progress in participation in a variety of professional fields. National Science Foundation data put the percentage of women receiving bachelor's degrees in science and engineering combined at 50 percent of the total in 2000. At first glance, one would think equity had been achieved, but upon closer scrutiny one sees that the definition of "science" in this case includes social and behavioral sciences, including psychology (in which women represented 76 percent of bachelor's degree recipients in 2000) and other fields where women are overrepresented. In 2000, women earned about 20 percent of bachelor's degrees in engineering, 33 percent in mathematical and computer sciences, and 56 percent in biological and agricultural sciences.

Furthermore, the apparent "gains" in percentages are more reflective of the lower percentages of men entering these fields than increases in percentages of women: In 1980, 1.3 percent of women earning bachelor's degrees majored in engineering vs. 11.1 percent of men. In 2000, 1.7 percent of women earning bachelor's degrees majored in engineering vs. 8.8 percent of men. The numbers of women beginning majors in science and math are much smaller than those for men, but once in these fields, women's attrition is not appreciably different from men's (Campbell et al., 2002), except at highly selective institutions (Strenta, 1993). Attrition and differential retention for women may still be a concern, however, since we would expect even stronger retention among women than among men, given their higher average academic performance (Seymour and Hewitt, 1997).

The gap in participation of minority groups is not as large as the gender gap (Campbell et al., 2002), but race and ethnicity are also key factors in understanding the full spectrum of women's participation in science and engineering. While the gender gap in preparation for higher education has closed, a gap in preparation persists for students of African-American, Hispanic, and Native American background compared with their white and Asian counterparts.

Most of the data reported, however, are not disaggregated by gender and race/ethnicity. Potentially even more problematic for educational equity is the lack of data on the relationship of socioeconomic status to entry and persistence in science and engineering education and workforce participation. The development of policy and practice to ameliorate the underrepresentation of various kinds of students and, later, workforce participants, is impeded by these limitations of available data. Because of the strong correlation, it's often not at all clear when differences in preparation, for example, reflect differences in socioeconomic status and when they reflect institutional or individual racism.

The situation of women's considerable underrepresentation in science and engineering cries out for remedy, but remedy is complex. Dramatic gains have proven elusive over the last three decades even though overt barriers to women's participation in these fields have fallen.

EXAMINING EXPLANATIONS FOR GENDER DIFFERENCES

Differences in aptitude, achievement, or preparation do not appear to explain women's lower rates of participation in engineering and science. Some may assume that women leave scientific and technical fields of study because they find them too difficult. Yet the achievement gap in mathematics between boys and girls is less than 1 percent (Campbell et al., 2002), and research suggests that women switching out of science and engineering majors in college have higher GPAs in these fields than do men who stay in such majors (Seymour and Hewitt, 1997; Adelman, 1998). Girls and boys appear to be taking math and science classes in high school at about the same levels.

The remaining area of gender difference as students prepare to enter college appears to be interest, with girls even less interested than boys in pursuing engineering and science in college and beyond. Women, to a somewhat greater extent than men, are apt to choose fields of study they believe will contribute to the social good, and engineering and related sciences are not widely perceived as professions making such contributions. Though examples abound of discoveries, inventions, and solid engineering work and scientific research that contribute to the health and welfare of people all over the planet, to environmental protection and improved quality of life, the links between this work and engineering and science are not obvious to those outside these fields, and the perception remains.

Lack of interest or misperceptions on the part of students are not the responsibility or domain of any one institution or system. They are prompted by a social fabric that pervades our society, represented not only within our educational systems but also in homes, within families, and in popular culture, which, by and large, stereotypes engineering and scientific fields as "geeky" and particularly inappropriate for girls and women. Targeted programs frequently attract only a portion of the students who could benefit from them, due to stigmas attached to participation, including peer backlash and harassment of those who participate.

We should be cautious about overemphasizing gender differences in seeking explanations and remedies for women's underrepresentation in science and engineering. Men and women are more alike than they are different. Women, like men, are not monolithic in nature; they choose to pursue or leave certain fields of study or employment for a wide variety of reasons. As a result, there won't be a "one size fits all" solution to increasing women's participation in scientific and technical fields, and many of the same strategies that work to encourage men's participation will encourage women's, and vice versa.

At the same time, we need to recognize that societal beliefs, attitudes, and behaviors still lead to differential perceptions of and expectations for women (see, for example, Valian, 1998). Expectations, in turn, strongly influence learning and behaviors (Steele, 1999). Mitigating differential expectations through deliberate encouragement of women, provision of mentoring, role models, internships and scholarships, and related strategies can be helpful.

Good educational practice, focused on improving the learning of all students without a particular focus on gender, frequently results in greater gender parity. Similarly, when special effort is put into understanding the causes and providing remedies for women's underrepresentation (e.g., through examination of institutional policies and practices, faculty development, or providing a stronger community of support), the resulting changes often benefit all students.

LESSONS LEARNED: STRATEGIES FOR CHANGE

Solutions to increase participation of women in science and engineering often initially focus on the problem of how to persuade more girls and women to enter and remain in these fields. These interventions have been characterized as efforts that focus on a "deficit" model, in which it is assumed that these individuals lack something—ability, experience, interest, inspiration, motivation—that they need in order to succeed. In this model, attention is paid to mitigating that deficit, typically by providing programs—summer camps, internships, remedial courses, special study groups, mentoring programs, social opportunities, seminars, evening programs, etc.

Program evaluation suggests that well-designed intervention programs can definitely make a difference in increasing the numbers of women in science and engineering, at least for some portion of the population in some environments. But even on college campuses with long-standing, comprehensive programs focused on women in engineering and/or science, the representation of women does not rise to parity. Some have criticized this approach for its development of "Band-aid" efforts that address symptoms rather than tackling the roots of the problem.

In the last decade, juxtaposed to the program intervention approach, many have suggested that we should instead address what needs to be changed in these fields, disciplines, and institutions so that more girls and women will be attracted to them. Within this framework, greater attention is paid to institutional and "systemic" features of the fields of study, modes of instruction, organizational policies, cultural practices, and structural elements that may impede women's full participation and success. Under consideration in this model, for example, are admissions policies, teaching practices, faculty rewards and incentives, faculty development, grading, testing, and other forms of assessment, curricular structure, and program and degree requirements. The appeal of this approach is strong. In theory at least, systemic change will address root causes and solve the problems so that they will not recur and will not need recurring treatment. It's also a bold, transformative approach with appeal to change agents who recognize and appreciate the serious limitations of program intervention.

At the same time, however, systemic change requires long-term investment to create measurable shifts in values, beliefs, attitudes, and behaviors, as well as structural changes in complex, interconnected organizations, professions, and practices. These changes are frequently challenging, complex, and time consuming, particularly if a comprehensive shift is desired, with measurable impact on the participation of currently underrepresented groups. There is a need to address interrelated systems and organizations in ways that are not under the control of any one single group of change agents.

Making a distinction between these two approaches is not always easy, and valuing one over the other is not altogether helpful either. We need to focus on changing systems, practices, and institutions, not on "fixing" the individuals who aren't choosing engineering and scientific fields, but support programs should not be tossed out even as we focus on critical systemic change. An analogy to consider is the treatment of disease: There are diseases for which the cause and cure are still unknown, but while research scientists are investigating the cause and cure, we don't withhold treatment to ameliorate the symptoms of the disease, improve quality of life, and extend life. Similarly, as we pursue systemic change, it is important to continue to measure the effects of good intervention programs and to offer as widely as possible those that are effective.

Programs that support and encourage individual girls and women, helping them to understand and thrive even within current flawed systems and organizational structures, are valuable. Such programs may also seed the process of longer-term shifts in institutional practices and culture. For example, in situations where men who are professional engineers and scientists serve as mentors to women students, they may learn more about the barriers women face in ways that lead to changes in their own beliefs, attitudes, and behaviors. In another example, faculty sponsoring research internships may have their erroneous assumptions about women students' abilities or other stereotypes dispelled.

There are already many strong programs in place, innovative as well as "tried and true," local, regional, and national, that help spark interest among young women; help to mentor students and emerging professionals at every level; provide "hands on" opportunities to explore the fun, challenge, and excitement of engineering and science; and offer role models and communities of support. Too often, however, these programs exist at the margins of our institutions, short on infrastructure for sustainability and scalability, the first to be cut when budgets are tight, vulnerable to leadership burnout or personnel changes. Leadership is needed to recognize the importance of this work, bring it into the mainstream of everyday educational practice, and create more ways to institutionalize, replicate, and scale effective efforts. Often, resources are needed to provide appropriate infrastructure for organizations or programs to ensure their sustainability, stability, and growth.

Too, the endless appetite of funding agencies, the media, and creative individuals who develop programs for the "new new thing" in programs for women and girls in engineering and science, may contribute to an overinvestment in "startups" at the expense of sustaining high-performing but more seasoned operations.

LESSONS LEARNED FROM MENTORNET

Mentoring is a frequently employed strategy for retention of women in engineering and science. The power of mentoring is sometimes poorly understood, and mentoring is not always effectively practiced (Zachary, 2000). At its weakest, mentoring is viewed as a somewhat offhand strategy to address deficits, providing some needed encouragement and advising of weaker and less confident students. Once in college, women are somewhat more likely than men to doubt their ability to succeed in scientific and technical fields, yet lack of confidence frequently influences women's decisions to persist in studies or postgraduate opportunities in these fields (Seymour and Hewitt, 1997). Mentoring appears to be a strategy that helps increase women's confidence in their abilities (MentorNet, 2002).

At its strongest, however, mentoring is understood as a powerful learning process, which assures the intergenerational transfer of knowledge and "know-how" on an ongoing basis throughout one's life (Clutterbuck, 2001; Zachary, 2000). Mentoring helps make explicit the tacit knowledge of a discipline and its professional culture. Whether or not such individuals are labeled "mentors," nearly everyone has one or more mentors in the form of more experienced guides and advisers as they grow and develop as individuals and professionals.

Both protégés and mentors learn from mentoring relationships (Zachary, 2000). Well-deployed mentoring can be highly effective in supporting systemic change and in creating positive, productive, equitable learning environments (Clutterbuck, 2001). When mentoring is understood as a serious and powerful learning process, complete with the need to establish learning objectives, measures, and discipline to achieve results, its potential can be realized (Zachary, 2000). Policymakers, funders, and program developers, however, need to understand better the elements of effective mentoring and to consider how best to construct mentoring experiences that can be valuable and powerful in their transformation of individuals and organizations.

MentorNet was specifically designed to take advantage of newly emerging widespread use of Internet technologies to create mentoring opportunities where they couldn't previously exist due to constraints of time and geography. It was also designed to leverage technology in support of scale of programs that can otherwise be very time consuming to manage well. Research-based program design, continuous improvement and feedback loops, and clever adaptation of technology-supported solutions have enabled an electronic mentoring program linking students with professionals in industry that is both scalable and cost-effective.

SUMMARY OF RECOMMENDATIONS

• Disaggregate data by sex, ethnicity, and socioeconomic status to ensure that program and change design will be influenced by data appropriate for all within the targeted population.

• Measure the effects of intervention programs, and offer those that are effective as widely as possible.

• Bring effective programs into the mainstream of everyday educational practice, and create more ways to institutionalize, replicate, and scale these efforts.

• Invest in infrastructure for effective programs to ensure sustainability, stability, and growth, creating high-performance organizations.

• Invest in both treatment (support under current systems) and cure (systemic change).

• Use research and practice to inform the development of effective mentoring programs for specific learning objectives for individuals and to support systemic change, measuring results against objectives.

• Explore ways in which technology can support scale and achieve efficiencies.

REFERENCES

Adelman, C. (1998). *Women and Men of the Engineering Path: A Model for Analyses of Undergraduate Careers.* U.S. Department of Education, The National Institute for Science Education, Washington, DC.

Campbell, P., Jolly, E., Hoey, L., and Perlman, L. (2002). *Upping the Numbers: Using Research-Based Decision Making to Increase Diversity in the Quantitative Disciplines.* A report commissioned by the GE Fund.

Clutterbuck, D. (2001). *Everyone Needs a Mentor.* Chartered Institute of Personnel and Development. London: CIPD Publishing.

MentorNet (2002). *2000-01 MentorNet Evaluation Report.* http://www.mentornet.net/Documents/About/Results/Evaluation/00-01/00.01.YearEnd.Eval.Report.appendices.pdf.

National Science Foundation. *Science and Engineering Indicators 2002,* Chapter 3: Science and Engineering Workforce—Women and Minorities in S&E. http://www.nsf.gov/sbe/srs/seind02/.

Seymour, E. and Hewitt, N. (1997). *Talking About Leaving: Why Undergraduates Leave the Sciences.* Westview Press, Boulder, CO.

Steele, C. (1999). Thin Ice: "Stereotype Threat" and Black College Students, *Atlantic Monthly,* August 1999. http://www.theatlantic.com/issues/99aug/9908stereotype.htm.

Strenta, C. (1993). *Choosing and Leaving Science in Highly Selective Institutions: General Factors and the Question of Gender.* Alfred P. Sloan Foundation, New York, NY.

Valian, V. (1998). *Why So Slow? The Advancement of Women.* MIT Press, Cambridge, MA.

Zachary, L. (2000). *The Mentor's Guide.* Jossey-Bass Inc., San Francisco, CA.

NACME, Engineering, and "Generation Next"

John Brooks Slaughter, President & CEO
Daryl E. Chubin, Senior Vice President
National Action Council for Minorities in
Engineering (NACME), Inc.

NACME AND THE NATION: NEED AND OPPORTUNITY

In 1974, NACME's founders estimated that it would take 10 years for minority representation in engineering graduates to mirror that of the college-age population. Twenty-eight years later, parity remains elusive. In 2001, African-Americans, American Indians, and Latinos—one-third of the college-age population—represented only 10 percent of all engineering graduates and only 6 percent of the engineering workforce.

Although enrollments soared through the mid-1990s, a persistent and significant achievement gap continues to grow. Only two of five minority students nationally who enroll in engineering graduate with a baccalaureate degree in engineering, compared to two of three nonminority students. A recent report by the GE Fund found that U.S. engineering institutions would need to graduate more than 250,000 minority engineers in the coming decade to reflect the ethnic and racial composition of the general population. The task is daunting, especially considering that those institutions have only graduated 116,000 since 1971.[1] The need is clear.

Over the next decade the traditional college-age population will swell by some 15 percent, producing 30 million 18- to 24-year-olds by 2015. But in sharp contrast to earlier generations, some 85 percent of this pool will be minorities, and 41 percent are likely to come from low-in-

---

[1]Campbell, P.B., Jolly, E., Hoey, L., Pearlman, L.K, *Upping the Numbers: Using Research-Based Decision Making to Increase Diversity in the Quantitative Disciplines.* A report commissioned by the GE Fund (January 2002), p. 2.

come families. Futurists call those born between 1980 and 2000 "generation next." They total almost 70 million, weaned on high-tech gadgetry and fast-paced routines at work and play. This generation is the nation's demographic future—and they are NACME's target audience.[2] The opportunity looms.

The findings and recommendations below derive both from NACME's first-hand experience and our distillation of national trends and studies. In what follows we are unabashedly self-referential as a minority-serving organization with a national mission, a recognized track record, and origins in the National Academy itself.

FINDINGS

Increasing Access and Retention

The concept of an "underserved community" refers to gaps in the necessary college preparatory coursework (notably mathematics and science) provided through K-12 education. Graduating from schools lacking experienced teachers, standards-based curricula and materials, and access to technology, students start behind and often stay behind. If they are first-generation college attendees from low-income families, the burdens of their circumstances can dwarf their aspirations. They often lack role models, information, and counseling. Yet they have potential that can be developed.

NACME has learned from its program operation experience that increasing opportunity for recruitment to undergraduate study requires a multifaceted strategy. Scholarships alone will not suffice. The sheer rigor of engineering coupled with the academic deficits that students of color from underserved communities often carry into college demands intervention. Barriers to minority student retention continue to be: the cost of education, isolating campus climates, a lack of peer and faculty engagement, and inadequate math and science preparation.[3]

Increasing the minority retention rate to that of nonminorities would raise aggregate baccalaureate production of underrepresented

---

[2]Symonds, W.C. "America's Future College Crunch—The Human Factor," *Business Week*, August 20-27, 2001. For a perspective on engineering's human resource needs for the next decade, see J.B. Slaughter, "Engineering Education for the 21st Century," Keynote presentation, Annual Conference and Exposition, American Society for Engineering Education, Montreal, Canada, June 17, 2002.

[3]Based on literature summarized at the Merck-NACME Think Tank on Retention, New York, NY, April 11, 2002. See "Attention to Retention," NACME Report, September 2002; and G.S. May and D.E. Chubin, "A Retrospective on Undergraduate Engineering Success for Underrepresented Minority Students," Journal of Engineering Education, forthcoming 2003.

minorities in engineering to ca. 10,000 per year. In other words, it would produce 100,000 over a decade, which is still less than half of the quarter million needed to reach parity with the minority presence in the general population. Increased access—through academic preparation and financial aid—must augment current enrollments rates. To enhance selection for college admission students with unconventional academic profiles, we provide financial assistance as well as intellectual support (e.g., mentoring, peer tutoring, internship experiences). Our goal is not only to boost retention to completion of the baccalaureate, but, moreover, to equip the neophyte engineer for success in the workplace.

Building Public Awareness

Informing choices motivated NACME's successful *Math Is Power* campaign. In 1995, realizing the need to cast a larger net to prepare students for engineering, NACME launched *Math Is Power,* a public service campaign that tells students about the importance of taking academic-track math courses. The good news, discovered through NACME's own follow-up surveys, is that students and parents *were* empowered to demand rigorous mathematics as the foundation to compete for admission to higher education. The bad news is that despite a multiyear multimedia campaign involving millions of dollars in pro bono radio and TV advertising, an 800 number, billboards, and kits for teachers and other allies of children, the campaign suffers from limited reach nationally.[4]

In May 2002, *GuideMeNACME: A RoadMap to Engineering* (www.guidemenacme.org) was launched at the National Academy of Engineering (NAE) as an antidote to what guidance counselors and other significant others in underserved communities often fail to provide.[5] Illuminating the pathways to a career in engineering, *GuideMeNACME* is targeted to middle and high school students of color, with easy-to-navigate sections and hundreds of links to local programs for students, parents, and educators. The site provides information on scholarships, applying to engineering school, and minority role models in various disciplines and industries.

---

[4]Markow, D., and K. Moore, "Progress Toward Power: A Follow-up Survey of Children and Parents' Attitudes about Math and Science," *NACME Research Letter*, vol. 9, October 2001.

[5]Today, the site features hundreds of links, audio and video, for parents, teachers, higher educators, and companies in a "one-stop shopping" mode. A Spanish-language version is in the works.

Influencing Career Choice

Historically, less than 10 percent of high school graduates—and six men for every woman—intend to pursue an undergraduate degree in engineering. Roughly half that proportion, 5-6 percent of college graduates, earn a degree in engineering. As the college-age population approaches 80 percent women and minorities in the next 15 years, the very groups historically neither recruited nor supported in S&E will represent the pool of talent for which all professions (including medicine and law) compete. As has been demonstrated, science fares poorly—even worse than engineering—in career prospects, lifetime earnings, and quality of student and professional life relative to its competitors.[6]

By reflecting a broader range of intellectual interest and work orientation, heterogeneity by race, ethnicity, and gender adds value in several ways. No more is this apparent than in engineering colleges, where only 2 percent of the faculty is minority. A diverse faculty is a sure sign to an increasingly diverse student body that a woman or person of color can indeed excel and achieve. Such role models are often disparaged, but they can make a difference between persistence in and departure from a science or engineering course of study.[7]

Assessing Institutional Production

The concentration of federal R&D funding, with 100 institutions accounting for 90 percent of federal R&D obligations and 30 institutions receiving the lion's share of that, is familiar to us all. The same applies to which universities produce the most Ph.D.'s. But how do these lists change when the output is *women and minority graduates*—B.S. and Ph.D.—in engineering? Size matters here. We should look for "critical mass" or some indication that within an institution a cadre across cohorts has been created and sustained.

Of ca. 300 institutions that award engineering degrees (according to the Engineering Workforce Commission), only 71 graduated half of the B.S. engineers in 2000. These same institutions, in the aggregate, produced engineers in the following categories: 35 percent of women, 47 percent of African-Americans, 57 percent of Latinos, and 53 percent of American In-

---

[6]Teitelbaum, M., "How We (Unintentionally) Make Scientific Careers Unattractive," in *Scientists and Engineers for the New Millennium: Renewing the Human Resource*, D.E. Chubin and W. Pearson, Jr. (eds.) (Washington, DC: Commission on Professionals in Science & Technology, 2001), pp. 71-79; and Seymour, E. and N.M. Hewitt, *Talking About Leaving: Why Undergraduates Leave the Sciences* (Boulder, CO: Westview, 1998).

[7]Chubin, D.E., and J.B. Slaughter, "Last Word: Right under Our Noses," ASEE Prism, September 2002, p. 72.

dians. Yet only *two* universities produced a baccalaureate engineer from all *four* of those categories. Fifty-two of the remaining 69 universities specialized in one group only. Except for B.S. degrees awarded to women in engineering, in institutions that awarded at least 500 such degrees in 2000, the top producers of minority B.S. engineers hardly overlap with the list of major research universities.

At the doctoral level, the results are even more skewed, though the universities are recognized R&D performers.[8] In all, only 45 institutions accounted for 60 percent of all the Ph.D.'s in engineering awarded to women and underrepresented minorities, with *no* university producing at least one in all four categories. One can argue that doctoral education is market *insensitive,* decentralized by department or program and driven by faculty interests and funding, *not* by demand for new professionals in particular disciplines who possess certain skills or industry or sector orientations.

RECOMMENDATIONS

The NACME portfolio is founded on four bedrock strategies that we believe will strengthen the nation's efforts to develop human resources for science and engineering: establish and grow partnerships, build institutional capability, learn from our programs, and transfer and adapt knowledge.[9] Our recommendations build on these strategies.

In 2001, NACME's history of college scholarship support for high-potential students of color became a more seamless approach—middle school to workplace. Student readiness for college may be revealed by college entrance exams and admission decisions, but an academic profile that includes rigorous mathematics and science courses bestows a true competitive advantage.[10] While few high school students take four years of math and science, nonminority students are twice as likely as their minority peers to have taken the requisite courses. Some of this is due to choice (students opt out of challenging coursework), but some is due to a lack of course offerings, especially as provided by experienced, certified teachers using standards-based materials and technology-laced pedagogy.[11]

---

[8]Of course, the threshold is far lower (at least 50 produced, with at least 20 percent female) because the numbers produced are far more modest.

[9]As elaborated in the Board-approved "NACME Program and Planning Strategy, 2001-2002," June 2001.

[10]Adelman, C., Answers in the Toolbox: Academic Intensity, Attendance Patterns, and Bachelor Degree Attainment (Jessup, MD: Education Publication Center, 1999).

[11]See, for example, articles in the debut issue of The NACME Journal: The State of Minorities in Engineering and Technology, 2001-2002, including "A Resolution [on College Admissions Policies] of the NACME Board of Directors to Presidents of U.S. Engineering Institutions" (pp. 36-37).

NACME's student support strategy relies on, indeed must grow the capacity of, its partner institutions. Individual scholarships, which NACME awarded in the 1990s through its successful Engineering Vanguard Program, served us as a demonstration model. To impact more institutions and students, we now favor a block grant mechanism that affords the partner institution the greatest flexibility in coverage and administration of student costs.[12] In July 2002, NACME sent a letter to the presidents of 277 Accreditation Board for Engineering and Technology (ABET)-accredited engineering institutions inviting them to indicate their interest in joining in the block grant program. We were heartened to receive 110 responses with supporting documentation (a 40 percent return).

Institutions committed to excellence in the undergraduate engineering education should exhibit outcomes that exceed national enrollment, retention, and graduation trends, and provide evidence of a campus culture that values and supports student success, particularly in recruitment, admissions, pre-matriculation enrichment, and community building.[13] Memoranda of understanding that establish guidelines and expectations for performance should seal partnerships between sponsors and higher-education institutions. *NSF could adopt these under Merit Review Criterion 2 and, under the rubric of "integrating research and education," make awards accordingly.*

Institutions of higher education must be made more accountable for outcomes. *U.S. News and World Report* rankings are reputational and rely on input variables such as endowment dollars and fraction of faculty with Ph.D.'s. An assessment of how the institution improves student access, knowledge, and skills would measure the *difference* between what students bring *to* the university and what they have attained as they exit

---

[12]Individuals selected as NACME scholars receive funds based on financial need (determined, for example, as eligibility for a Pell grant). We aim to fill financial aid gaps, replace "self-help," and leverage other sources of support—primarily the nontaxable costs of tuition and books—on behalf of the student, which is consistent with the partner institution's intention to meet student need. Given the variability in tuition, fees, and books, we want to stretch scarce resources and at the same time increase the number of students that can be supported under the block award.

[13]*Recruitment* refers to institutional leadership committed to recruiting and admitting promising students from high schools in underserved communities and two-year colleges; *admissions* to published policies and procedures that goes beyond SAT/ACT scores and high school GPA in evaluating student potential to succeed in engineering; *pre-matriculation enrichment* to summer programs designed to enrich intellectual exchange and socialize students for participation in the life of the university and the engineering community); and *community-building* to a campus community and institutional support structure for faculty, students, and administrators designed to increase student engagement and grow the capability to graduate more students of color in engineering prepared for entry to graduate school and the workforce.

degree in hand. Student performance should become a metric for faculty and department performance to be judged alongside research productivity and grantsmanship.[14] *Universities could be required to show how they add value in converting raw SAT-certified talent, as well as those with two-year college experience, into skilled science-based professionals.*

As attempts to "grow our own" stall, we continue to import talent—a sacrosanct value in this democracy and especially in the history of U.S. science—and rely on ad hoc measures such as H1-B visas. This may be necessary, even as the threat of terrorism narrows our thinking, but is no substitute for a national human resource development policy. Only a strategy of investment in native talent will prepare the population to ascend to positions of leadership in and outside the academic sector. *Institutional leaders should make departments accountable for succeeding in growing the S&E workforce instead of relying on the importation of talent.*

Public sector organizations with which NACME personally collaborate— such as BEST, NAE, AAAS, and NSF—are dedicated to the proposition stated at the outset: Generation Next is the nation's demographic future. It is our collective responsibility to nurture, develop, and guide it—not only by directly supporting the financial and intellectual needs of students, but also by activating institutional allies who can bring full campus resources to bear on the development of human resources for science, engineering, and the national workforce.

---

[14]Hersh, R.H., and R. Benjamin, "Assessing the Quality of Student Learning in Undergraduate Education: An Imperative for State Policy and Practice," *CAE Policy Papers*, Council for Aid to Education, New York, NY, 2001.

Skills for a 21st Century Workforce: Can We Meet the Challenge?

Phyllis Eisen, Vice President
The Manufacturing Institute
National Association of Manufacturers (NAM)

While it appears that everything has changed in our economy over the last two years, in reality some things have not changed. Productivity remains high despite the slow economy, and the demand for skilled workers in the high-tech world of manufacturing is still very real.

In NAM's latest workforce survey of U.S. manufacturing employers, 80 percent of respondents said that they had a serious problem finding qualified candidates for the highly technical world of modern manufacturing. Over 60 percent said they could not continue the levels of productivity and satisfy customers with today's workforce. The lack of workforce readiness, math and science competencies, and ability to work in a problem-solving, critical-thinking atmosphere was hampering their ability to stay competitive. In a disturbing response, manufacturers reported for the first time that the quality of their engineering and research professionals concerned them. And always, their attitude about U.S. schools preparing a future skilled workforce was negative and despairing. This was not a pretty picture.

Certain powerful economic, social, and demographic forces underlie and contribute to the persistent skills shortages in the manufacturing workforce. These same forces will continue throughout the next two decades and beyond.

First, the relentless advance of technology is immutable. New technologies, primarily computers and the Internet, but also new materials and new processes, have infused manufacturing—from design to production, inventory management, delivery, and service. These technologies increase both productivity and product quality. In most respects, manufacturing jobs are technology jobs, and workers at all levels must have a degree of technical competency required by their equipment and processes. The bar is continuously rising. Employees at all levels must be continually re-skilled, and students in the education system and new entrants must be technologically prepared if the U.S. economy is to retain its competitive edge in a global economy.

The good news is that manufacturers have been aggressively training and educating their employees in new technology skills during the last five years. The NAM survey was clear: Less than 45 percent said they need employees with computer skills, and the need for IT workers has significantly diminished. This was a big change from 1997 when over 70 percent said they were desperate for these skills. An important note is that the business community spent over $100 billion in workforce education and training per year over the last couple of years. No small chump change.

The rub is that young people are taking less and less rigorous math and science, starting with middle school, than ever before—at the same time that math and science and technical skills are increasingly necessary for the high-tech world of manufacturing. This is further complicated by the fact that engineering and manufacturing is an honored profession in other parts of the global economy as it was in the U.S. post-World War II through the 1970s. We are hollowing out the core of what has been the mainstay of U.S. economic growth. This is a grave error. As a result, the NAM and the Department of Commerce, and now joined by the Department of Labor, created GetTech, a multimedia and education initiative to help guide young people, educators, and parents on the necessity of taking science and math to be prepared for the 21st century workforce. Please see www.gettech.org for more information on this career exploration site.

A second force is the demographic imperatives we all face. We are simply getting older. We know that the massive cohort born between 1946 and 1964—the so-called baby boomers—are moving toward retirement. They have been the most skilled generation in U.S. history. By 2020, most will have left the workforce. Their retirements will peak in 2010—only seven years away. The average skilled employee in most manufacturing firms is between 55 and 60 years of age. What is less obvious is that the native-born U.S. population has, for all practical purposes, achieved zero population growth. As a result, current and near-term growth in the labor force will come from immigrants and their children. Some of these immigrants are skilled; many are not. This is a numbers game with serious consequences unless we fill our workforce pipeline now.

Finally, global pressures continue to dominate both our business and our personal lives. The rest of the world matters as never before. Although manufacturing is still the greatest contributor to our growth and productivity and U.S. workers are still the most productive in the world, in a global economy, manufacturers face unprecedented challenges. Even small companies in rural areas might now compete with, sell to, or receive supplies from companies and markets half a world away. To continue to succeed, U.S. manufacturers must compete less on cost than on product design, productivity, quality, and responsiveness to customer needs. These competitive mandates put a high premium on the skills, morale, and commitment of workers.

The nation's fixation on four-year college attendance intensifies. An educated citizenry and workforce is a nation's greatest asset, and education is a key to personal and economic fulfillment. But manufacturers are not alone in pointing out that a fixation—among high school teachers and counselors, students, and parents—on a four-year university education immediately following high school makes young people shun other attractive options, leaving alternative career paths starved for attention and resources. While manufacturers strongly support a world-class university system (and pay heavily for research and scholarships) as well as work-based learning and internships, they also point out that many satisfying, remunerative jobs in the future will increasingly require a technical certificate or an associate degree beyond a high school diploma. These options deserve equal time from school guidance counselors and curriculum designers and equal consideration by students and parents.

A more serious skills gap looms. These technical skills, with a strong math/science background combined with problem-solving, critical-thinking, and teamwork skills are sorely needed by modern manufacturing as well as by other sectors. The challenge before us is how to close the gap. One way is to have more U.S. workers, native-born or immigrant, receive the right amount and level of training and education to enter and succeed in the workplace. Or we could bring more skilled immigrants into the U.S. or continue to take our jobs off shore. The choice is ours.

And we do not have a choice. This is a national shame, which should be at the top of all our to-do lists. Until that changes, we will continue to tinker around the edge of workforce excellence in the U.S. and our dominant place in a global economy.

The skills gap we have identified in our studies and surveys is the result of long-term forces. They will yield only to long-term solutions. Right now, the sluggish economy needs to be helped by policies that promote economic growth. Economic growth is, of course, the predicate for a skilled workforce. In addition, people displaced by the slow economy need their traditional supports by our workforce and compensation system. But while these short-term responses are necessary right now, long-term solutions must also be forthcoming if the U.S. hopes to achieve a real and lasting solution to the skills shortage.

Next, it is imperative that our young people should expect and parents should demand a rigorous, disciplined K-12 experience with world-class standards. It is also a necessity to improve our technical training systems and attract jobs—challenging careers in manufacturing with high pay and full benefits—that require an education level between high school and a four-year college.

A long-term vision of a skilled and productive technical workforce in modern manufacturing is what is required today—from the government, from the educational system, from every company and every CEO and employees making the things that make America work. The U.S. economy has always rested on the bedrock of manufacturing: This remains so despite the fact that U.S. manufacturing is in transition in a global industrial economy. The choices made today in education and public policy will affect the competitive strength of the U.S. tomorrow and well into the future.

Transforming the Academic Workplace: Socializing Underrepresented Minorities into Faculty Life

Saundra D. Johnson, Executive Director
Cecilia Lucero, Ph.D., Grants and Research Specialist
The National Consortium for Graduate Degrees
for Minorities in Engineering and Science (GEM)

INTRODUCTION

The National GEM Consortium is a nonprofit, tax-exempt corporation founded in 1976. Our mission is to enhance the value of the nation's human capital in science and engineering fields by increasing the participation of underrepresented minorities—African-Americans, Hispanic Americans, and Native Americans—in master's and Ph.D. studies in these fields. GEM accomplishes its mission by identifying and attracting exceptional students to graduate schools, matching their interests and talents with the needs of GEM member universities and company sponsors, and providing them full financial support as well as academic and professional development opportunities to help them achieve their potential as scientists and engineers.

STATEMENT OF POSITION

While it is crucial to address the need for greater diversity of scientists and engineers in industry and government, it is GEM's position that diversity in the academic workplace is an even more exigent issue that requires the attention of not only the academic community, but corporations and government agencies as well. Industry and local, state, and federal governments are stakeholders in the academic enterprise as much as universities and students themselves are. They, too, must make diversity in the professoriate a priority.

Increasing diversity among science and engineering faculties is critical because women and minority professors challenge the prevailing stereotypes that females and certain racial and ethnic groups are not suited for the more prestigious and rigorous "hard" disciplines (Eisenhart and Finkel, 1998). They serve as role models and mentors to female and minority students by affirming their presence and providing a positive outlook about school and about the future (Gregory, 1999; Smith, 1989).

Because faculty create and legitimize knowledge, they determine the quality of the scientific enterprise within academia as well as in industry and government research laboratories. As the world becomes more highly technological and wrestles with more complicated scientific challenges, the need for minority scientists and engineers among the faculty grows more urgent, especially to mentor the next generation of scientists and engineers. It is essential that the American academy, particularly research institutions, cultivate the best scientific minds and ensure full participation in the scientific/technological enterprise, not just to enhance U.S. economic prospects, but to address global health and environmental issues (Essien, 1997). "If science is to continue to prosper and move forward," the National Academy of Sciences (2000) states, "we must ensure that no source of scientific intellect is overlooked or lost" (p. vii). Given the dramatic demographic shifts in the population, "a science establishment run primarily by white males runs the danger of alienating our nation and our people from science" (National Academy of Sciences, 2000, p. 4).

Higher-education policies, therefore, must be more responsive to the problem of underrepresentation of minorities in science and engineering faculties of American colleges and universities. The current context of the academic workplace presents all stakeholders, including organizations like GEM, with a prime opportunity to shape policies that can make the science and engineering professoriate truly diverse.

THE CURRENT CONTEXT OF THE ACADEMIC WORKPLACE

During the 1990s, as the academy braced itself for the 21st century, the daunting challenges arising from the explosion of information technology, the constraining of financial resources for postsecondary education, and the burgeoning of a multicultural society led higher education researchers and practitioners to devote increasing attention to the recruitment, hiring, and career development of the "new academic generation" (Finkelstein, Seal, and Schuster, 1995). College and university departments had virtually suspended customs associated with these activities during the 1970s and 1980s, due to shortages of funding and faculty prospects (Boice, 1992). In the late 1980s, the urgency to replenish the pool of faculty who were expected to retire in the coming decades—nearly 340,000 by the year 2004 (Schuster, 1990)—revived recruitment and hiring efforts.

Ongoing research about faculty life, however, continued to find that stress, isolation, and myriad other ills were debilitating new professors (Dunn, Rouse, and Seff, 1994). Thus, because new faculty are expected to be on the "front lines" determining "on a daily basis how well the [higher education] system adapts to new realities" (Finkelstein, Seal, and Schuster, 1995, p. 1), scholars began to sharpen their focus on new faculty socialization.

Because multiculturalism has become one of the exigent realities of the academy, colleges and universities have been making concerted efforts to enlist more minorities and women into the ranks of the new academic generation. A 1996 American Council on Education (ACE) report found, for example, that the number of full-time faculty of color grew by 43.7 percent during the 1983-1993 period (Carter and Wilson, 1996). The most recent ACE report shows that minority faculty continue to make gains, their numbers having increased by more than 28 percent during the 1991-1999 period (Harvey, 2002).

Despite the progress of women and minority professors, however, the proportion of them who are employed full-time and/or awarded tenure remains abysmally low, especially relative to their white male counterparts. This is especially true in science and engineering. While women and faculty of color are concentrated in disciplines such as education, social work, and nursing, they are "practically invisible" in engineering and science (Gregory, 1999, p. xi). Furthermore, although the life sciences and civil engineering have become more feminized, sex segregation persists in physics, mathematics, computer sciences/technology, and engineering in general (Glover, 2000). Referring to science and engineering fields, Turner and Myers, Jr. (2000) indicate that "at the critical juncture at which doctorates move to faculty tenure at four-year colleges and universities, there is a [considerable] drop-off among *all* minority groups, including Asians, who are adequately represented at earlier points along the pipeline" (p. 183). Turner and Myers, Jr. (2000) analyzed National Science Foundation (NSF) data that illustrate trends from 1977 to 1991. Recent NSF (2000) statistics show that the presence of minority Ph.D. scientists and engineers in the academy has not improved much in the last decade.

The current NSF (2000) data, which describe science and engineering employment trends between 1993 and 1997, show that Asian/Pacific Islanders, non-Hispanic Blacks, Hispanics, and American Indian/Alaskan Natives represented only 18 percent of all Ph.D. scientists and engineers employed full-time in four-year colleges and universities. Minority women are especially underrepresented. A comparison of the total number of tenured and tenure-track women of color to all tenured and tenure-track Ph.D. scientists and engineers (not just their particular gender and racial/ethnic groups) underscores the reality that female faculty of color are practically invisible in academic science and engineering.[1] Black women, for example, represented nearly 0.8 percent of the total and 3.5 percent of all female academic scientists and engineers at these institutions. By comparison, white non-Hispanic males represented 64 percent of the total, and white non-Hispanic females represented 81 percent of all women and 18 percent of the total. Furthermore, Black, Latina, and Asian women were less likely than white women or men of any racial/ethnic group to be tenured. Twenty-nine percent of African-American women, 29 percent of Latina women, and 17 percent of Asian women had tenure in 1997, compared to 38 percent of white women, 63 percent of white men, and between 43 and 53 percent of Latino, Black, and Asian men (NSF, 2000). This "ghettoization"[2] limits the presence of faculty of color in the higher education system; worse still, it hinders individual human potential.

THE IMPORTANCE OF FACULTY SOCIALIZATION FOR UNDERREPRESENTED MINORITIES

Higher-education researchers have considered various explanations for the underrepresentation of minorities among college and university faculties:

• The pipeline issue—the lack of qualified minority candidates for tenure-track appointments
• Market forces—low faculty salaries and the lure of lucrative industry positions that compel minorities to choose careers outside of academia
• The "chilly climate" factor—racial, ethnic, and gender bias; isolation and an unsupportive work environment; lack of information about tenure and promotion; language or other communication barriers; lack of mentors and lack of support from superiors
• The turnover problem–the failure to promote and retain minority faculty despite successful recruitment of excellent candidates. Turnover is often related to the absence of adequate mentorship, the ambiguity of the tenure and promotion process, and other institutional circumstances that

---

[1]Asian/Pacific Islander, Black non-Hispanic, and Hispanic women account for nearly 2 percent of all tenured, and 6 percent of all tenure-track, scientists and engineers at four-year colleges and universities. Black women are 0.4 percent of all tenured and 1.6 percent of all tenure-track science and engineering faculty. There is a preponderance of minority female Ph.D. scientists and engineers in non-tenure-track positions or in institutions with no tenure system for their position (NSF, 2000).

[2]Reskin and Roos (1990) use this term to refer to gender segregation, but it may also apply to minority faculty, who, like female academics, are concentrated in lower-ranked positions and shoulder a disproportionate amount of service and committee work.

neglect minority faculty development (e.g., "cultural taxation" of minority junior faculty who are expected to serve on minority-serving committees and advise minority students in addition to fulfilling their other teaching and research responsibilities) (Midwest Higher Education Report, 1995).

Just as universities, government agencies, corporate and private foundations, and various other educational associations have done, GEM has addressed—and continues to address—the pipeline issue through its graduate fellowship programs. Diversity initiatives, however, must consider more than just the numerical representation of various racial, ethnic, and gender groups. They must also consider the psychological climate (the perceptions and attitudes between and among groups) and the behavioral climate that is characterized by intergroup relations (Hurtado and Dey, 1997).

Policies must be directed toward eliminating the "chilly climate" and solving the problem of turnover in order to enrich the lives of minority faculty, and to make academic careers attractive to minority graduate students. These may be accomplished through structured opportunities for faculty socialization—"learning the ropes," adoption of or identification with the behaviors, values, beliefs, and attitudes of the academic profession—which begin in graduate school.

Mentoring is an essential component of faculty socialization. Thus, for many years now, GEM has also provided mentorship training for graduate students' faculty advisers, company internship supervisors, and other mentors. More recently, GEM's programming has evolved to address more comprehensively the factors that create a "chilly climate" and contribute to turnover of minority science and engineering faculty. For example, GEM's Faculty Bridge Seminar, a weeklong workshop designed to inform graduate students about faculty careers and to socialize novice professors into their roles and responsibilities, helps to demystify the processes of developing a research agenda, publishing one's scholarship, preparing a tenure portfolio, etc.

RECOMMENDATIONS FOR POLICY

Developing policies and implementing change to create a multicultural campus is a complex undertaking within colleges and universities. We believe, therefore, that government, industry, and other stakeholders must collaborate with campus communities to develop policies that encourage more innovative, more creative faculty socialization that fulfills the needs of minority academic scientists and engineers.

In a timely *Change* magazine article that reconsiders the purposes and future of doctoral education, Nyquist (2002) identifies various groups who have a stake in graduate education, what their contributions are or might be in re-envisioning the Ph.D., and what issues they will navigate. Using Nyquist's summary as a guideline, we outline the following recommendations to various stakeholders as possible areas of policymaking. While these recommendations are merely a sketch of the possibilities, we offer them in order to begin the process of change.

- *To university leaders, college deans, department chairs, and others involved in preparing the "new academic generation"*—policies should be directed at investing more time and energy in the recruitment and retention of underrepresented minorities for graduate science and engineering studies. This involves thoughtful design of the doctoral education experience, more meaningful mentoring, more rewards for mentoring, and making expectations and requirements (e.g., of tenure and promotion) explicit. Issues such as opportunity costs, time-to-degree, family responsibilities, etc., should be explicitly addressed. Policies should also encourage critical self-examination of how departmental cultures hinder or help the socialization of minority graduate students and novice professors into faculty life (e.g., how professional practices, interactions among colleagues, etc., may be gendered or racialized).

- *To government agencies, business and industry foundations, and others who fund doctoral education*—policies should be directed at increasing outreach to minority communities and their participation in doctoral education; redirecting monies toward research and practice associated with faculty socialization (e.g., fund projects like the highly successful Preparing Future Faculty program); and helping universities to enhance faculty reward structures to encourage senior colleagues to mentor novice professors.

- *To colleges and universities, government agencies, nonprofit organizations, and business and industry*—policies should encourage communication about teaching and research as exciting and rewarding career options. The idea that minority Ph.D.'s have to make a choice between low-wage faculty appointments and lucrative industry careers should be disabused.

- *To professional societies, educational associations, and others who influence doctoral education*—policies should be directed at encouraging collaboration among stakeholders to establish programming for faculty socialization, and maintaining conversations about career options for Ph.D.'s, especially in academia. Professional societies, educational associations, and organizations like GEM should highlight the personal and professional benefits that a faculty career presents to minority scientists and engineers.

- *Finally, to graduate students, working professionals, and other prospective graduate students who aspire to the Ph.D.*—their own personal policies should be directed at ownership of their graduate school and subsequent career experiences. This requires taking the initiative to ask questions, identifying mentors and role models with whom they can develop productive relationships, and making sure they are aware of the full spectrum of careers (and the required roles and responsibilities) that is at hand once they earn their doctorate.

REFERENCES

Boice, R. (1992). *The New Faculty Member*. San Francisco: Jossey-Bass.

Carter, D. and Wilson, R. (1996). *Minorities in Higher Education 1995-1996: Fourteenth Annual Status Report*. Washington, DC: American Council on Education.

Dunn, D., Rouse, L., and Seff, M. (1994). "New Faculty Socialization in the Academic Workplace." In J.C. Smart (ed.), *Higher Education: Handbook of Theory and Research, Vol. X* (pp. 374-416). Bronx, NY: Agathon Press.

Eisenhart, M., and Finkel, E. (1998). *Women's Science: Learning and Succeeding from the Margins*. Chicago: University of Chicago Press.

Essien, F. (1997). "Black Women in the Sciences: Challenges along the Pipeline and in the Academy. In L. Benjamin (ed.), *Black Women in the Academy: Promises and Perils* (pp. 91-102). Gainesville, FL: University of Florida Press.

Finkelstein, M., Seal, R., and Schuster, J. (1995). *The American Faculty in Transition*. Paper prepared for the National Center for Education Statistics, NSOPF93, Washington, DC.

Glover, J. (2000). *Women and Scientific Employment*. New York: St. Martin's Press; London: Macmillan.

Gregory, S. (1999). *Black Women in the Academy: The Secrets to Success and Achievement*. Rev. ed. Lanham, MD: University Press of America.

Harvey, W.B. (2002). *Minorities in Higher Education 2001-2002: Nineteenth Annual Status Report*. Washington, DC: American Council on Education.

Hurtado, S., and Dey, E. (1997). "Achieving the Goals of Multiculturalism and Diversity." In M. Peterson, D. Dill, L. Mets, and Associates (eds.), *Planning and Management for a Changing Environment* (pp. 405-431). San Francisco: Jossey-Bass.

Midwest Higher Education Report. (1995). *MHEC Minority Faculty Development Project Final Report*. Minneapolis: Midwestern Higher Education Commission.

National Academy of Sciences. (2000). *Who Will Do the Science of the Future?* Washington, DC: National Academy Press.

National Science Foundation. (2000). *Women, Minorities, and Persons with Disabilities in Science and Engineering: 2000*. Arlington, VA (NSF 00-327).

Nyquist, J. (2002, November-December). "The Ph.D.: A Tapestry of Change for the 21st Century." *Change*, 34(6): 13-20.

Reskin, B., and Roos, P. (1990). *Job Queues, Gender Queues*. Philadelphia: Temple University Press.

Schuster, J. (1990). "Faculty Issues in the 1990s: New Realities, New Opportunities." In L.W. Jones and F.A. Nowotny (eds.), *An Agenda for the New Decade*. New Directions for Higher Education, no. 70. San Francisco: Jossey-Bass.

Smith, D. (1989). *The Challenge of Diversity: Involvement or Alienation in the Academy*. ASHE-ERIC Higher Education Report no. 5. Washington, DC: George Washington University School of Education and Human Development.

Turner, C., and Myers, S., Jr. (2000). *Faculty of Color in Academe: Bittersweet Success*. Needham Heights, MA: Allyn and Bacon.

Mathematics as a Foundation for a Productive Science and Engineering Workforce

Johnny W. Lott, President
National Council of Teachers of Mathematics

With an increasingly competitive global marketplace and changing demographics of the workforce, there is understandable concern for our country's future productivity and our ability to keep pace. This concern has sometimes been translated as a need for functional literacy for all students. Functional literacy is in some respects too simple a term for a significant challenge posed to our educational system and a very real concern for the populace of tomorrow.

Two primary components of functional literacy are reading and mathematics. Just as reading is fundamental for a sound education and success in any academic or career path, mathematics is the foundation for achievement in science and engineering. The sustained vitality of our scientific workforce and the education of future workers are dependent upon the mathematics education of today's students and the quality of their teachers.

Thus, any workforce strategy must rest on a solid foundation of quality K-12 instruction in mathematics and science. K-12 students must have the light of creativity and imagination sparked and nurtured in their formative years. Hence, K-12 math and science education must be a priority for the National Academies, the government, and the American people. As a priority, the National Academies, the National Science Foundation, the Department of Education, and all other interested parties must support the continual evolution of the mathematics curriculum in schools. Just as the needs of the workforce are changing, so must the curriculum, teaching strategies, and tools needed to deliver instruction in the schools.

A key to quality K-12 education is a highly knowledgeable and enthusiastic teaching force. In the 1998 report, *Every Child Mathematically Proficient: An Action Plan of the Learning First Alliance*, we find, "All students of mathematics should be taught by teachers who have been well prepared in the content of mathematics and the techniques of teaching mathematics" (p. 5). Thus a high priority integral to the future workforce must be the professional development and pre-service training of all teachers of mathematics, especially those teaching in grades K-6. As a nation, we must continue to push both for more mathematics to complement the pedagogy of these teachers and for more mathematically capable students to become teachers. If this means recommending different certification programs for the nation, then let us work together to determine what those programs must be.

Teacher quality should be a concern for all of us. It is a special concern of the National Council of Teachers of Mathematics, an organization of nearly 100,000 members committed to mathematics education of the highest quality for all students. The Council's members include both classroom teachers from kindergarten through grade 12 and teacher educators and researchers in academia, with the majority being teachers. The mix with teachers and academia has enriched the Council's work, including the development of its *Principles and Standards for School Mathematics*, which describes a vision of mathematics from pre-kindergarten through grade 12. Teaching mathematics with understanding is the basic tenet of the Council and it is a philosophy that infuses all we do, from the professional development institutes we offer teachers to the range of publications and other forms of professional development we provide classroom teachers. All classroom and university teachers need both a solid foundation in mathematical content and a broad understanding of how students learn mathematics.

TEACHER PREPARATION AND SUPPORT

The growing public discourse about new paths for teachers to enter the profession seems to have engendered a growing assumption that content knowledge alone is enough for one to be a teacher. Or, that if one simply has enough content knowledge, quality teaching will follow naturally. For mathematics teachers, deep understanding of *how* one knows and learns mathematics is vitally important. And how one comes to know mathematics is a vital element in developing the mathematical learning of students. The certification of new teachers through either traditional means or alternative routes must attend to the critical elements: content and pedagogy.

Regardless of the method of certification, it is critical to the success of our education system that classroom teachers are adequately prepared for the classroom, and then it is equally critical that teachers are adequately supported once they are in the classrooms. School systems should develop structured induction programs that include mentoring. University teacher-preparation programs should partner with school districts in induction programs by participating in the training of mentors, continuing communication with their graduates, and serving as a resource. Mentor teachers should be provided with significant and consistent training and be given additional remuneration or release time for their services. Schools should set aside time specifically for the collaborative efforts of the beginning teacher and the mentor. And finally, district and school administrators should recognize the added demands on beginning teachers and their mentors and should be sensitive in making teaching assignments.

Teachers' needs do not end when they have completed their induction programs. Once a part of the workforce, they should have professional development opportunities provided by districts and universities that include a strong focus on content knowledge, pedagogical knowledge, and a knowledge of *Principles and Standards for School Mathematics* and its applications to the classroom.

DOCTORAL PROGRAMS

A key to training and certifying teachers is high-quality faculty at the college and university level. The worsening shortage crisis at this level matches the problems of the entire science and engineering workforce. Thus the recruiting, training, and retention of these professionals must be one of the major initiatives of an overall program.

A significant percentage of mathematics doctoral students will become postsecondary faculty. Many have no training for teaching positions; yet many will become teacher educators. We should ensure that all those who are completing doctoral degrees, and not in a research or business track, take some pedagogy coursework to be prepared to be the teacher educators of the future. Because our colleges and universities must supply our K-12 classrooms with highly qualified teachers in every sense of the word, identifying core elements of doctoral programs in the United States that will prepare these postsecondary educators is a challenging and evolving process. As this development continues and as research helps us learn more about effective practices in the preparation of graduates, the more the profession of mathematics education will ultimately benefit. This in turn will benefit our students, and the improved education of today's students will provide us with a better workforce tomorrow.

As a discipline that is vital to the future scientific and engineering workforce, doctoral programs in mathematics education should be included in the National Academy of Sciences doctoral programs review. This is not a simple matter because mathematics education doctoral programs cut across disciplines, but it is a necessary step for future quality and productivity.

The issues of the science and engineering workforce affect us as individuals and strike at the heart of our nation's leadership position in the world. At a time of uncertainty and anxiety, we owe it to our country, its future, and future generations to make a thoughtfully considered, concerted commitment to better prepare for a tomorrow we can only imagine. Making an increased commitment to education and mathematics education is a basic and fundamental investment in revitalizing the science and engineering workforce of tomorrow. We must focus attention at the start of the education pipeline, K-12 mathematics education, but we must not fail to consider the other end of the pipeline, teacher educators, if we are to achieve the desired result: more scientists and engineers and a more knowledgeable and productive workforce in the future.

The mission of the National Council of Teachers of Mathematics is to provide the vision and leadership necessary to ensure a mathematics education of the highest quality for all students. With nearly 100,000 members and more than 250 affiliates, NCTM is the world's largest organization dedicated to improving mathematics education in grades pre-kindergarten through grade 12. The Council's Principles and Standards for School Mathematics are guidelines for excellence in mathematics education and issue a call for all students to engage in more challenging mathematics. NCTM is dedicated to ongoing dialogue and constructive discussion with all stakeholders about what is best for our nation's students.

Utilization of African-American Physicists in the Science and Engineering Workforce

Keith H. Jackson, President
Lawrence Norris, Treasurer
National Society of Black Physicists (NSBP)

Throughout the 1990s the National Society of Black Physicists (NSBP) had been concerned about the lack of utilization of African-American physicists in national laboratories funded by the Department of Energy (DOE). In the context of this paper, utilization refers to the number of Ph.D.-level African-Americans with career-level appointments, on the scientific research staff of the laboratory. The NSBP had collected some preliminary data but in 1999 approached the Committee on Minorities (COM) in Physics of the American Physical Society (APS) for additional assistance. COM responded favorably to our request and formally took up the topic and sought to update and confirm the data. COM enlisted and received the full support of the NSBP.

The data-gathering process was basic and straightforward. First, we simply telephoned the laboratories with a request for data. We also called the DOE field offices that oversee the labs, thinking they might have the data as well. We encountered insurmountable bureaucratic difficulties with both the laboratories and the field offices. We discovered that there is a huge chasm between the contractors and the federal government employees. In the end our study was greatly helped by the American Physical Society, which expended much personal and professional capital by writing personally to the lab directors. To their credit the laboratory directors mobilized their respective staffs and provided the data we requested in an intelligible form.

Our data show that, in general, African-American Ph.D. physicists represent less than 1 percent of the Ph.D. physicists employed at the DOE laboratories. By comparison, African-Americans make up nearly 2 percent of

TABLE 1 Number of African-American Ph.D. Level Physicists
Employed in Career Positions at DOE-Funded National Laboratories

DOE-Funded Laboratory	Total Number Ph.D. Physicists on Staff	Total Number African-American Physicists	Percent of African-American Physicists
Argonne	223	0	0.0
Brookhaven	335	1	0.3
Fermilab	472	1	0.2
Idaho National Engineering	27	0	0.0
Jefferson	79	0	0.0
Lawrence Berkeley	187	2	1.1
Lawrence Livermore	642	5	0.8
Los Alamos	686	2	0.3
Oak Ridge	182	0	0.0
Pacific Northwest	66	0	0.0
Princeton Plasma Physics	94	0	0.0
Sandia	264	0	0.0
Stanford Linear Accelerator	115	0	0.0
Totals	**3372**	**11**	**0.3**

Note: This table does not include those with postdoctoral appointments. For comparison, African-Americans receive 2.5 percent of Ph.D.'s awarded to U.S. citizens in physics each year.[1]

the physics faculties across the United States. These data include African-American faculty members at Historically Black Colleges and Universities (HBCUs).

These are the numbers, but what do they mean? On their face it appears that the laboratories are not nearly as successful as academia in recruiting African-American scientists. Let me offer just a few thoughts as to reasons:

- The nature of research and graduate training, the whole culture of what makes a successful career, is biased toward getting a faculty position. We want to be *Professor* Brilliant, instead of *Staff Scientist* Brilliant.
- Many African-American physicists have a commitment to the idea of teaching at an HBCU. While this is undoubtedly true, it is also the case that the HBCU might be the only opportunity for an African-American pursuing an academic career.

---

[1]Patrick J. Mulvey and Starr Nicholson, Enrollments and Degrees Report, AIP Pub. # R-151.38 (College Park, MD: American Institute of Physics, 2002), pp. 7-8.

- But the bottom line is that the laboratories have shown little if any enthusiasm in recruiting domestic African-American scientific talent from HBCUs, or from majority institutions for that matter.

It is important that we understand the relationship between the national laboratories and the universities, which are responsible for the day-to-day management operations. DOE laboratories are government- owned but contractor operated (GOCO) or federally funded research and development centers (FFRDC). Thus the utilization of African-American physicists at the national laboratories is merely a reflection of their utilization on the contracting university campus. The human resources function at the laboratory mirrors that of the university:

- Many contractor university scientists have joint appointments with the laboratory.
- The contract between the laboratory and the university recognizes the "special relationship" between the university and the laboratory.
- The human resources function at the laboratory mirrors that of the university regarding scientific appointments.

As a result of the above, personnel from established collaborations with university researchers are the first to learn of, and the first to benefit from, postdoc and staff scientist positions at the laboratories. Those not from that closed population have much less chance of obtaining a position. In other words, the institutional structure reinforces established "old boys' networks" that have not historically—and still do not—utilize African-American physicists, and by extension African-American scientific talent in general.

As evidence to support our position, NSBP has compiled a portfolio of cases demonstrative of what can happen to an African-American job applicant at our national laboratories. Some of these cases are described here:

One of our young members who completed a Ph.D. in computational physics at an HBCU applied for a postdoctoral position at a national laboratory. A secretary, upon seeing the Ph.D. institution, dismissed his application out of hand. NSBP became involved, but, after numerous discussions, was unable to have the applicant considered for an interview.

In another case, a recent Ph.D. from one of the top five physics departments in the United States was similarly rebuffed when he applied for a career-level position. Of interest here was that the applicant's experience and expertise were an excellent match for the posted job requirements. In fact, the applicant had some value-added skills. He was not granted the courtesy of an interview. When a member of NSBP spoke on the candidate's behalf, the scientist responsible for hiring stated that he had

"200 applicants for this staff position, some with over seven years of postdoctoral experience." It is well known that almost any scientific job posting results in a flood of résumés; most are from international applicants looking for positions so they can remain in or come to the United States. This example puts to rest the idea that affirmative action gives an African-American job candidate some preference in the scientific job market. His or her application is evaluated on the same basis as the 200 candidates that applied for the position. In the end the laboratory considered offering our applicant a postdoc, a position that was several steps below the candidate's skills and accomplishments.

Also, in the summer of 2000, one of our most senior and distinguished members ran into exceptionally severe difficulties just trying to obtain a summer visiting appointment at one of the national laboratories. His application was treated in a manner inappropriate for a physicist with his credentials. NSBP speculates that it was because he was from an HBCU, though, ironically, he once worked at one of the laboratories where he completed what is considered outstanding research.

These types of incidents are not isolated to the national laboratories. They also occur at the managing universities. In March 2001, Stanford University hosted the annual meeting of the NSBP and the National Conference of Black Physics Students. Stanford itself has graduated more African-American Ph.D.'s in physics than any other university, and the university made a special effort to host a reunion of all its African-American physics graduates at this event. Ironically, although members of the Stanford faculty spent a lot of time at the conference talking about all of the opportunities for a physics career, they apparently initiated no discussions of employment possibilities with some of our junior members nearing the end of their graduate programs or postdoc appointments. No invitations to return to Stanford to give a seminar or colloquia were extended. In fact, Stanford has not aggressively recruited its own graduates, who they cannot credibly say are not sufficiently trained for faculty positions.

Before moving to our proposed solutions and actions, we ask a rhetorical but important question: What should be the role of the DOE national laboratories in terms of training and developing American human scientific talent? At the April 2001 APS meeting, Dr. Millie Dresselhaus (who had just finished a term as director of the DOE Office of Science, which manages and directs the DOE scientific research effort) mentioned that when DOE tries to do a major workforce development program they are told by either Congress or the Office of Management and Budget (OMB) that that is not their mandate. But there are three important reasons why the DOE laboratories should have diversity, workforce utilization, and science education as some of their fundamental mandates:

- There is a major U.S. taxpayer investment in the laboratories, and yet a significant fraction of the taxpaying public is not being afforded the opportunity for employment at the laboratories.
- The laboratories are a fundamental part of the informal scientific apprentice system. A letter of recommendation from a scientist at a DOE laboratory can make the difference between acceptance or rejection for a student applying to graduate school. These recommendations are particularly important for those who do not come from research-intensive institutions.
- These institutions, by their research, define the critical scientific skills and hence the job opportunities of the future. Every attempt should be made to ensure that citizens of the United States can take advantage of their investment.

We turn finally to proposed solutions and actions that should be taken to address the utilization problem at the national laboratories. First, the laboratories should become intimately involved with the NSBP, which has been in existence for over 26 years. NSBP generally meets in February or March. These meetings are attended by serious scientists with whom the staff of national laboratories can form collaborations, partnerships, and student exchanges. Also in attendance are many students looking for opportunities and mentorship. The laboratories could also benefit from a site visit by a team composed of members of COM and NSBP to review the recruitment and hiring practices, workplace environment and equity, and quality of scientific outreach activities of these DOE laboratories. NSBP members possess considerable scientific expertise and are well informed about science resources within minority communities.

Second, the laboratories should aggressively seek out and form research partnerships with faculty at HBCUs, Hispanic Serving Institutions (HSIs), and tribal colleges. American Institute of Physics (AIP) statistics confirm that most African-American students who earn a baccalaureate degree do so at an HBCU, and most African-American physics professors teach at HBCUs. Research partnerships between research-intensive institutions and HBCUs have historically paid great dividends in increasing the number of minority Ph.D. physicists. Each DOE lab, if not each division at each lab, should have a set of rich, active, vibrant collaborations with HBCUs, HSIs, and tribal colleges that include staff exchanges, i.e., sending lab personnel to the schools as visiting professors, and inviting professors to the laboratories as guest scientists, along with their students as fellows. Importantly, each laboratory has a Laboratory Directed Research and Development Fund (LDRD), i.e., funds under the control of the lab director meant to achieve lab-wide goals or pursue hot research projects that could be used to finance these initiatives.

The laboratories should ensure that minorities participate on advisory committees and on annual divisional review committees at all levels. This is particularly true of laboratory divisions that operate publicly financed national user facilities. Diversity of the division staff and facility users should also be a topic to be reviewed.

On this point, and upon the announcement of this year's Nobel Prizes, there is an important observation to be made. By ignoring interactions with HBCUs, as many of the lab divisions do, the laboratories are in effect enforcing a form of scientific apartheid. Nobel laureates (and I have actually worked with two) cite as key to their success the fact that they have always been connected with good people and good facilities. To have a career marked with tremendous research success, participation in overall policy and funding direction of the science and engineering enterprise, and large program management, somehow one must be connected to mainstream researchers. NSBP believes the DOE national laboratories are one entry ramp for African-Americans to enter the mainstream research community.

Given the recalcitrance and intransigence of the laboratories in working with HBCUs, the NSBP recommends that Congress require 10 percent of the operating budget of the DOE laboratories be used to establish scientific relationships with HBCUs, HSIs, and tribal colleges, with the main rationale being that DOE should play a role in American science training.

Third, the laboratories should make sure that bench scientists are given the responsibility of hiring and program direction to increase minority participation. Too often too much is left to the human resources or lab diversity officer. In our survey and follow-on research we have found that this is a fundamental disconnect at the laboratories. Diversity officers often are not scientists and have few contacts amongst working scientists. NSBP has found that most of their job content involves protecting the laboratory from lawsuits from current employees, not the recruitment of future employees.

In fact, we found that relegating minority concerns to a diversity officer is seriously hindering diversity efforts. The amount of paperwork and FTE resources devoted to processing this paper gives only an illusion of effort in recruiting and diversity workforce development. The anecdotal evidence suggests many searches are not truly open, and often a candidate is identified before the job is posted. This pre-identified candidate is drawn from the small pool of students and fellows of established collaborators; i.e., outside the pools of minority researchers. This situation needs to be remedied; it has a deleterious effect on diversity efforts. Moreover, the resources applied to generating diversity reports and plans could be better applied to establishing the true personal connections necessary to embrace the minority community, as recommended in the preceding text.

Many senior laboratory personnel somehow think that K-12 science outreach efforts will solve the problem. The laboratories will bring in kids for a day of show and tell, but will not invite serious African-American scientists to serve on review panels and policy boards. Furthermore, the laboratories are not committed to programs to improve the scientific skill sets of not only professors and students from HBCU's, HSI's, or tribal colleges, but of all U.S. students of science. There is no intensive program to train undergraduates and graduate students in the use of neutron sources and synchrotron light sources for scientific research, yet the DOE is investing a large portion of the budget of the Office of Science in the construction and operation of these facilities.

Finally, we assert steadfastly that the Congress must exercise some oversight. It was stated previously that we endured a tremendous amount of frustration in getting data from the laboratories and the DOE field offices. We were sent data that were cryptic, unintelligible (e.g., with undefined acronyms), and in some cases so obviously outdated that they constituted a bad faith effort if not absolute fraud. There is little external motivation for the contractors, e.g., University of California, University of Chicago, University of Tennessee, to comply with outside requests for these data. Their contract to run the laboratories is not at risk over diversity issues. While the management contracts require a *diversity plan*, there are few, if any, sanctions for failure to adhere to the plan. Congress must ensure that diversity performance in the crucial regard is strongly and explicitly stated in the management contracts, and oversee that performance as only Congress can.

Now is the time for bold action. Enough data gathering, audits, and assessments have been done to diagnose the problems. DOE, the contractors, and the scientists that manage and direct the laboratories know what the numbers are, and they are unsatisfactory. We are dealing with very small numbers that perhaps defy rigorous statistical analysis and control grouping, but that does not excuse the singular lack of improvement in the numbers. It is possible for the situation to change—but only if the motivation for change is high. NSBP calls for bold congressional action because the time for commissions, reports, diversity plans, and statements is past. The Congress ultimately is the board of trustees for the laboratories, and the ball is firmly in its court.

Building a Federal Civil Service for the 21st Century: The Challenge of Attracting Great Talent to Government Service

Joan Timoney, Vice President for Programs
Partnership for Public Service (PPS)

THE MISSION OF THE PARTNERSHIP FOR PUBLIC SERVICE: ENSURING A STRONG CIVIL SERVICE

The Partnership for Public Service is a new nonpartisan, nonprofit organization dedicated to recruiting and retaining excellence in the federal civil service. Through an aggressive campaign of agency reform, legislative advocacy, focused research, and educational efforts, the Partnership encourages talented people to choose federal service for some or all of their careers and works with the government to help retain high-achieving federal employees.

The mission of the Partnership is to help ensure that the federal government has the workforce it needs to meet the economic, social, and security demands of the 21st century. There are a number of areas of concern. High among them is the challenge of recruiting and retaining a highly skilled technical and scientific workforce.

The Partnership looks forward to working with the members and supporters of the Government-University-Industry Research Roundtable (GUIRR) to encourage young scientists and engineers to consider federal service. We appreciate that a critical first step is to encourage more young people to pursue careers in engineering and science so the country has the talent pool required to meet its public- and private-sector needs. One way the Partnership can help is by working with GUIRR and others to educate young students about the important and often exciting work that is carried out each day by scientists and engineers working for the federal government. Exposing students to the work, and to the committed federal employees engaged in it, may have the dual benefit of drawing more students to the profession and encouraging some number of them to embrace a public service that sorely needs their skills.

THE NEED FOR ACTION

The need for the federal government to recruit and retain talented workers is ever more urgent as many of its most experienced workers prepare for retirement. In the next five years, over 50 percent of the federal workforce may qualify for retirement and 70 percent of its senior managers will reach retirement age.

It is a graying workforce among federal scientists and engineers as well. According to data from the U.S. Office of Personnel Management, nearly 40 percent of the physical scientists and 30 percent of the biological scientists in cabinet-level agencies are over the age of 50. Among federal engineers, 32 percent of those working in the cabinet agencies are over 50.

The urgency of the issue at just one agency was brought home recently by National Aeronautics and Space Administration (NASA) director Sean O'Keefe who said earlier this year in testimony before the Congress, "In an agency where the expertise is not as deep as we would like it to be, even a few retirements can be critical. Everywhere I go across the NASA Centers, I hear the same story: we're only one deep; we can't afford to lose that skill."

KEY FINDINGS ON RECRUITMENT AND RETENTION BARRIERS

As it seeks to replace its most experienced employees, the federal government is entering a recruitment marketplace that even in today's economy is characterized by keen competition for top talent in most professions. That competition will only intensify as the U.S. labor force continues to shrink. And there are additional factors that often add up to a competitive disadvantage for the federal government.

TROUBLING ATTITUDES TOWARD FEDERAL EMPLOYMENT

The government has the burden of promoting its opportunities to a public that considers the private and nonprofit sectors to be much more attractive employers. A poll conducted by the Partnership last year about attitudes toward federal employment found the following:

• By 40 percent to 9 percent, college-educated Americans believe the private sector offers more interesting and challenging work.

- By 62 percent to 5 percent, the private sector is seen as better rewarding outstanding performance; 60 percent of those polled believe the private sector does a better job of allowing employees to take initiative.
- Among those who consider "contributing to society and making a difference," the nonprofit sector won out over government as the employer of choice by a startling 52 percent to 10 percent.

Added to these perception problems is the issue of compensation. While salary is not always the determining factor in career choice, for certain professions the disparity between public- and private-sector salaries can spell too much sacrifice to talented young job seekers. This is particularly true for younger Americans who graduate with significant student loan debt.

A LACK OF INFORMATION ABOUT FEDERAL OPPORTUNITIES

The perceptions about federal employment are set against a backdrop of a general lack of information about the civil service and the opportunities that abound across government. Many college-educated Americans know very little about the civil service or the varied work of federal employees. Only 29 percent of those the Partnership polled felt well informed about federal government opportunities; a mere 20 percent could recall seeing a federal recruiter on their campus.

The good news is that these findings should improve over time as many federal agencies are working hard to reconnect with college campuses and becoming more sophisticated in their education and recruitment campaigns. The more information college-educated Americans receive about the civil service, and the more effective the communications, the greater the chances that the unfounded perceptions about federal employment can be changed.

BROKEN HIRING PROCESS

The sometimes impenetrable federal hiring process remains a real barrier to recruitment. In a study conducted by the Brookings Institution last year, federal employees themselves, by very large percentages, described the process as too slow, too confusing, and unfair. And these are people who are reasonably familiar with the system. For outsiders, the process can be incomprehensible. Talented people with multiple options are unlikely to make the effort or wait the six months that it can sometimes take to hear back from an agency. The director of the Office of Personnel Management has taken this issue head on and there are proposals pending before Congress that could help. Some agencies have also made great strides and can serve as a model for others. But there is still a great deal of work to be done across government to make the federal hiring process a 21st century system.

UNDERUTILIZATION OF INTERN PROGRAMS: A MISSED RECRUITMENT OPPORTUNITY

Internships have long been recognized as a particularly valuable recruitment tool. According to a 2001 Employer Survey conducted by the National Association of Colleges and Employers, internships were rated as the most effective means of bringing in new talent, particularly technical talent. Other studies have shown that recruits who were originally interns tend to stay with their employer longer than their counterparts hired off the street. And interns who have enjoyable and productive experiences are walking advertisements for their employers—a boost the federal government clearly needs on campuses.

Unfortunately, as the Partnership found in its research on internship opportunities in the federal government, internships represent a missed recruitment opportunity for many agencies. Despite the anticipated need for new talent, there has been almost no growth in the government's career-oriented Student Career Experience Program in the last seven years. Further, the federal government falls significantly behind the private sector in the percentage of interns it converts to employees. The federal government converted only 12 percent of its career-oriented interns, while the private sector typically converts 36 percent of its program participants.

We also found that, over the past five years, seven agencies account for approximately 70 percent of federal interns in the career-oriented program. Therefore, there is a great deal more that could be done across government to expose younger Americans to the rewards of public service through internships.

And much more could be done to better inform students about the opportunities that do exist. Currently, there is no central source of information on internship opportunities across government. For younger Americans who know very little about the civil service, it is a high hurdle to search agency by agency for opportunities.

RECOMMENDATIONS

1. Organizations that share a concern about the availability of skilled scientists and engineers to meet public- and private-sector needs in the new century should work together to help educate the Congress about

the issues and to support funding for scholarships and other incentives to encourage students to embrace those careers.

2. Federal agencies, schools, and other interested organizations should work together to better inform young people about opportunities that exist for scientists and engineers in the civil service. By more aggressively publicizing the exciting, often state-of-the-art, work being done in federal laboratories and research centers across the country, agencies can counter erroneous perceptions about the federal work environment. This education and outreach effort should start at least at the high school level. University students must also be given the tools they need to pursue federal employment opportunities once they are made aware of them. The Partnership can be of assistance through its campus-based initiative A Call to Serve: Leaders in Education Allied for Public Service. This is a joint initiative of the Partnership and the U.S. Office of Personnel Management. Launched last April, the network has grown to over 380 schools and 58 federal agencies that have agreed to work together to educate students about the importance of a strong civil service and the opportunities to serve.

3. Federal agencies should also make student employment programs part of their strategic workforce planning and use them as a critical tool for building the talent pool for future hires. The agencies, the Office of Personnel Management, and other organizations providing student employment and internship opportunities should work together to improve the visibility and quality of the information made available to students about those opportunities.

4. Federal offices around the country should begin to work more closely with their local high schools to afford young students the opportunity to experience firsthand the important and varied work of the civil service. This is particularly important in the hard-to-recruit professions such as science and engineering where there is a need to interest many more young people in these careers and in public service.

5. Agencies should make it a priority to ask for funding to implement the various recruitment and retention incentives that will help attract top talent to the federal service, and Congress should provide those funds. This includes funding scholarship for service programs, loan repayment assistance programs, recruitment and retention bonus programs, and continuing education programs.

6. Federal agencies must make much better use of existing tools and authorities to improve the federal hiring and selection process. And where legislative changes are required, Congress, the agencies, and other interested organizations should work together to bring about needed reforms.

Position Statement on the U.S. Science and Engineering Workforce

Jeanne L. Narum, **Director**
Project Kaleidoscope (PKAL)

INTRODUCTION

From experience with institutions active within Project Kaleidoscope,[1] we offer recommendations that reflect our conviction that "doing science" in a research-rich environment is a powerfully attractive mechanism to motivate students to persist in the study and practice of science, technology, engineering, and mathematics (STEM) fields. Doing science as scientists do science—puzzling out a problem, exploring solutions, collaborating with colleagues, linking to the work of others, communicating results—is a transforming experience. It is a critical first step in drawing students into science and technology fields. Thus expanding and enhancing research opportunities for students is the logical point from which to address the concerns of this summit.

We are also convinced that research experiences within and beyond the campus must be embedded in the total academic experience for each student, not included as an extra or an add-on. This becomes a complicating factor in a national effort to attract more students into S&T careers. It requires a combination of (1) faculty with the right expertise and commitment, (2) an academic program designed to engage students as scientists from their first day

---

[1]Project Kaleidoscope (PKAL) is an informal national alliance involved in the growing effort to strengthen undergraduate programs in science, technology, engineering, and mathematics. Since 1989, PKAL has sponsored 150 workshops and other events, bringing faculty, administrators, and other STEM leaders together to focus on what works, and to outline agendas for individual and collective action. http://www.pkal.org

through graduation, (3) a physical infrastructure that accommodates such research-rich learning experiences, and (4) a supportive community beyond the campus. All four of these dimensions must be in place.

A second complicating factor is that the S&T world—the context for doing science—is changing rapidly. This places heavy demands on all stakeholder communities (government, university/college, industry) to keep how science is learned in sync with how science is practiced. This is somewhat more difficult for predominantly undergraduate institutions than research universities from the faculty perspective, but all academic institutions are faced with the challenge to keep the academic program and the physical infrastructure up to date and serving 21st century science and technology.

Data from National Science Foundation (NSF)[2] suggest almost 60 percent of current faculty are 45 years and older, thus with 20-25 years of service ahead of them and 15 years from graduate school behind them. Employment in S&E occupations is expected to increase about three times faster than the rate for all occupations.[3]

A third factor to consider is the educational distribution of the S&E workforce. Nearly 50 percent of those in nonacademic S&E occupations have bachelor's degrees, with 20 percent having master's degrees. Thus the key intervention point in addressing pressing current needs in the nation's S&E workforce is at the undergraduate level. According to *Science Indicators*, in 1998, liberal arts colleges and comprehensive universities (masters I&II) graduated 38 percent of the total number of baccalaureate degrees in STEM fields (78,700 out of 205,330 total).

The experiences of colleges and universities active in PKAL over the past decade suggest that insufficiencies in the scientific workforce at the national level can be addressed, in the context of a greater focus on student learning and motivation. Many of these institutions are now graduating more than 30 percent of their majors in STEM fields. How they have achieved those numbers can inform the development of a broader national agenda.

Based on those experiences, we present an answer to the question: If we assume that a shortage exists, what are your recommendations to mitigate the shortage?

RECOMMENDATIONS

1. Expand and support collaborative efforts between research laboratories in business and industry; government agencies at the local, state, and national level; and colleges and universities that are closely integrated

---

[2]*Characteristics of Doctoral Scientists and Engineers in the United States:* 1999 (NSF 02-328).
[3]*Science and Engineering Indicators 2002.* Volume 1. NSB-02-1.

to the academic experience of students, the scholarly responsibilities of faculty, and the needs of our nation, including:

• Summer-length research projects to be undertaken by teams of undergraduate students and faculty (and perhaps high school science teachers) on a campus or in an industrial or government research lab
• Experiential projects such as "clinics" and service learning in which students solve a real-world problem for a business or government agency, working with faculty on their home campus
• Summer or sabbatical research opportunities for faculty to keep abreast of new directions in the field, particularly midcareer faculty some years away from graduate school
• Sharing data and instrumentation from major research centers with the undergraduate community for the analysis of that data on site or electronically
• An array of opportunities that link the undergraduate research community to global science and technology issues
• A national electronic catalog of undergraduate research opportunities (for students and faculty) in laboratories in federal and state agencies, business and industry, and other major research centers
• Regional advisory groups of government/university/industry colleagues.

In developing a broader set of collaborative opportunities, the following must be recognized:

• The unique contributions of different types of educational institutions (ranging from K-12 schools, community colleges, and liberal arts colleges to large research universities). Failure to fully explore the potential of each type of institution by industry and community leads to the underutilization of the nation's talents and resources. Particular attention should be given to community colleges, as they enroll 47 percent of the nation's first-time freshman, as well as to the institutions with historic and current strength in these fields.
• Existing models of best practices in government/industry/academic collaborations.
• Recommendations from the many recent reports addressing this issue.[4]

_____

[4]*U.S. Commission on National Security/21st Century.* 2001. "The inadequacies of our systems of research and education pose a greater threat to U.S. national security over the next quarter century than any potential conventional war that we might imagine. American national leadership must understand these deficiencies as threats to national security. If we do not

2. We further recommend coherent efforts—at the campus, regional, state, and national level—to establish an environment supportive of the first two recommendations, including consistent and targeted support for the following:

• Ensuring that spaces for research and research-training in the undergraduate setting can accommodate new technologies and interdisciplinary approaches to learning, teaching, and research in STEM fields
• Scholarships and other opportunities such as mentoring programs for students from groups currently underrepresented in the study and practice of science so they can be active members of the research communities described in recommendation #1
• Scholarships and other opportunities for undergraduate students and faculty to make global connections through their study of STEM fields
• Focusing on admissions policies that serve to attract and retain graduates of two-year colleges in baccalaureate programs
• Incorporating career counseling into the undergraduate STEM program
• Programs that encourage and enhance collaborative efforts to use information technologies to build and sustain a 21st century research-rich learning environment

These recommendations are based on the experiences of institutions succeeding in attracting students to the study of STEM fields and in moti-

---

invest heavily and wisely in rebuilding these two core strengths, America will be incapable of maintaining its global position long into the 21st century."

Analysis to Action. National Research Council. 1996. "Advisory councils from industry can help shape educational programs in colleges and universities. The education of future technicians highlights a major challenge facing higher education: placing content in context. Student and faculty internships in industry, industrial involvement in designing and teaching college courses, and cooperative projects in undergraduate education all promote continuous interaction between educational and industrial partners. An emphasis on flexibility and core competencies would help ensure that institutions of higher education balance broad education with specific training. Hands-on learning, project-oriented courses, distance learning, and the delivery of courses at industrial sites would tie learning to the application of knowledge. Inquiry capabilities, including problem solving, critical thinking, communication, and teamwork, are all basic to lifelong technical careers."

"Faculty members and departments are responding to the new needs of the workplace with a variety of innovations. Close links between the offerings of different departments are enhancing understanding of the connections among subjects. Majors in some departments are doing senior projects grounded in real-world problems that instill skills they will need in their careers.

vating them to persist and pursue careers in these fields. These are learning environments in which students

- are given responsibility to shape their own learning in a research-rich environment;
- come to understand that what they are learning in the classroom and lab has some relevance for the world beyond the campus and thus can be a foundation for a career upon graduation;
- are expected to succeed and given appropriate support to do so; and
- have repeated and persistent opportunities, from the very first day through capstone courses for majors, to have hands-on engagement with doing science as scientists do science.

These are also places where significant investments have been made:

- In faculty, so they keep abreast of
    - advances in their scholarly field, connecting student learning to those advances
    - emerging technologies and pedagogies that enhance undergraduate learning
- In an academic program, so that it
    - connects to real-world issues and problems
    - reflects contemporary science and technology, specifically its interdisciplinarity
- In the physical infrastructure, so that
    - state-of-the art instrumentation can be accommodated
    - interdisciplinary programs can be nurtured
    - faculty and student research can be enhanced.

BACKGROUND

Attention to building and sustaining a strong undergraduate STEM community has been on the national agenda since the mid-1980s. Early attention to this effort emerged from a perception that America's interest would be served better if the number of students pursuing graduate programs were increased. This single objective drove the work of academic leaders and stakeholders as they shaped policies and budgets, facilities and faculties. But even then, as important as that work was, concern about numbers of coming generations of Ph.D. professionals was linked to concerns about how undergraduate STEM programs were serving the national interest more broadly.

Recent reforms, building on earlier efforts, have led to profound changes in the undergraduate learning environment. In addition to preparing the next generation of Ph.D. professionals, colleges and universities now recognize the responsibility to offer programs that motivate students to consider a wide range of careers that require scientific and technological capabilities, including that of a K-12 mathematics/science teacher. Perhaps most important, academic institutions now accept their responsibility to ensure all their graduates are science-savvy, ready for responsible citizenship in a world increasingly dominated by science and technology.

CONCLUSION

The need to increase the nation's technically trained workforce has an immediacy that should not override the continuing and critical need for first-rate undergraduate STEM programs grounded in the traditional liberal arts. Such programs—as they challenge all students to be respectful of diversity and to engage as creative problem-solvers, critical thinkers, intelligent communicators, effective collaborators, and lifelong learners—are solid grounding for a career as a STEM professional, whether in business, industry, or academe. It is the creative energy of the innovators with such skills that will drive our nation's prosperity over the long haul, coupled with a public that understands the role of science and technology in shaping the future of our society.

Is There a Shortage of Scientists and Engineers? How Would We Know?

William P. Butz, Gabrielle A. Bloom, Mihal E. Gross,
Terrence K. Kelly, Aaron Kofner, Helga E. Rippen
Science and Technology Policy Institute
RAND

This paper has the following objectives:

- To clarify the concepts of "shortage" and "low production" in the context of scientists and engineers
- To suggest answers to the questions in the paper's title
- To point toward strategies for increasing the science and engineering (S&E) workforce

WHAT WOULD A "SHORTAGE" OF SCIENTISTS AND ENGINEERS LOOK LIKE?

Over the last half-century, numerous alarms have sounded about looming shortages of scientists and engineers in the United States. What is meant by "shortage" has not always been clear. Further, the population under discussion, the scientists and engineers themselves, has not always shared the perspective of those sounding the alarm. Regardless, the implications of a shortage of skills critical to U.S. growth, competitiveness, and security are significant. So are the implications of the continuing low entry of female and minority students into many S&E fields. These implications justify closer examination of the nature and sources of the over- or underproduction of scientists and engineers. Improved understanding of

Note: The views expressed here are those of the authors and not necessarily those of the Science and Technology Policy Institute of RAND.

the definition and nature of the problem can point toward relevant data and useful questions.

As a starting point, consider the different circumstances in which the production of any good or service, new S&E Ph.D.'s being one, might be called "low":

1. If production is lower than in the recent past (steel is a recent example)
2. If competitors' share of total production is growing (electronic component manufacturing, shoe manufacturing, and oil production are increasingly foreign)
3. If production is lower than the people doing the producing would like (automobiles, best-selling novels, blockbuster movies)
4. If less is produced than the nation is deemed to need (well-trained K-12 teachers, community volunteers, clean urban air)
5. If production is not meeting market demand, as indicated by a rising price (nurses, Washington-area housing).

Each of these concepts of "shortage" has a place. The pain of steel workers and their communities is real when production falls and plants close (concept #1). The nation's concern about reliance on Mideast oil is justified (concept #2). And so forth. However, one of these five concepts of "shortage" is fundamentally different from the others in a manner crucial for the question at hand. Only the fifth concept integrally embodies a corrective mechanism that solves the problem, that induces increased production of its own accord.

To see this, consider the S&E workforce. If production of scientists and engineers is insufficient to meet market demand—that is, if each new crop of American scientists and engineers is too small to fill the growing number of jobs offered by academic, industrial, and government employers—then salary offers will tend to increase and unemployment or underemployment of the S&E workforce will tend to diminish. As young people observe this tightening labor market and consider lifetime employment prospects along with the many other factors influencing their career choice, some of them will opt for S&E, rather than for clinical medicine, law, business, or another profession. As these people complete their education and join the workforce, total production of scientists and engineers will accelerate. The shortage will diminish.

To the extent that production is "low" in any sense other than this fifth sense, production will tend to stay low. For example, the fact that competing countries are manufacturing more electronic components while America produces less (concept #2) may constitute a "shortage" of American-produced components. But there is nothing about this kind of shortage that will induce American companies to reverse the move off-shore.

Indeed, in whichever other respect there is a "shortage," policy actions to relieve it will be effective to the extent that they operate to increase demand for the good or service (concept #5). Policy can also induce increased production by lowering the costs of production, regardless of the manner of shortage that exists.

IS THERE A SHORTAGE OF SCIENTISTS AND ENGINEERS?

Diverse data from the National Science Foundation, the RAND RaDiUS database, the U.S. Census Bureau, the U.S. Bureau of Labor Statistics, the National Research Council, and scientific associations can characterize the production of S&E Ph.D.'s, indicate the respects in which such production may be low, and point to causes of observed patterns. Accordingly, we briefly focus such data on the five different concepts of "shortage," indicating the particular respects in which the production of S&E Ph.D.'s indeed appears to be low. This overview points to the fifth concept, unsatisfied demand, as the key both to understanding and to correcting whatever shortages are thought to exist according to the other concepts.

Unfortunately, the uneven detail, varying definitions, and inconsistent time periods in the available data make possible only the teasing out of "stylized facts"—hypotheses awaiting empirical testing. That data more recent than 1999 or 2000 are generally not yet published is especially unfortunate, as the S&E workforce situation has arguably changed significantly since then. Hence, we conclude this analysis not with positions or solutions, but more modestly, with four possible strategies for increasing the production of S&E Ph.D.'s in whatever fields might be deemed low, by whatever criteria.

To begin, consider whether the United States is experiencing a shortage of S&E Ph.D.'s in either of the first two senses—decreased production or gains by competitors. Figure 1 shows that the number of American Ph.D.'s awarded in each major area of science and engineering has been increasing, beginning in the 1980s. These gains were interrupted in the late 1990s, an interruption that has apparently continued in some fields, although confirming data are not yet published. Hence, at least until very recently, American Ph.D. production has not been declining in the broad S&E fields. There has been little or no shortage of the first type.

What about the second concept of shortage—competitors gaining ground? Figure 2 shows that S&E doctorate production turned up in many other countries during the 1980s as in the U.S., but the numerical increase has been larger here than in any of these "competitor" countries.

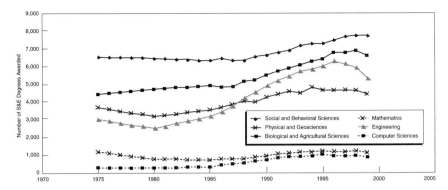

FIGURE 1 S&E Ph.D. Degrees Awarded by Broad Field, 1975-1999. *Source*: *Science and Engineering Doctorate Awards (2002)*. The American Bar Association (2002).

From two other angles, however, the situation vis-à-vis our "competitors" does not appear so sanguine. Figure 3 reports the ratio of S&E first degree holders to the total population of 24-year-olds in the so-called G7 countries in 1975 and 1999. Think of the height of each column as representing the probability that a representative young person will complete an S&E degree. That probability for American youth grew from .04 in 1975 to .06 in 1999, a notable increase corresponding to the numerical growth evident in the first two figures. In 1975, this probability in America was exceeded only in Japan, among countries shown. After 1975, however, the picture is radically different. Each of the other countries has experienced a much larger increase, measured in either absolute or percent-

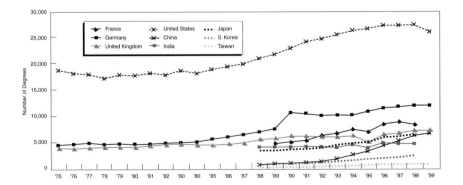

FIGURE 2 S&E doctorates awarded in nine countries, varying years 1975-1999. *Source*: *Science and Engineering Indicators (2002)*.

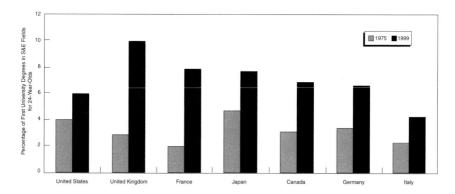

FIGURE 3 Ratio of natural science and engineering first university degrees awarded to 24-year-old population, by G7 country, 1975 and 1990. *Source: Science and Engineering Indicators (2002).*

age terms.[1] Although their young-adult populations are growing less rapidly than ours (not shown), the proportion of their young people opting for university degrees in science and engineering is rising faster.

Figure 4 examines from another angle the question of whether our competitors are gaining. Here, doctorate recipients from American institutions are divided into U.S. citizens and non-citizens.[2] The latter's share has grown rapidly indeed, from 23 percent of the total in 1980 to 42 percent in 1994. Even with the subsequent decline in noncitizen degree awards,[3] this longer-term rise, combined with the increasing propensity of students abroad to enter S&E fields (Figure 3), buttresses the case that the American S&E workforce is low in the sense that our competitors are gaining (concept #2 above).[4]

Consideration of the third and fourth concepts of "shortage" is best deferred until we have taken up the fifth and last concept: Is growth of the S&E workforce insufficient to satisfy market demand? If such growth is insufficient; that is, if the numbers of American scientists and engineers are too small to fill the new jobs offered by academic, industrial, and government employers, then employers will be bidding to fill their empty positions. Job openings, lab facilities, salaries, advancement opportuni-

---

[1]Other countries can be seen in the source table to have experienced even larger increases, notably Mexico and Spain.

[2]The underlying data for this figure include M.D.'s. Permanent residents are counted with noncitizens.

[3]Since September 2001 the number of foreign students enrolled in graduate S&E programs in the U.S. has apparently decreased even more markedly.

[4]Of course, many foreign recipients of U.S. degrees choose to remain and work here.

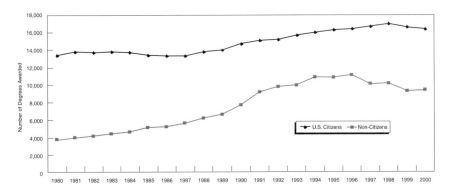

FIGURE 4 S&E and Health Doctorates Earned by U.S. Citizens and Noncitizens, 1980-2000. *Source*: *Science and Engineering Indicators (2002)* and *Science and Engineering Doctorate Awards—2000.*

ties, and other components of career satisfaction will be on the rise, while unemployment and underemployment[5] will be falling.

Alternatively, if the rewards to other careers—perhaps clinical medicine, law or business—are higher and are growing relatively to S&E, and if it is instead the costs of training for a job that are growing for S&E, then there is no shortage of scientists and engineers in this important fifth sense. Indeed, in this latter case, the "shortages" that others discern may well look more like discouraging surpluses to young people considering career choice. In the sense that matters for spurring production, they indeed are.

Is there in fact unsatisfied demand for scientists and engineers in the American job market? Available data are sketchy but they are consistent. We consider two indicators of S&E career opportunities: earnings and unemployment. Where data allow, we compare these opportunities and costs to those facing budding holders of professional degrees—M.D., D.D., D.V.M., J.D., and M.B.A. These comparisons are instructive to the extent that bright ambitious young people consider other challenging alternatives while deciding whether to become scientists or engineers.

Figure 5 compares a measure of annualized earnings for Ph.D.'s (all Ph.D.'s are included in this measure, not just S&E)[6] with earnings of pro-

---

[5]Prevalence of postdoctoral appointments, particularly successive appointments, might be considered an indicator of underemployment.

[6]These highly aggregated data cannot reveal salary trends for just the S&E workforce, much less for particular disciplines and subdisciplines that may have experienced unusual salary growth or decline. For comparison purposes, about 60 percent of Ph.D. degree holders were in S&E fields in the period covered by these data.

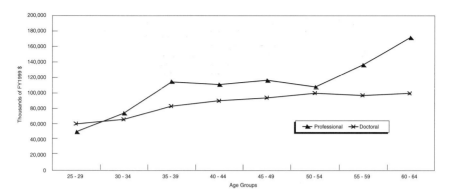

FIGURE 5 Synthetic estimates of work life earnings for advanced degree holders by age, 1997-1999 period. *Source*: *Census*—The Big Payoff.

fessional degree holders (those listed just above).[7] Professional degree holders earn more at nearly every age and considerably more over an entire career, as measured by the summed difference between the lines. This is no surprise.

Our purposes here would be better served by this same earnings measure calculated separately for the S&E workforce and repeated for a decade or so earlier. This comparison would reveal whether the professional degree premium is falling; that is, whether the relative attractiveness of an S&E career is rising, indicating a shortage in that crucial fifth sense. Alas, this measure is not yet available separately for S&E or for earlier periods. Still, the data at hand give no indication of the kind of earnings premiums for scientists and engineers that would signal the existence of a shortage.

Unemployment rates are another indicator of market conditions. Rates that are falling or lower than in alternative occupations also suggest shortages in the fifth sense—unsatisfied demand. Unemployment rates are available and plotted in Figure 6 for chemists, recent mathematics

---

[7]Called by the Census Bureau "synthetic estimate of work life earnings," this measure calculates for the 1997-99 period the annual earnings of persons in each indicated age range. A young person today might interpret the lines connecting these age points as the expected career profile of annual earnings on into her future. That interpretation requires several strong assumptions. An alternative measure of the career earnings profile would report annual earnings of the same group of people as they age over the years. As those data must necessarily refer entirely to the past, even to the deep past when the group of people was young, they also are a flawed proxy for looking at the future. However, lacking real data about the future, people and organizations use information about the past and present to make decisions, including career decisions.

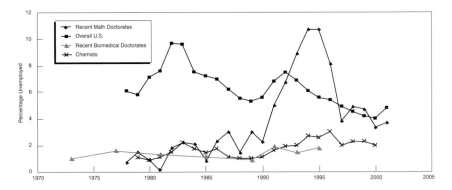

FIGURE 6 Unemployment rates of the United States and selected S&E fields. *Sources*: ASM-IMS IAAA Annual Survey 2001. ACS Annual Salary Survey. *Chemical & Engineering News 77*: 28-39. NRC *Trends in the Early Careers of Life Scientists.*

Ph.D.'s, and recent biomedical Ph.D.'s and M.D.'s.[8] Although not fully comparable in population or time period, these three rates, when compared to the overall U.S. unemployment rate, suggest a general increase or leveling in the 1990s, while the general unemployment rate was falling substantially. Rising unemployment in one sector, while the overall economy is doing well, is a strong indicator of developing surpluses of workers, not shortages.

Hence, neither earnings patterns nor unemployment patterns indicate an S&E shortage in the data we are able to find. Altogether, these data in Figures 5 and 6 do not portray the kind of vigorous employment and earnings prospects that can be expected to draw increasing numbers of bright and informed young people into science.

We return now to the third concept of shortage: Is production lower than the people doing the "producing"—in this case the young people making career choices—would like? More young people today may arguably enjoy doing science or engineering than plan actually to prepare for such careers. Instead they may choose a professional degree but only reluctantly. In a market economy, even one characterized by rigidities, regulations, and unequal opportunity, qualified people tend toward career paths whose rewards and satisfactions are becoming more attractive and/or whose preparatory costs are becoming less onerous.

---

[8]The American Mathematical Society and American Chemical Association publish more extensive data (including unemployment rates) on their members than are available for most other S&E communities.

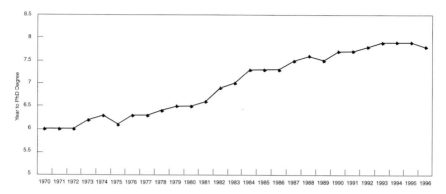

FIGURE 7 Average registered time to Ph.D. in the biomedical life sciences (postbaccalaureate study). *Note:* Includes all graduate education. *Source: Trends in the Early Careers of Life Scientists* (1998).

We have seen that broad fields of science and engineering do not appear particularly attractive from the earnings and unemployment perspective. What about the cost side? Figure 7 points to a sobering part of the answer. Average time from bachelor's degree to Ph.D. in the life sciences has increased by two full years since 1970. Professional association staff in several other sciences informally confirm similar increases. If, as is likely, the variance in time-to-degree has increased along with the mean, then prospective life scientists face not only more years out of the labor market, but also more uncertainty about the number of years. Complaints about perceived subjectivity and arbitrariness of the postgraduate process—its length and the prospects of eventual completion—are also not infrequent.

All this might not matter so much if the brightest young people lacked alternative training and career paths. But consider the paths to the M.D., D.D., D.V.M., J.D., and M.B.A. The number of years to degree has stayed absolutely constant in these programs for decades,[9] and the prospects for successful completion, once begun, remain high. Have the amount and complexity of material to be mastered expanded so much more in biology or mathematics than in medicine, the law, or finance? This would seem hard to argue. Then why does it take longer and longer to be ready to begin one's career in most of the sciences, but not in the professions?

Finally, what about the fourth concept of shortage, unmet national needs? Will particular subfields of science or engineering soon become critical, perhaps for national security, for health care, for feeding the world, or for national competitiveness? Perhaps some fields are already

---

[9]Flexible training alternatives that can extend time to degree have arisen in each of these fields, but these are optional, serving to increase the attractiveness.

critical but somehow without the corresponding inducements that attract qualified young people. Where would these inducements come from?

GENERAL STRATEGIES FOR INCREASING THE SCIENCE AND ENGINEERING WORKFORCE

We have seen that the production of American scientists and engineers is not low in the sense that it has fallen over some years from previous heights, nor in the sense that employers are driving S&E earnings up and unemployment rates down in a scramble to hire more. However, in another sense of shortage—that of competitive foreign gains—American production does appear low.

Whether from unmet national needs, foreign competition, or any other source, a perceived shortage of U.S. S&E talent must be expressed in terms that motivate young people, or the shortage will persist. If such perceived shortages do emerge, the story loosely told by these data points toward four general strategies to relieve them. Two of these strategies involve government actions to increase the returns and rewards to be expected from a career in science. The other two strategies—somewhat less amenable to direct government policy—would reduce the costs of preparing for such a career. A fifth strategy points to data improvements.

1. *Steadily and predictably increase federal research obligations for the S&E fields of concern.* This strategy, though not easy, is straightforward. There is nothing so directly under control of the federal government as its budget, and probably little that has so direct an effect on the attractiveness of an S&E career. Federal grants, contracts, and other S&E expenditures are a major determinant of fellowship support, job opportunities, lab facilities, and salary growth. Figure 8 shows that federal obligations for total research, in constant dollars, have increased more than fivefold since 1970 in some fields, but hardly at all in others. The substantial growth in federal support for the biological sciences seen in Figure 8 is likely a major reason for the corresponding growth in biological science Ph.D.'s seen in Figure 1. If national needs now (also) point in other directions, substantial and predictable federal budget enhancements in those directions can be expected to call forth the same kind of response on the part of young people (or midcareer people) contemplating their careers.

However, growth in Ph.D. production without corresponding growth in available jobs for Ph.D.'s may cause more harm than good. There is evidence that this has occurred in the past. Anecdotal evidence suggests recent widespread underemployment of some biology specialties, indicating possible "overshooting"—too many new Ph.D.'s to satisfy the demand. Goldman and Massy (2001), in particular, argue that funding increases natu-

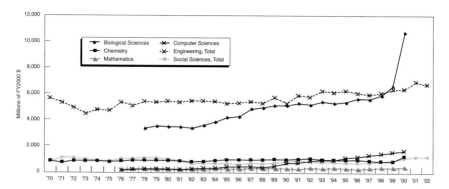

FIGURE 8 Federal obligations for total research, by field of science & engineering, FY 1970-2002. *Source*: NSF Federal Funds for Research and Development Fiscal Years 1951-2001.

rally lead to greater increases in Ph.D. production than in Ph.D. employment, without specific policy interventions. Romer (2000) calls for a system of portable national fellowships as a means of increasing funding for S&E, while allowing market forces a role in matching supply and demand.

2. *Increase incentives for private investment and hiring in the priority fields of science and engineering.* This strategy, while less straightforward, falls also in the federal bailiwick. Subsidies, patent and intellectual property protection, and regulatory changes can be effective tools for encouraging private investment and jobs in industries that employ particular types of scientists and engineers. Often, jobs fallout is a byproduct of policy intentions toward some other goal, but job growth in particular professions can just as well be the explicit policy target. In either case, young people and others in midcareer can be expected to respond. Although not primarily driven by federal policy, the boom in computer science and engineering degrees during the 1990s was fueled by rapidly increasing private sector demand.

3. *Adopt the "professional school model" for S&E Ph.D. programs.* This strategy aims not at increasing later career rewards but at reducing the early costs and uncertainties of training for an S&E career. The acceptance of this strategy in academe, even any resolve toward attempting it, seems remote. Still, more young people would surely be lured away from professional schools to S&E doctoral programs, if the years to S&E Ph.D. completion were rolled back, say, to 1970 levels, if this term were predictable and standard, and if the subjective and arbitrary aspects of the Ph.D. path were curtailed.

4. *Introduce two new professional doctoral degree programs for science and engineering, built on the M.D. model.* This fourth strategy would also reduce

training costs and uncertainties, but specifically for those whose career goals focus on professional practice rather than cutting-edge research. Graduates would have a firm grounding in a broad set of skills, understand how their skills fit in with other skill sets, and be able to keep up with the cutting edge. These new programs would feature a structured curriculum with well-defined completion criteria and a definite term, perhaps of four years. Their faculty would be practitioners with other sources of income, as in medical schools. The rapid growth of industrial parks, corporate-like technical centers, and corporate partnerships would facilitate this arrangement. As with existing professional degree programs, students would not normally rely on grants and fellowships, but would instead look to substantially higher lifetime earnings to pay their own way. The attractiveness of this strategy depends partly on whether the current employment of S&E Ph.D.'s could be partly satisfied instead by holders of these new professional doctoral degrees.

5. *Expand content and improve timeliness of S&E workforce data.* To know whether shortages of scientists and engineers are in fact developing and whether strategies to encourage their production are succeeding, specific additional data should be collected. In addition, a subset of indicators could be developed to provide early warning, some two years or more before full data become available.

Logic as well as repeated experience counsels caution in pursuing these strategies, particularly the first two. Young people's career decisions do not shift instantaneously when the relative attractiveness of their various choices begins to change. Having begun to shift, their choices do not then emerge in the employment market for as long as their graduate training takes—and undergraduate training, too, for the many who choose when they are younger. Government actions to raise opportunities and earnings in one field must be sustained for many years or they do more damage than good. To see this, consider that such a policy must be sustained for substantially longer than the lag between the policy's initiation and the labor market entry of the last new crop of graduate scientists and engineers. In this last crop are the first high school students who jumped (and were encouraged to jump) in the newly favored direction. Hence, 8 to 10 years is the absolute minimum period of sustained government investment before those young people who responded can begin to reap the reward, much less begin to repay their investment. Policy that cannot be sustained for more than a decade will therefore be destabilizing and harmful to bright young people's careers and lives, to the extent that they and their advisers trusted the policy.

These important caveats notwithstanding, sustained strategic movement in any of these first four directions could reduce the costs and uncertainties of postgraduate S&E training and increase the job opportunities, earnings and satisfaction of graduates, whether in priority fields of science and engineering or across the spectrum. In response, the young people who are bright enough to drive 21st century American science and engineering (but also bright enough to work its clinics, courts, and businesses) would increasingly do so.

REFERENCES

American Bar Association. (2002) *Statistics.*

Berger, Mark C. (1988). "Predicted Future Earnings and Choice of College Major." *Industrial and Labor Relations Review* 41(3): 418-429.

Current Population Surveys. (1998-2000). U.S. Census Bureau.

Day, Jennifer C., and Newburger, Eric C. (2002). "The Big Payoff: Education Attainment and Synthetic Estimates of Work-Life Earnings". U.S. Census Bureau.

Federal Funds for Research and Development: Fiscal Years 2000, 2001, and 2002. National Science Foundation, Division of Science Resources Statistics.

Federal Funds for Research and Development Detailed Historical Tables: Fiscal years 1951-2001. National Science Foundation, Division of Science Resources Statistics.

Goldman, Charles A., and Massey, William F. (2000). *PhD Factory: Training and Employment of Science and Engineering Doctorates in the United States.* Bolton, MA: Anchor Publishing.

Loftsgaarden, D. O., J. W. Maxwell, et al. (2002). "2001 Annual Survey of the Mathematical Sciences (Second Report)." *Notices of the AMS* 49(7): 803-816.

National Research Council (1998). *Trends in the Early Careers of Life Scientists.* Washington, DC, National Academy Press.

National Science Foundation. *Science and Engineering Doctorate Awards (1995-2002).* Arlington, VA, Division of Science Resources Statistics.

National Science Foundation (2002). *Science and Engineering Indicators (2002)* Arlington, VA, National Science Board.

Romer, P.M. 2000. "Should the Government Subsidize Supply or Demand in the Market for Scientists and Engineers?" NBER Working Paper 7723. Cambridge, MA: National Bureau of Economic Research

Salary and Employment Survey. (1999) Chemical and Engineering News 77 (31): 28-39.

Salsberg, E. and G.J. Forte (2002). "Trends in the Physician Workforce, 1980-2000." *Health Affairs* 21(5): 165-173.

Position of the Board of Directors on the U.S. Science and Engineering Workforce

W. Frank Gilmore, President, Sigma Xi, the Scientific Research Society
Chancellor, Montana Tech, The University of Montana

BACKGROUND

Sigma Xi, the Scientific Research Society, is the international honor society of research scientists and engineers. Founded in 1886, Sigma Xi is a nonprofit membership society of nearly 75,000 scientists and engineers who were elected to the Society because of their research achievements or potential. The Society has more than 500 chapters at universities and colleges, government laboratories, and industry research centers. In addition to publishing the award-winning magazine, *American Scientist*, Sigma Xi bestows more than 600 grants annually to promising young researchers, holds forums on critical issues at the intersection of science and society, and sponsors a variety of programs supporting excellence in science and engineering, science education, science policy, and the public understanding of science.

Many of the recommendations in this position paper have been abstracted from Sigma Xi documents,[1] while others represent a synthesis of Sigma Xi positions and recommendations from other governmental and nongovernmental organizations. Taken together, these documents, produced by the full range of stakeholders, present a compelling message. Science, technology, engineering, and mathematics (STEM) education in the United States needs to be thoroughly reformed from elementary school through graduate school if we are to meet this country's workforce needs. Moreover, these reforms must center on improving STEM teaching, dra-

---

[1]Sigma Xi publications on science education are listed at http://www.sigmaxi.org/resources/publications/index.shtml#sciencee

matically improving access to STEM education for all young people, and providing understandable science information for all Americans.

Recently, there have been many promising initiatives designed to respond to concerns about STEM education.[2] However, we have seen many other programs of similar promise come and go over the past 20 years. None of these efforts has had a systemwide effect. Student performance in STEM fields has continued to decline, as has interest in STEM careers. From this experience it is clear that sustained restructuring of both K-12 and college level instruction is necessary.

Scientists and engineers must play a central role in this reform process. We know that many of the best researchers are also excellent and committed undergraduate teachers, and that there are colleges and universities that encourage and support high-quality teaching among their STEM faculty. Balance between education and research must be the standard career expectation for STEM faculty. Over the years, the very forces that have made research universities so successful have drawn vital energy away from teaching. Yet, excellence in both teaching and research is clearly compatible and they are often mutually supportive activities. Our goal must be to develop new approaches to STEM education that build on the remarkable success of our research programs. Undergraduate STEM instruction is potentially the most effective leverage point for improvement in the quality of education in STEM fields at all levels. Many in the workforce, including K-12 teachers, are formally exposed to STEM courses for the last time in their undergraduate coursework, and research universities are the largest producers of STEM-trained college graduates. Those who teach at the undergraduate level have rich academic backgrounds and close ties with current research. They understand modern science, mathematics, and engineering. Effective teaching by STEM faculty can meet the needs of students preparing for careers in nonscientific fields as well as those students who are preparing for graduate and professional

---

[2]The Burroughs-Wellcome Fund has announced the creation of the North Carolina Science, Mathematics and Technology Education Center. The Center is based on the recommendations in *Before It's Too Late*. NSF has announced grants to the University of Georgia, Washington University in St. Louis, and the American Association for the Advancement of Science (AAAS) ($9.9 million) to develop new centers for improving K-12 education in science and mathematics. *Chronicle of Higher Education* 10/25/02 "NSF Awards $50-Million to Support 5 New Centers for Science and Mathematics Education." http://chronicle.com/daily/2002/10/2002102504n.htm and http://www.aaas.org/news/releases/2002/1024nsf.shtml

The NSF Criterion 2, an evaluation requirement for research grant proposals has received considerable attention as a vehicle for encouraging research scientists to actively convert research discoveries to educational tools. A summary of the Criterion 2 can be found at http://www.nsf.gov/od/opp/opp_advisory/oaccrit2.htm

programs in STEM fields. For endeavors of such significance, the magnitude of the task cannot be an excuse for inaction.

Fortunately, current circumstances present a variety of opportunities to improve STEM education at all levels. Over the last decades, we have gathered a great deal of valuable information about what works in math and science education. Enormous demographic changes anticipated over the next decade will dramatically alter the ranks of teachers and university faculties. The substantial replacement of the workforce presents a unique opportunity to inject new energy into mathematics and science teaching in the form of new recruitment, training and supportive structures that can strengthen teaching at all levels.

RECOMMENDATIONS

1. Improving K-12 Science Education

In their 2000 report *Before It's Too Late*, the National Commission on Mathematics and Science Teaching for the 21st Century identified three major goals and associated strategies for bringing about the changes that are necessary. Sigma Xi recommends the approach taken in *Before It's Too Late* and endorses the three principal goals of their program.

- To establish an ongoing system to improve the quality of mathematics and science teaching in grades K-12
- To increase significantly the number of mathematics and science teachers and improve the quality of their preparation
- To improve the working environment and make the teaching profession more attractive to K-12 mathematics and science teachers. STEM-trained teachers have ample options elsewhere in the labor force. Quite simply, to attract and retain these teachers the teaching environment needs to be made more appealing.

In the short term, programs are urgently needed to address the pressing current needs created by shortages in mathematics and science teachers.

- Science-trained individuals should be actively recruited for teaching careers. This recruitment effort should be supported with a well-crafted media campaign to attract teachers and a range of incentive-based strategies like teaching fellowships and scholarship programs.
- The link between research and education training should be flexible and fluid. New graduates and graduate students with an interest in teaching should be able to participate in relatively short-term commit-

ments to teach through programs like Teach for America (TFA)[3] that place college graduates with content-rich training in underserved schools. Many TFA corps members make a long-term commitment to teaching. Those who do not typically return to graduate or professional careers with a deeper appreciation for issues in education.

• These programs must be supported through government and industry funding, but STEM departments must also endorse them so that their graduates consider teaching as a genuinely rewarding career option. Possible mechanisms for targeted support include scholarship and fellowship programs for new graduates.

• Similarly, programs that ease the transition from midcareer and postretirement years to teaching, like the army's Troops-to-Teachers Program,[4] should be expanded to recruit seasoned scientists and engineers to work in classrooms and provide professional training and support. These programs offer an excellent opportunity for businesses and industries to fund short-term awards for employees and new retirees to enter the teaching field.

• Action must be taken to support and encourage teachers in order to stem their loss to other professions. Teachers must be given the time they need within the school day to keep up with new developments in their fields, teaching aids, and materials. They must have the opportunity to collect the feedback necessary to reflect on their teaching. Teachers must receive the respect they deserve and be rewarded accordingly, including salaries that appropriately value science and mathematics training.

2. Undergraduate Education

Sigma Xi fully endorses the 10 recommendations contained in the Boyer Commission Report. The following recommendations emphasize points made by the Boyer Commission and in other reports:[5]

• The reward system for excellence in undergraduate teaching should be commensurate with reward systems for excellence in other STEM faculty activities, including research.

• Funding sources should be arranged so that tenure-track faculty positions have a clear teaching component and a clear research component.

---

[3]Teach For America is the national corps of outstanding recent college graduates, of all academic majors, who commit two years to teach in public schools in low-income communities. http://www.teachforamerica.org/

[4]http://voled.doded.mil/dantes/ttt/index2.htm

[5]These recommendations were adapted from the Sigma Xi Report, An Exploration of the Nature and Quality of Undergraduate Education in Science, Mathematics and Engineering. A Report of the National Advisory Group of Sigma Xi, The Scientific Research Society. (1989) (The Wingspread Report)

• Successful reinvention experiments, curricula, and other related projects should be collected and disseminated so as to provide a blueprint for other universities and departments.

• Congress and the National Science Foundation (NSF) should continue to support and facilitate scholarly research related to learning at the undergraduate level.

• Funding agencies must continue to encourage and expand the participation of STEM majors in undergraduate research.

• Funding agencies, universities, and professional societies must actively support, facilitate, and provide incentives for the entry and sustained professional development of women, underrepresented minorities, and the physically disabled in STEM programs.

Government agencies, foundations, industries, and professional organizations can provide essential help. It is, however, university faculties that must initiate and bring about change. Achieving fundamental change is a slow, difficult, and expensive process. Our nation's future justifies the investment.

3. Diversity in the Science and Engineering Workforce

While equal opportunity for participation in higher education for all citizens is a long-term social goal achievable only with consistent national commitment and investments, current demographic changes are affecting our ability to produce scientists and engineers now. Based on a review of successful programs,[6] Sigma Xi recommends the following:

• Programs that encourage human interactions between more experienced STEM professionals and women and minority students through mentorship, internships, and research experience, should be expanded and widely supported via government funding, professional association programs, and private funding. All STEM departments at colleges and universities should consider peer and mentor support programs for minority and women majors at undergraduate and graduate levels aimed at retaining a larger proportion of these students through graduation.

• Educational reforms at the K-12 and undergraduate levels must address the difficulties that lack of access to good academic preparation poses for poor and underrepresented minority students.

• Access to information about college-level training needs to be improved. There is early evidence that "coaching" on how to apply for college admission and financial support for students in high schools, espe-

---

[6] A good source of information on successful programs is Building Engineering and Science Talent (BEST) http://www.bestworkforce.org

cially those schools where few graduates normally attend college, can increase the number of students who apply for postsecondary training.[7]

• The cultural experience in many poor and minority communities does not support the common practice of incurring thousands of dollars of loan debt for college training. Access to information about financial aid and the process of obtaining aid needs to be streamlined to retain minority students in college programs.[8]

• Educational institutions need to reassess how the general climate in STEM fields discourages the participation of women and minorities at their institutions and introduce appropriate changes.[9]

• Policymakers and funders must direct more attention to assisting two-year colleges. These institutions have large numbers of students from underrepresented groups. Programs are needed that encourage students to move on to teaching or science research careers, and help them to make the transition to four-year institutions.

4. Graduate Training and Beyond

The most reliable way to attract a diverse and talented range of people to STEM research careers is to make those fields attractive relative to others that involve similar time commitments and educational costs. At the moment, there is very little reward for the uncertainty and long commitment that we require of STEM graduate students, and not surprisingly, graduate school attrition rates are high.[10]

Sigma Xi endorses the recommendations related to improving graduate student experience in science and engineering contained in the congressional report, *Unlocking Our Future*.[11] These recommendations focus on the following:

---

[7]Bridging the Gap: Two Experts on Higher-Education Policy Go to a Low-Income High School to Test Their Ideas on How to Get More Students Into College." *Chronicle of Higher Education,* August 9, 2002; p. A22.

[8]For example, a recent study by the Pew Hispanic Center found that financial difficulties are a significant factor in the poor retention rates of Hispanic students. Initially, Hispanics are actually enrolling in postsecondary education at higher rates than are their white counterparts. Financial support rather than academic preparation is the likely explanation for the trend. http://www.pewhispanic.org/site/docs/pdf/final_joint_college_release-suro_edit.pdf

[9]The Association of Women in Science has developed a Web site that offers guidance and assistance in the process of evaluating campus "climate" issues. http://www.chillyclimate.org/

[10]http://www.aaup.org/publications/Academe/00nd/ND00LOVI.HTM

[11]Unlocking Our Future: Toward a New National Science Policy. A report to Congress by the House Committee on Science, September 24, 1998 http://www.house.gov/science/science_policy_report.htm

• Increasing the size of individual grants for doctoral and postdoctoral training. The National Institutes of Health (NIH) has substantially increased postdoctoral salaries in recent years. This increase should be expanded to students in the physical sciences and engineering. In general, federal funding for research in all scientific fields should be more balanced among broad disciplinary areas.

• Expanding funding opportunities targeted at scientists early in their careers to offset funding shifts away from young researchers that have developed over the past two decades.[12] In the present climate, young researchers see no viable career structure between postdoctoral and tenured professor appointments.

• Developing appropriate university policies to control the length of time spent in graduate and postdoctoral program study.

• Continuing to expand on initiatives to make STEM graduate training programs more flexible. Specifically, graduate students should be permitted to pursue coursework and gain relevant experience outside of their specific area of research.

The significance of the supply of talented STEM researchers to the health of the economy warrants coordinated and well-funded research into the dynamics of the scientific labor market. This research should be directed at the collection of data and the design of models that can be used to predict more accurately the future demand for, and supply of, STEM-trained individuals.

The climate for women and underrepresented minorities in STEM graduate programs has improved at many colleges and universities. There is considerable research on this topic, and many institutions have begun to experiment with programs explicitly designed to address this situation. Progress that has begun to improve the climate needs to be supported. Ultimately, the ability of institutions to attract and retain women and minority students will be the test of their success.

• Continued funding should be made available to universities, diversity-oriented organizations, and professional organizations that disseminate new information, facilitate dialogue on the climate issues, and evaluate their success.

5. Communicating Science—Public Understanding and Participation

There is a large gap with respect to understanding of scientific issues between the scientific community and the general public, and it is the

---

[12]"NIH Grantees: Where Have all the Young Ones Gone?" *Science*, 298:40-41, October 4, 2002.

responsibility of the scientific community to bridge that gap.[13] The better the citizens and the officials on whom researchers rely for their essential support are educated and trained to understand the nature of process and progress in scientific research, the better the prospects will be for restoring a more productive partnership with science, society, and government. Not only should scientific literacy for informed democratic participation be encouraged, but also the scientific community should improve its capacity to listen to and incorporate public concerns.

• Institutions that encourage the interactions of scientists and the public in making technical decisions should be encouraged and actively supported by professional organizations, universities, and funders.

• Programs that advance the public understanding of science through popular culture, books, plays, films, and radio programs, like the programs of the Alfred P. Sloan Foundation, should be encouraged and expanded.

• Joint journalism—STEM academic programs and coursework should be encouraged through grants and other incentives.

• Sigma Xi and other professional organizations should expand their existing services to journalists to provide information and contact with scientists so that news stories can be covered with greater accuracy.[14]

• Scientists and engineers at any level, including tenure-track faculty, with an aptitude and an interest in public speaking, should be encouraged to take time away from academic work to participate in programs designed to communicate science to the public, without penalty to their careers. Funding agencies, journals, and the media can support these scientists through grants and fellowships.

---

[13]National Science Foundation, *Science and Engineering Indicators 2002,* Chapter 7: "Science and Technology: Public Attitudes and Public Understanding," reports on a variety of polling information about attitudes to science. http://www.nsf.gov/sbe/srs/seind02/c7/c7h.htm

[14]Sigma Xi's Media Resource Service (MediaResource) is the oldest referral service for journalists in existence. It is a public understanding of science program that helps journalists to strengthen their science-related stories by providing independent expert sources. The sources are good communicators of science who provide journalists with the context and commentary necessary for clear and balanced reporting of science and technology. Experts range from researchers at academic institutions and corporations to government scientists and policymakers to those ethicists and historians of science based in our nation's broad collection of think tanks and associations.

U.S. Science and Engineering
Workforce: Equity and Participation

Maria Elena Zavala, President
Society for Advancement of Chicanos and
Native Americans in Science (SACNAS)

INTRODUCTION

Science, technology, engineering, and mathematics (STEM) are cornerstones for the future of this country. Current U.S. global economic and political dominance is based in great measure on the success of this country's investment in and development of technology. Invention, technology development, and its transfer are part of the American fabric. Advancements occur because *people* work to create a better tomorrow with their ideas. *People* are a natural resource that is often forgotten in the formula of success, and there are groups of our people who are most likely to be overlooked: Chicanos/Latinos, Native Americans, and African-Americans. We cannot afford the continued neglect and underutilization of a large and growing portion of our nation's citizens, especially now, at a time of heightened competition and global unrest.

The science workforce shortages in our nation's recent past have been met by raiding other countries for their nearly mature to mature scientists. This has had many effects: it has allowed us to ignore significant problems of science preparation in our own educational system. It has limited job prospects for many Americans. It has caused a significant brain drain in less developed countries. This brain drain has serious negative consequences for less developed countries because it represents the loss of their investment in human capital, a loss of potential scientific leadership that is desperately needed in those countries, and the loss of teachers and scholars for the next generation (Bagla, 2002). If global raiding has caused a brain drain abroad, it has led to even more serious consequences for educational development within our nation.

It is relatively easy for America to take well-trained or partially trained people from other countries to fill our scientific workforce needs. A majority (63 percent; 34,930 out of 55,444) of recently awarded foreign Ph.D.'s (1988-1999) expects to stay in the United States (NSF 99-304). Filling many of the positions in higher-education science careers and industry with foreign students is a shortsighted lack of national policy that increases our national security risks while at the same time overlooking the human treasures here at home. Members of minority groups, especially Chicanos and Native Americans, are foremost among the forgotten here at home; they are the passed-over treasures rarely seen, heard, or valued. A recent study shows that, while minorities make up nearly 25 percent of the population of our nation (Delaker, 2001), Chicanos, Latinos, Native Americans, and African-Americans make up less than 6 percent of all our Ph.D.s in STEM (NSF 00-327). Underrepresentation of these groups in the scientific enterprise is a serious national problem with many factors contributing to this state.

A skilled scientific workforce is critical to the progress and maintenance of our country's position in the world. Our purpose here is to arrive at a rational approach for developing our nation's scientific workforce.

WHY WON'T AMERICANS BECOME SCIENTISTS?

A recent report clearly shows that only women and minorities are showing increasing participation in science careers (NSB 02-01). While we can see a positive increase in their participation, it is very clear that this increased participation does not fully match in numbers the loss of white males in the scientific workforce. It is not likely that a baby boom of white male children will suddenly emerge to fill the steadily increasing need for scientists. The usual pool from which scientists have been traditionally drawn is not expanding as fast as the need.

The youngest, fastest-growing segment of the American population is Chicanos/Latinos (Delaker, 2001). Chicanos/Latinos, Native Americans, and African-Americans represent an untapped and underdeveloped source to meet future workforce needs. How, then, can we as a nation accept the now pitiful underrepresentation of these groups in the scientific endeavor? One important caveat is that not all Latinos are *equally* underrepresented in science, although they are *all* underrepresented. Thus, studies that disaggregate "Hispanic" data are particularly useful for developing sound science policy (Quintana-Baker, 2002). For example, Puerto Ricans are about 10 percent of all Latinos but make up 29 percent of the Latino Ph.D.'s. In contrast, Mexican Americans/Chicanos make up

59 percent of all "Hispanics" but only 24 percent of STEM Ph.D.'s (Quintata-Baker, 2002). It is also not clear whether there is a difference in success of "Island" vs. "Mainland" Puerto Ricans in STEM.

The level of participation in higher education of Chicanos/Latinos and Native Americans is about 10 percent of the 18-24-year-olds. This is compared to 25 percent for the same age bracket of whites. Part of this low representation of minorities in higher education is explained by the fact that Native Americans and Chicano/Latinos have high secondary school dropout rates, which essentially precludes them from higher education (Delaker, 2001). However, if we look at those that *do* attend college we find that they are still underrepresented in science and technology majors (NSB, 02-01). Underrepresented minority children are most likely to come from families with low educational attainment and low socioeconomic status (Delaker, 2001). They are more likely to attend schools where the teachers are not well prepared to teach science and mathematics and/or who have few resources to enhance their teaching and learning. These children are at a significant disadvantage from the very start of their educational careers, and they continue to fall further behind. They are less likely to take college preparatory courses that would allow them to enter college and prepare them for college-level science and mathematics courses (College Board, 1999). These minority students attend a more affordable school, such as a community college, before entering a four-year college or university. If they decide to continue in graduate school, they will often enter an M.S. program before making the commitment to a Ph.D. program. These educational choices are often based on finances, family social constraints, a lack of academic preparation, and a fear of the unknown (since few of their family or friends may have gone to college). The educational choices these students make result in educational career paths that take between 12 and 14 years to complete, often far longer than those of more privileged students. When they finish the Ph.D. in a STEM discipline, they will work as a postdoctoral researcher for another two to five years.

Minority-serving institutions (MSIs) continue to be the chief producers of students who pursue advanced degrees in STEM (NSB 00-01; Borden, 2002). Because STEM uses the apprenticeship model for training scientists it is important for these institutions to receive financial support for such activities. Comprehensive colleges and universities provide training for K-12 teachers. It is critical that talented students are supported to become excellent teachers for our minority youth and that they take content-rich courses to prepare them to teach our future scientists.

Graduate school represents a difficult transition for all students. Intellectual independence is one of the goals of Ph.D. programs. Intellectual independence often comes with feelings of cultural and social isolation. While science and technology fields are objective in their methods, the conduct of science, like all other endeavors, is completed in a social milieu, and this social world in which the minority student is even more of a minority, means that the students may not know how to act. These students often lack "scientific cultural capital," and they may not know how to accrue it. Minority professional organizations and their members play an important role by serving as resources and role models for these students. However, all scientists, agencies, and corporations need to take an active role in developing scientists.

To become scientists, minority students may have spent more than 24 years in pursuit of their science education. Minority students may generally be more in debt than their white counterparts, face years as poorly paid postdoctoral researchers, remain uncertain of employment or advancement in their field, and have a starting salary that will not allow them to participate in the American dream of homeownership. Finally, when they land their first "real" job they will earn less than their white or Asian counterparts (NSB 02-01). Is it any wonder why there is a shortage of minority scientists?

It has taken many years to establish systems that are excellent in failing to educate our youngsters. We can expect that it will take at least that long to recover. We need multifaceted systemic approaches that will enhance achievement and encourage excellence in students.

WHAT IS SACNAS?

SACNAS was started by a handful of Chicano and Native American scientists attending an American Association for Advancement of Science (AAAS) meeting in 1972. When they realized at that point in time that they represented all of the Chicanos and Native Americans with Ph.D.'s in the U.S., and that they could all fit in one elevator, they moved into action. SACNAS was incorporated in 1973. It is among the oldest and largest minority science societies in the country. It is a professional society with a student focus. The Society is dedicated to increasing the representation of these underrepresented groups in science, to advocating for better opportunities for minority scientists in all facets of scientific endeavors, and to improving science education. SACNAS is a national, nonprofit, professional science organization striving to increase the numbers of Chicano/Latino and Native American Ph.D.'s in all science, mathematics, technology, and engineering disciplines. While the focus of the Society is to promote Chicano/Latino and Native American achievement and excellence in science, SACNAS has provided opportunities for African-Americans, Pacific Islanders, Asians, and Euro-Americans as well.

The mission of SACNAS is to increase the number of Chicano/ Latino and Native American students pursuing graduate education

and obtaining the necessary degrees for research careers and science-teaching professions at all levels. SACNAS works on a national level to close these gaps in educational opportunities and high achievement by creating partnerships and initiatives that increase representation of Chicanos/Latinos and Native Americans in the sciences. To address the needs of minorities in the sciences, SACNAS provides creative approaches to improving science education and equalizing opportunities in the national scientific workforce. SACNAS delivers high-quality mentoring and professional development to its members through its national conference, summer research programs, and publications. The Society's strengths lie in the active involvement of its members, a dedicated board of directors, and a strong multilevel network between federal agencies, professional scientific societies, universities, and the private sector.

SACNAS is nationally recognized for its leadership and effective programs in science and education. It has received the National Science Board's Public Service Award. The National Science Board (NSB) established the Public Service Award in November 1996. "The annual award recognizes people and organizations who have increased the public understanding of science or engineering." Its members have been recognized nationally for their effective mentoring programs. Seven of the past winners of the White House's Presidential Award for Excellence in Mentoring in Science, Engineering and Mathematics were SACNAS presidents, board members, or active SACNAS members.

SACNAS seeks to change the woeful state of science-education minority youth by encouraging all underrepresented groups—while focusing on Chicanos/Latinos and Native Americans—to pursue advanced degrees in science, mathematics, and engineering.

RECOMMENDATIONS

Based upon 30 years of experience in working to advance the status of minority students in science careers, SACNAS proposes the following recommendations:

1. High-quality education is the right of all children and it is the responsibility of society to ensure that it is available to all. Education begins in preschool. It is clear that high-quality early education is a key to success (Headstart). These programs must be fully supported and the most successful practices replicated.

2. While SACNAS's mission has focused on graduate education, we understand that K-12 teachers hold the keys that open the doors to college. There must be expanded efforts to train teachers not only in peda-

gogy but also in science content and mathematics and to promote teachers' lifelong learning.

3. Teachers must encourage achievement and excellence from *all* students.

4. Funds to support the number of rigorous hands-on/minds-on math and science at middle and high schools must be provided for schools with high minority student enrollments.

5. Information about college, especially application requirements, and financial aid, must be readily available. This information needs to be given to parents and students often. Colleges and universities must begin their outreach to children in elementary school.

6. Financial aid for students must be expanded to meet the needs of students. Although recently increased aid for college was a step in the right direction, it still does not meet the needs of many students who most need the support, students from economically challenged families. Scholarship programs to support economically disadvantaged students must be expanded.

7. All scientists must be involved in community outreach. Often, only minority faculty are required to take on special work focusing on minority outreach, minority mentoring, and advisement. However, this work should be spread among all faculty.

8. There are many successful features of the SACNAS annual conference that can be replicated elsewhere. These are meant to address the needs of our students, to encourage their academic achievement and their professional success. We are explicit in informing the participants what we expect of them. Many students have never been to a scientific conference; indeed, have never been out of their state nor slept away from their families. So we have a required orientation session for all sponsored students. The Society also provides professional development workshops on how to negotiate graduate school, job interviews, presentations, and publication, and, for faculty, tenure. We promote excellence in science by providing students with opportunities to listen and meet with outstanding scientists, many of whom are themselves members of an underrepresented minority group. We invite parents and family members of local participants and high school students to attend our "Community Day" at the conference.

9. Support for programs that provide opportunities for undergraduate research should be enhanced and expanded. Stipends for students in these programs must be sufficient to allow them to pay for tuition, fees, books, and living expenses.

10. Graduate fellowships and traineeships should provide support that permits graduate students to survive, so that they do not have to take out thousands of dollars of loans just to get by. These tax-derived funds should benefit our citizens and resident aliens.

11. Colleges and Universities must seek to diversify the professoriate. Many colleges are currently providing incentives for scientists who are also interested in K-12 science education. Can private/public partnerships be created to increase the diversity of the professoriate?

12. Partnerships between private corporations, federal agencies, and nonprofits must be encouraged and strengthened to promote diversity in the scientific workforce.

13. A federal committee should be formed to determine a national policy that will encourage greater development of our country's youth to seek science careers and lessen our dependence on foreign nationals.

REFERENCES

Bagla, P. 2002. Missing Generation Leaves Hole in Fabric of Research. *Science* 298: 773-74.

Borden, V. 2002. The Top 100. *Black Issues in Higher Education* 19:40-49.

College Board. 1999. *Reaching the Top: A Report of the National Task Force of Minority High Achievement.* College Board Publications, New York, NY.

Dalaker, J. 2001. *Poverty in the United States: 2000.* U.S. Census Bureau, Current Population Reports, Series P60-214, U.S. Government Printing Office, Washington, DC, 2001.

National Science Board. *Science and Engineering Indicators 2000.* Arlington, VA: National Science Foundation, 2000 (NSB-00-01).

National Science Board. *Science and Engineering Indicators 2002.* Arlington, VA: National Science Foundation, 2002 (NSB-02-01).

National Science Foundation. Division of Science Resources Studies. *Statistical Profiles of Foreign Doctoral Recipients in Science and Engineering: Plans to Stay in the United States.* Arlington, VA: National Science Foundation, 1998.

National Science Foundation. *Women, Minorities, and Persons with Disabilities in Science and Engineering: 2000.* Arlington, VA: National Science Foundation, 2000 (NSF-00-327).

Quintana-Baker, M. 2002. A Profile of Mexican American, Puerto Rican and Other Hispanic STEM Doctorates: 1983-1999. *Journal of Women and Minorities in Science and Engineering* 8: 99-121.

WEPAN Position Statement

Jan Rinehart, President
Susan Staffin Metz, Immediate Past President
Sherry Woods, President-Elect
Women in Engineering Programs and
Advocates Network (WEPAN)

STATEMENT OF ORGANIZATION AND MISSION

WEPAN is a not-for-profit, 501(c)(3) organization founded in 1990. WEPAN is dedicated to catalyzing change to enhance the success of women of all ethnicities in the engineering profession.

STATEMENT OF POSITION

Demographic trends indicate that by the year 2005, women will represent 62 percent of new entrants into the United States' labor force, and underrepresented minorities will represent 51 percent (Judy and D'Amico, 1997). In addition, employment opportunities for science, mathematics, engineering, and technology (SMET) jobs during 1998-2008 are expected to increase by about 51 percent or about 1.9 million jobs. It is WEPAN's position that policies must recognize these demographic shifts and must address systemic changes to meet the national need for engineers. Without addressing the lack of women studying engineering and the underrepresentation of women in the engineering workforce, the gap between the national need and the supply of engineers will not change. In essence, we put the nation at risk.

A principal effect of these population changes based upon recent trends and projections for coming decades, is that engineering's traditional talent pool of Caucasian men is rapidly becoming insufficient to meet future demands in both industry and academia. It is therefore imperative that greater emphasis be placed upon preparing the women and minorities who will be a majority of the available workforce to enter these fields—and whose representation within engineering has grown steadily, if slowly, in recent decades.

Women remain severely underrepresented at all levels in the U.S.: representing 9 percent of the engineering workforce; 20.5 percent of baccalaureate degree recipients, 22 percent of master's degree recipients, and 14.7 percent of doctoral degree recipients (Engineering Workforce Commission of the American Association of Engineering Societies, Inc., *Engineering and Technology Degrees* 2001).

The response by policymakers must, therefore, be viewed as a national priority. Policies must go beyond simple encouragement, which thus far has proven inadequate in bringing women to the engineering classrooms, laboratories, and workforce. Beyond numbers, women represent a vital source of intellectual talent that can no longer go untapped.

RECOMMENDATIONS FOR POLICY

WEPAN recommends the adoption of national, state, and local policies that serve significantly to enhance science and mathematics education at all grade levels, while aggressively implementing initiatives that will increase enrollment and retention of women in engineering at the college level. We need to increase the public awareness of the role and mission of engineers so that "being an engineer" means something tangible to the general public. To encourage girls and women to consider and pursue careers in engineering, WEPAN believes that policies must address two broad areas:

- The popular understanding of what engineering is, who engineers are, and how they contribute to society
- The "culture" in which engineering is taught at the university level.

POPULAR UNDERSTANDING OF ENGINEERING AND PRECOLLEGE OUTREACH

Only 8 percent of all students taking the SAT intend to major in engineering. Of this group, 19 percent are girls of all races and ethnicities. Girls are taking the necessary math and science classes in secondary school to major in engineering. Over 40 percent of high school physics and calculus students are girls (NSF, 1999; American College Testing, 1998). Girls are prepared for engineering majors. They are just not interested. Engineering is currently failing to interest students, male or female, in becoming engaged in the profession. This general lack of interest may be attributed to a lack of awareness. In a 1998 Harris poll,

61 percent of Americans described themselves as "not very well informed" or "not at all informed" about engineering and engineers. Among women, the percentage increased to 78 percent; among college graduates, 53 percent.

Addressing problems of how engineers and engineering are understood and perceived could be addressed, at least partly, through simple interaction (by students and their teachers alike) with representatives from within the field. Another avenue is reaching out to media- and tech-savvy youth of the early 21st century in ways they can understand. Depictions of science, engineering, and technology in movies and television are more present than ever before in medical and crime shows. September 11, 2001, has been accompanied by heightened visibility and increased public discussion and debate, both of which create opportunities for expanded understanding of the role of science and engineering in our daily lives. Educators and practitioners should capitalize on these opportunities that are relevant to young people.

Programs that supplement the science and math curricula in lower grades, provide mentoring at all levels, enlighten students about the importance of science and technology to society, and educate students about the broad range of career opportunities in engineering, need to continue to increase the representation of women in engineering. However, outreach alone is not sufficient to effect meaningful change. After-school programs or summer camps, while a valuable component, are not going to increase participation in numbers adequate to address the problem on a national scale.

What is called for, instead, is a systemic shift toward engagement with teachers, schools, and entire school systems. Educators from kindergarten through graduate school must join with professional engineers in developing an innovative approach that is dynamic, systemic, and synergistic. For example, Massachusetts has taken the lead by incorporating engineering principles as part of the state's educational standards, a first in the U.S. Texas has also taken a step in this direction by accepting an engineering-based course as a science credit at the high school level.

UNIVERSITY CULTURE

Addressing issues of the engineering "culture" in the university environment is imperative to ensure the long-term success of women who enter the field. The difficulties women students experience in attempting to retain their intrinsic interest in science and engineering in environments that undercut their confidence, motivation, and sense of belonging in the field, pose formidable obstacles to their completion of academic training and/or satisfactory performance in engineering careers.

Research strongly suggests that factors unrelated to academic performance are largely to blame for a disproportionate drop-out rate among women engineering students:

- According to the 1998 report, *Women and Men of the Engineering Path*, women and men earn similar grades in engineering courses, and women who leave engineering have higher grades than men who stay. It is not, therefore, poor academic performance that drives women out of engineering, but higher levels of dissatisfaction.
- The persistence rates for women in math, science, and engineering programs range from 30 to 46 percent, depending on the type of institution—far below the 39 to 61 percent rate for their male counterparts (Adelman, 1998).

A 1998 national pilot climate study by WEPAN found that, although male and female students responded similarly in many cases, perceptions of their college experience differed widely. Women, for example, generally rated their experience lower in areas relating to feelings of self-confidence, such as comfort level with lab equipment, the sense that engineering is the "right" major, and participation in classroom discussion. Many institutions participating in the pilot study have recommended changes at their institutions based on its results (Brainard et al., 1999).

The recently released Goodman Research Group's (GRG) final report on the *Women's Experiences in College Engineering (WECE) Project (2002)* provides comprehensive quantitative evidence that women's assessments of (1) their self-confidence in their academic abilities, (2) the engineering department environment, and (3) the engineering classroom environment are vital factors in their persistence in engineering majors. The study also demonstrates that women who participate more frequently in engineering support activities, particularly those combining social and academic interaction, are less likely to leave engineering majors. As both Adelman (1998) and Goodman (2002) have documented, women students are not leaving engineering because they cannot make the grade or because they find the curriculum too challenging. Instead, it is the lack of social interaction and sense of community within the field of inquiry, and the divorce of curriculum from real-work application (Goodman, 2002).

Margolis and Fisher's 2001 book, *Unlocking the Clubhouse*, asserts that confidence issues for women in computer science require and deserve institutional responses of attention, intervention, and remediation. In their well-structured, longitudinal study, Margolis and Fisher explore multiple dimensions of this issue in careful detail. Their findings also counter casual myths (e.g., about the so-called natural distribution of interest and aptitude) that have inhibited or misdirected earlier remedial efforts. Further, their model of undergraduate recruitment and retention raises the enrollment of women in undergraduate computer science from 7 percent in 1995 to 42 percent in 2000. And Fisher's work at Carnegie Mellon University provides a host of recommendations on how institutions can change the quality of the student experience to further promote gender equity in STEM (science, technology, engineering, and mathematics) education.

Identifying recommendations and policies that can affect the culture within universities is no small task. WEPAN proposes the following:

- Link research funds to first- and second-year retention of engineering students in the researcher's home institution.
- Require that universities collect and publish data that are disaggregated by race and gender. A standard definition of first- and second-year retention would need to be defined and observed.
- Evaluation criteria for research grants should include status or improvement in enrollment, retention, and graduation rates of undergraduate and graduate women and underrepresented minorities.
- Performance evaluation for department heads within universities should include status or progress of recruitment, retention, and promotion of women faculty.
- Funding agencies should review guidelines and expand criteria to include the replication of tested programs and initiatives, not just a focus on new and original ideas.

WEPAN's final recommendation bridges public awareness, pre-college outreach, and university culture of engineering. At this time, the focus continues to be the pipeline. How do we get more kindergarten students to develop and sustain their interest in engineering? Most students do not have an opportunity to fully explore engineering until they reach college. All students, but girls in particular, are not ready to narrow their choices and select a major such as engineering that precludes study in other areas. When students are asked to declare a major, given the stereotypes, lack of awareness, and male-dominated environment, the choice to major in engineering loses far too often, particularly among women and people of color. It is time to develop alternate pathways and frameworks at the college level that can engage students in engineering beyond the first or even second year of college. Given the rigorous curriculum, this is a challenge. But engineers always meet challenges and we implore them to do so. Too many creative minds are being lost in the current process.

Since 1990, WEPAN has taken the lead in promoting change to increase the number and success of women in engineering. Our impact has been significant; yet the systemic change now needed will require collaborative efforts and, more importantly, policy changes that have the real power to positively impact the demographics of tomorrow's engineering and science workforce.

REFERENCES

Adelman, C. (1998). *Women and Men of the Engineering Path: A Model for Analyses of Undergraduate Careers*, U.S. Department of Education and The National Institute for Science Education, Washington, DC.

American College Testing. (1998). *Are America's Students Taking More Science and Mathematics Coursework?* ACT Research Report Series 98.2. Available online at: http://www.act.org/research/briefs/98.2.html

Brainard, S., Gilmore, G., and Metz, S. (1999, June). *National WEPAN Pilot Climate Survey: Exploring the Environment for Undergraduate Engineering Students*. WEPAN National Conference Proceedings, San Antonio, Texas.

Engineering Workforce Commission of the American Association of Engineering Societies, Inc. (2001). Washington, DC.

Goodman, et al. (2002). *Women's Experiences in College Engineering (WECE) Project 2002,* http://www.grginc.com/WECE_FINAL_REPORT.pdf

Judy, R., and D'Amico, C. (1997). *Workforce 2020: Work and Workers in the 21st Century.* Hudson Institute, Indianapolis, IN.

Margolis, J., and Fisher, A. (2001). *Unlocking the Clubhouse: Women in Computing.* MIT Press, Cambridge, MA.

National Science Foundation. (1999). *Women and Minorities and People with Disabilities in Science and Engineering, 1998*: National Science Foundation, Arlington, VA.

Strenta, C. (1993). *Choosing and Leaving Science in Highly Selective Institutions: General Factors and the Questions of Gender*: Alfred P. Sloan Foundation, New York, NY.

Concluding Remarks

Marye Anne Fox, Chancellor,
North Carolina State University

This Summit revealed what many participants already knew: the U.S. science and engineering workforce includes too few native-born Americans, with particular underrepresentation among women and minority groups. Most young Americans are choosing careers outside of science, mathematics, and engineering, which are the basis for innovation in the development of new technologies that drive our economy. Our K-12 schools graduate only 27 percent of their students with training in precalculus,[1] the first stepping-stone to an S&E career. Half of college freshmen intending to major in S&E abandon that major before their sophomore year[2]—one reason our universities rank 61st out of 63 countries in converting college undergraduates to B.S. degreed graduates in the natural science and engineering disciplines.[3] Existing workers in several fields—notably electrical engineering and computer science—find there is only weak supporting infrastructure for the constant retraining required to keep up with their fields (IEEE).[4] At every level of education and em-

---

[1]National Center for Education Statistics. *National Assessment of Educational Progress.* Washington, DC: Dept. of Education, 2001. Also available: http://nces.ed.gov/pubs2001/2001498.pdf.

[2]Nancy M. Hewitt and Elaine Seymour. Talking About Leaving: Why Undergraduates Leave the Sciences. Boulder CO: Westview Press, 1999.

[3]U.S. students graduating with degrees in the natural sciences or engineering as a percentage of total degrees ranks 61st in a list of 63 countries. National Science Foundation. Science and Engineering Indicators 2002 [Appendix Table 2-18]. Arlington, VA: NSF, 2002. Also available: http://www.nsf.gov/sbe/srs/seind02/start.htm.

[4]From Instititute for Electrical and Electronics Engineers (IEEE) position paper within.

ployment, women and minorities are significantly underrepresented in S&E positions.[5] By 2010, these "underrepresented" groups will constitute 72 percent of the college-age cohort.[6]

Yet, despite these shortcomings, American science is still strong and innovative. The combined effects of foreign S&E workers entering this country[7] and the ability of U.S. industry to outsource or relocate to other countries[8] have meant—on a global scale—that demand has often adjusted to supply, and vice versa. But the national loss remains: lost jobs and lost opportunities for new businesses and national leadership. Without broader participation, the technological superiority that has served the U.S. so well may be held captive in the future to an inefficient S&E labor system that threatens our continued ability to lead in scientific innovation.

This Summit has been held in order to showcase and consolidate community views on policy directions regarding this complex and urgent issue. For over a year, the Government-University-Industry Research Roundtable (GUIRR) has sought to define a common ground on which existing organizations might combine resources to mobilize and tackle areas of mutual interest. Summit presenters identified at least nine such areas of common interest and concern (see introduction). This outcome should help policy leaders focus on those approaches currently receiving the most community support.

-----

[5]National Science Foundation. *Science and Engineering Indicators 2002* (pp. 3-12 to 3-16). Arlington, VA: NSF, 2002. Also available: http://www.nsf.gov/sbe/srs/seind02/start.htm.

[6]In the year 2010, current trends project that 37 percent of the college-age U.S. population will be from minorities of both sexes and another 35 percent of that population will be nonminority women. U.S. Bureau of Census. Projections of the Resident Population by Age, Sex, Race and Hispanic Origin: 1999 to 2100. Washington, DC: Government Printing Office, 2000. Also available: www.census.gov/population/estimates/nation.

[7]Foreign-born, S&E-trained U.S. scientists and engineers represent 12.2 percent of the total S&E workforce. National Science Foundation. Science and Engineering Indicators 2002 (Text Table 3-24). Arlington, VA: NSF, 2002. Also available: http://www.nsf.gov/sbe/srs/seind02/start.htm.

[8]U.S. Department of Commerce. Office of Technology Policy. Globalizing Industrial Research and Development. Washington, DC: Government Printing Office, 1999.

Appendix A—
Keynote Speaker Addresses

A Critical Mass for Making a Difference

Shirley Ann Jackson, Ph.D.
President, Rensselaer Polytechnic Institute

Good afternoon.

If, ever, there was a time at which one might be in danger of preaching to the choir, this may be that time.

I find myself in the happy circumstance of being surrounded by like minds and comparable interests. There are more than 30 organizations participating at this summit, and even more in attendance—each concerned with, and working on, the issue of developing the United States' scientific and technological workforce of the future.

I currently serve with three of these organizations:

• With our hosts, the Government-University-Industry Research Roundtable (GUIRR)—I am a member of the Roundtable, and chair the Working Group on the Science and Engineering Workforce.
• With Building Engineering and Science Talent (BEST)—I serve on the Board of Directors' executive committee, and chair BEST's Blue Ribbon Panel on Higher Education.
• With the Committee for Economic Development—I am co-chair of the Subcommittee on the Supply of Scientists and Engineers.

So you can discern the level of my interest in, and commitment to, this issue. And to be in this company—to be a member of this choir, if you will—is an abundance of riches.

One would wish only that the topic were neither so serious nor so urgent. I am sure that most of you saw in yesterday's *Chronicle of Higher Education* that the number of doctorates awarded by American research universities in 2001 fell to a level not seen in nine years—a decline of 4.5 percent over 1998, the all-time high. The decrease in doctorates in the science and engineering disciplines, which fell by 6.5 percent since 1998, is responsible for a major portion of the decline. Fields outside science and engineering, on the other hand, saw a decrease of less than 1 percent over 1998.

Is there a more apt, or more timely, incentive for our work at this summit? Obviously not.

Nevertheless, I am buoyed and encouraged because what I sense, overwhelmingly, is that this summit may represent an approaching critical mass—a coming together of enough good minds, good work, and good research on the issue. With critical mass, we can begin to make a real difference.

To make a difference, this issue must capture the full and serious attention of lawmakers, policymakers, educators, corporate executives, government officials, the media, and, ultimately, the public, for these are the constituencies that, in the end, will address and resolve it. And to have that happen, we will want to work in concert with each other, supplementing our research data and pressing conjointly for the points upon which we agree.

So, as I have said, I am buoyed that there are so many organizations that take this issue seriously, each approaching the situation with its own perspectives, having positions that reflect the issue's urgency to them, and actively working for change. For although we may differ on some aspects, and although we may differ on approach, we are moving in essentially the same direction. And, that is the important thing.

For, surely, we all understand that if the United States is to continue to be a world leader, a nation without peer—a position Americans have enjoyed for decades and now take for granted—the nation must make a substantial investment in its scientific and technological capital, its intellectual capital.

As we all know, the source of our innovative capacity and technological ability, which has given us heretofore unknown richness, choice, and leadership, is thinning.

• We know that the average age of the science and engineering workforce is rising. And we know that the total number of retirements among science- and engineering-degreed workers will dramatically increase over the next 20 years.

• We know, too, that the college-age population has declined, that fewer U.S. students are electing courses of study in the sciences (especially the physical sciences) and engineering, and that growth in doctorates awarded has been to students from overseas, not to U.S. recipients.

The net of these and other factors is that U.S. production of science and engineering professionals is at risk of not being sufficient to maintain the status quo, which puts the United States in danger of relinquishing its world leadership to other nations—leadership important not only to our economic status and security but to the world.

For years we have avoided confronting this issue, shielded by importing the advanced talent that we need on H-1B visas. International scientists and engineers have been, and remain, a valuable reservoir of talent for the U.S.

But several factors make this no longer a viable option for the long term. With new homeland security concerns, many science and engineering positions (especially in government and with regard to certain dual-use technologies) must be held by U.S. citizens, and only by U.S. citizens. Moreover, the United States finds itself amid nations fast becoming peers in science and engineering. Centers of technology-based activity, training, and entrepreneurial activity are spreading rapidly throughout the globe. China, for instance, which used to send students to the United States for advanced training, has increased its domestic Ph.D. production by a factor of 60 over the last 15 years. Those students who used to come to the United States to earn advanced degrees and then stay to work in our industries, now have a viable choice to return home, where they can find both employment and the satisfaction of building and contributing to their own nations. We are not the only game in town. What we are considering is occurring, and must occur, within the global context.

Other nations have put into place strong national strategies to promote and expand their core technological strengths. These countries recognize that national superiority, security, and economic status in a global economy rely on technological capacity and their ability to muster a technologically trained and literate workforce. Yet, despite the obvious need, the United States has no national plan for "growing and sustaining our own" technological talent.

This is a general consideration and overall risk.

There are areas of specific concern, however. I already spoke of governmental needs. The situation with regard to nuclear science is another case in point. As in the other science and engineering disciplines, the nuclear workforce is approaching retirement age without a corresponding influx of appropriately qualified younger personnel to replace them. Fewer young people are studying nuclear science, nuclear engineering, and related fields at the university level, and a growing number of universities are giving up their nuclear education programs altogether, due to a lack of interest and perceptions that the nuclear power industry is fading.

Yet, ironically, the nuclear power industry is recording better performance than in any time in its history. The safety, performance, and economic competitiveness of the nuclear industry are at an all-time high. The questions are, Who will maintain and enhance existing nuclear technology? and Who will design the new—in nuclear power, and beyond?

On the security front, there are new threats from rogue nations and groups that have, or are developing, weapons of mass destruction. Homeland protection has taken on new importance, and if the United States is to engage in credible monitoring, inspection, and mitigation roles, it must have the trained nuclear scientists who can perform those duties.

This is but one example. To maintain our economic standing and our national security, we must examine the scale and severity of the current shortfall in "succession planning" for the science and engineering workforce, as a whole, and identify educational and training initiatives that will help to ensure the nation's human reservoir of scientific and technological knowledge and expertise.

Now, there are varying needs. I am not talking about predictions of numbers of specific jobs in specific fields, but rather, national capacity— national capacity that has brought the United States, and I dare say, the world, to the degree of advance and progress we have reached today— national capacity to ensure our future and to provide hope to those beyond our shores.

I will not presume to suggest specific answers, or even to summarize all good ideas—after all, that is what this summit is about.

Rather, as we collaborate at this summit, and in the future, to resolve these issues, there are two key elements that I would urge you to keep uppermost in your minds.

The first concerns demographics. The population of our nation now reflects a "new majority" made up of women and minority groups, which together account for more than half of our numbers. As an example, women now outnumber men in undergraduate enrollments. This "new majority" will continue to grow throughout this century. But although they now make up more than half of the nation's workforce, these groups long have been underrepresented in the science and engineering disciplines. They are the underrepresented majority. Moreover, there is no tradition for them to follow, and few examples for them to aspire to. So, for some time to come, students pursuing these career paths will be pioneers, breaking a new path.

This is a change with enormous implications for the future of the science and engineering workforce. It means that, although this is where significant talent resides—and it is from these sectors that we must draw our future scientists, mathematicians, engineers, and technologists—we are not doing so. This really must change. There is no other choice. The talent that we have as a nation lies within all of our young people, including this new majority talent pool. And, it is there. And, it can, and must be, mined.

To do this, we will have to find new ways to interest and attract these nontraditional pioneers into science and engineering. We will have to find new ways to educate them. We will have to find new ways to mentor them. We will have to value intellectual agility, if we want intellectual agility. We may have to alter workplace cultures to assure that these non-traditional pioneers feel comfortable and welcomed in their new careers.

It is a huge undertaking, which will require new ideas, new concepts, new ways of thinking. But in the end, we are lucky because our nation has a rich vein of talent that can be mined and refined.

The second element I ask you to keep in mind, and to which we must sensitize others, is the element of time. The challenge to building a new cohort of scientists and engineers is that this is not subject to a "quick-fix." The kind of investment that is required takes many, many years, as we all know. If we wait until we discover that we do not have a science and engineering workforce sufficient to meet our needs—if we wait until that crisis actually is upon us—it will be too late, by several decades, to remedy. That is why the crisis is today.

I could not help but notice that last month the public schools of the District of Columbia endured a $30 million dollar budget cut. To accommodate this cut without closing schools or furloughing employees, the school board postponed, by a year, the re-opening of McKinley Tech, a school in Northeast Washington, DC, that is to re-emerge as a technology high school. I am a product of the DC public school system. The generation of students studying and learning now in DC classrooms constitutes our talent pool, and each time we delay engaging them, nurturing them, educating them, teaching them, we delay our future.

The case could be made that delaying McKinley Tech sets back homeland security, postpones increased nuclear safety and security, delays energy production, curtails nuclear medicine and industrial radiology, and strikes at the heart of our economic security and global competitiveness.

Nevertheless, there are indications that we are approaching critical mass in addressing these issues. Corporations have long understood the need to invest in programs for both students and their teachers—programs that build their future workforce. These help us to tap into the full talent pool.

The National Science Foundation recently awarded grants amounting to $50 million over the next five years to support new centers for improving K-12 and postsecondary science and mathematics teaching and for research on learning. This will help us to tap into the full talent pool.

We have new "No Child Left Behind" legislation, which encourages proven teaching practices and promotes the concept that every child is valuable. This helps us to tap into the full talent pool.

And we have the participation of so many groups here today at this GUIRR Pan-Organizational Summit on the U.S. Science and Engineering Workforce. Your commitment and your efforts have a cumulative effect. This, too, helps us to tap into the full talent pool.

When we are all moving toward the same goal, the nation is in the strongest possible position, with the capacity to maintain our economic security, national homeland security, and the American way of life.

Building science and engineering talent is a cumulative process requiring commitment and participation over time, but beginning now, of all elements—government, industry, education, the media, the public, everyone. We need to engage *all* these elements to create critical mass, which is what is needed for action and progress.

And so—since I am addressing the choir, since I am a member of the choir—I urge you to sing, and to sing loudly, to sing in harmony, and to sing long. We need all our voices.

Thank you.

Transportation Workforce Issues and Opportunities

Joseph S. Toole
Associate Administrator for Professional Development
Federal Highway Administration,
U.S. Department of Transportation

INTRODUCTION

America's transportation workforce has become a major issue for all facets of industry. Faced with a shrinking pool of qualified workers, the public and private sectors have begun to advance a variety of strategies focused on dealing with this critical problem. Because all of these entities are competing with each other for the same pool of candidates, there is a clear need to advance strategies in a coordinated and comprehensive manner to address the workforce issue.

There is a particular concern and focus on the need for scientists and engineers in developing the workforce. Engineering is at the core of the industry's ability to design and deliver the nation's transportation system. It is also clear that an increasing dependence on technological advancements in transportation will be necessary to keep pace with the country's growing demand for mobility, and science and engineering will make a critical contribution to that technological innovation.

Many factors impact the industry's ability to recruit qualified individuals into the workforce. A critical issue is the increasing competition among professions for skilled workers. Today, individuals have a broad range of options available to them including positions in the information technology, health, and environmental industries. Overall, this means there is a decreasing pool of skilled workers available to the transportation industry. The industry is also changing. The new transportation reality requires technical and managerial skills, and abilities beyond traditional backgrounds.

Many organizations and individuals have attempted to address the workforce issue in transportation. National associations have embarked on programs specifically designed to attract individuals into the workforce. These efforts have enjoyed modest success, but not to the extent that they have put in place permanent solutions to the problem. More must be done, and greater industry-wide efforts must be embraced.

To address the critical issue of transportation workforce development, the U.S. Department of Transportation hosted the National Workforce Summit in May 2002 during National Transportation Week. Transportation leaders representing federal and state transportation agencies, academia, industry, labor unions, professional associations, and consulting firms participated in the program. The National Workforce Summit was the first ever, fully coordinated workforce initiative focused on developing the people necessary to preserve and advance our nation's transportation system.

FRAMING THE CHALLENGE

U.S. Department of Transportation deputy secretary Michael P. Jackson noted that the industry as a whole faces serious challenges of an aging workforce with the potential of more than 50 percent of the transportation workforce eligible to retire in 5 to 15 years. Mr. Jackson commented that cooperation and creative partnerships with educational and academic institutions; professional organizations; and state, local, and international transportation agencies are the key to effectively addressing the transportation workforce challenge. The deputy secretary referred to the process as "building the pipeline," which has become a metaphor for addressing workforce issues.

Deputy Secretary Jackson also participated in a discussion with industry leaders concerning their perspectives on the transportation workforce issue. Participants identified institutional concerns that the industry must overcome if it is to find and retain effective employees:

- Potential employees don't perceive transportation as an attractive, rewarding career option.
- The industry is burdened with an "engineers-only" image that contradicts the wide range of technical and managerial skills necessary to operate successful transportation organizations.
- Transportation agencies offer inadequate career development opportunities, which makes it difficult to retain qualified employees at all levels.

DATA NEEDS

One obstacle is the lack of workforce data. Cinde Weatherby Gilliland, senior project manager/Transit and Transportation Planning for URS

Corporation, reviewed research concerning the challenges facing the transportation workforce. The General Accounting Office (GAO) views the projected human capital shortfall as providing serious programmatic problems and risks for the industry. In addition to the anticipated loss of the industry's technical expertise in the next five years, data indicate that 71 percent of federal career senior executive service workers will be eligible for retirement by 2005. Transportation Research Board (TRB) data research reinforce the GAO data, citing institutional constraints, human resources, and an aging population as critical issues. To further emphasize the changing face of the industry, TRB also sees computer support specialists as the greatest occupational area for growth, predicted to increase by 97 percent. By comparison, the projected change for civil engineers is 10 percent, while occupational growth for environmental engineers is expected to increase 26 percent. Gilliland concluded by pointing to the lack of real numbers of transportation workers compared to need (demand), and the number of projected workers (supply).

OPPORTUNITIES FOR INTERVENTION

Cheri Marti, assistant director for the Minnesota Local Technical Assistance Program/Center for Transportation Studies, and who chairs an ad hoc Workforce Framework Group, reported on the group's work to date. The group has identified important societal and cultural factors affecting the decision-making process about career choices. Members also developed a life-cycle continuum, a graphic that identifies opportunities for intervention to create awareness, influence choice, and "brand" transportation as an attractive career goal. The continuum reinforces the necessity to create learning paths for fundamental skills that also satisfy workforce needs. In addition, statistics indicate that two thirds of employees change occupations during their work life. This information reinforces the need to look beyond the entry-level employee and include recruiting midlevel professionals as a workforce strategy to capture the richness of professional experience. Marti also emphasized the need to promote a collaborative and coordinated approach to address the issue throughout the transportation industry.

ADMINISTRATORS' PERSPECTIVES ON THE
WORKFORCE CHALLENGE

Three U.S. Department of Transportation administrators participated in the Summit: Ellen G. Engleman, administrator for the Research and Special Programs Administration (RSPA); Jennifer L. Dorn, federal transit administrator; and Mary E. Peters, federal highway administrator.

Ms. Engleman noted that, whether we move goods, people, or information, transportation is the pipeline to the nation's prosperity. Jennifer Dorn commented that three principles should guide the initiative: (1) all recruitment is personal, it requires individuals who can motivate and inspire others; (2) knowing how to think is more important than knowing what to think, a multidisciplinary approach is necessary; and (3) flexibility can be difficult, but it's not impossible; organizations must pilot new approaches and identify new ways to engage and reward those in the system. Mary Peters supported the need to help young people understand that they can have a role in making change happen in their communities. Education is key, but educating the transportation workforce requires a variety of skills and disciplines in the new transportation environment.

ISSUES AND PRIORITIES

The Summit participants focused on three critical components of transportation workforce development:

- Workforce Pipeline: identify new opportunities and approaches to ensure a trained, motivated, and diverse workforce to deliver transportation programs.
- Training and Professional Development: characterize processes to ensure that transportation workers are able to apply new technologies and bring new skills to effectively manage projects in a more demanding work environment.
- Institutionalize Workforce Development: improve and coordinate training and development programs industry-wide by institutionalizing procedures and resources to prepare a skilled, technically proficient, and motivated workforce.

These themes reflected an awareness that the workforce development effort needs to reach beyond current efforts and be more strategically oriented in addressing the issues. While there was a desire on the part of the public agency, private sector, organized labor, and academia representatives to develop a workforce strategy, there was also a definite call for the U.S. Department of Transportation to exercise its leadership, particularly as a convener and an advocate.

WORKFORCE PIPELINE

Participants focused on the multidisciplinary aspects of transportation and the need to develop communication and marketing strategies that speak to potential, current, and retired employees throughout their education and professional lives. Working with the life-cycle continuum graphic, the group identified the problem as both supply and demand, highlighting the need to involve industry, locally led partnerships, and academic institutions at all levels throughout the process. Participants noted that the pipeline analogy was perhaps too rigid, that in reality it was much more porous because employees tend to move in and out of the system. They reinforced the need and value of lifelong learning that welcomes a diverse workforce competent in an array of academic disciplines and technical skill levels. The group identified the need for industry partners to coordinate closely with educational institutions—K-12, technical schools, community colleges, and universities—to raise the awareness of transportation as a rewarding career. These cooperative programs must be complemented with an aggressive marketing and outreach campaign to create excitement about transportation careers beyond the traditional engineering focus.

The challenges to the group's recommendations involve identifying current partners and leaders to champion the effort. Additionally, while the participants focused on the need for lifelong learning and professional development, they are concerned about the current workforce and its ability to meet the demands of a changing transportation environment. There was a feeling among the Summit participants that it would take a sustained commitment on the part of the transportation community to assure that the youth of today are attracted to the transportation jobs of the future. Specifically, this included

- stronger partnerships with educational systems to reach students in K-12;
- a concerted effort to show the contributions that transportation makes to society, the career opportunities transportation offers, and the importance of transportation to the United States;
- development of an integrated program of outreach activities that would support students through ongoing activities (e.g., awareness programs that might lead to internship opportunities, which would lead to scholarships); and
- a much greater tie between the transportation community and universities, colleges, and community colleges to support transportation-related programs, and the need for the transportation and education communities to be much more proactive in attracting students into transportation.

TRAINING AND PROFESSIONAL DEVELOPMENT

Group members considered better ways to invest in skills development and training of transportation agency employees. They agreed that professional development encompassed more than traditional training and should include mentoring programs and other opportunities available throughout the industry. They noted that training needs must respond to the organization's core competencies and ensure that the employee and the organization benefit from the instruction. Participants also recognized the need to modernize organizational structures so that they can respond more quickly and accurately to employee training needs.

There was also a focus on the need to cultivate a public/private partnership to foster cooperative programs and activities. These partnerships should also help develop a consistent definition of transportation training objectives and outcomes, and promote the need for broad training that incorporates both professional and technical skills. For example, an engineer must be able to explain projects and schedules to communities affected by transportation projects. There was a recognition that there needs to be continuing investment in the transportation workforce to (1) assure workers are using the latest technologies and practices to improve transportation, (2) better equip the workforce to meet the challenges of today, and (3) help attract and retain the best and brightest workers for the future. Approaches would include:

- developing a clearinghouse of transportation-related training, educational and developmental programs that can be shared and used by the entire community;
- developing programs that use the latest training and development technologies (e.g., Web-based training, distance learning) to make training more accessible and effective;
- investing in existing programs that have served as successful mechanisms for providing new skill development in the transportation sector; and
- finding ways to support programmatic and cultural changes in the transportation industry that encourage investment in learning and development.

INSTITUTIONALIZING WORKFORCE DEVELOPMENT

Participants reiterated the need for a coordinated approach to recruiting, retaining, and developing the transportation workforce throughout the professional life cycle. With the impending retirement of more than half of the industry's engineering and technical employees, the group discussed the need to encourage those who are retiring to choose partial retirement rather than full retirement. They pointed to the number of 55-year-old retirees who are interested in second and third career choices, and the need for organizations to capture their years of experience.

There was also agreement that the industry is larger than a single mode, and it requires a broad range of technical and professional skills. Participants regard partnerships with educational institutions and professional associations as vital to the success of any workforce development initiative. This includes partnering with the Department of Education. Participants also discussed the need for accurate, critical data about the transportation workforce. The group linked workforce development with economic development issues, which can be translated into political support. In the short term, these data will be key to reauthorization. In the long term, having a better understanding about the status of the current workforce will help managers project future staffing needs.

In addition to data, the participants saw a need for a better, more systematic way to identify best practices across modes. The challenge is to adapt innovations and create new initiatives to address workforce problems. This will require champions from the transportation community who can advocate for resources to support the effort. Advancing initiatives to the institutional level will require start-up resources and the commitment of key decision makers if they are to be linked to agency capital programs. A key to these actions is partnering, and the value of the partnerships must be reflected in all aspects of the workforce development effort. Likewise, any barriers to such partnerships need to be removed. Specifically, there needs to be

- an institutional framework for coordinating these efforts and bringing the transportation community together to more effectively address the workforce issue, and
- greater ties between government, industry, and academia to share and pool resources and data for the workforce effort to be truly effective.

A NATIONAL PARTNERSHIP

The National Workforce Summit was designed to create an industry-wide partnership and foster the cooperative spirit that will carry forum results to implementation. The Summit concluded with each partner—transportation agencies, industry and association representatives, academics, and union representatives—signing a charter: "A Partnership for Educating, Training and Developing the Nation's Transportation Workforce." With this charter, the participants committed their support to an effort that will improve workforce development through new initiatives in the academic and transportation communities and may have implications for reauthorization. As a next step in support of the Summit initiative, a steering committee is being formed to guide and coordinate activities and to ensure that they complement government, industry, and academic community efforts.

Appendix B
Nonprofit Organizations Participating in the Pan-Organizational Summit on the U.S. Science and Engineering Workforce (November 11-12, 2002)

Alfred P. Sloan Foundation
Alliance for Science and Technology Research in America
American Association for the Advancement of Science
American Institute of Chemical Engineers
American Institute of Physics
American Society for Biochemistry and Molecular Biology
American Society of Civil Engineers
American Society of Engineering Education
American Society of Mechanical Engineers
Building Engineering and Science Talent
Business-Higher Education Forum
Coalition of the Concerned
Commission on Professionals in Science and Technology
Council on Competitiveness
Educational Testing Service
Global Alliance
Industrial Research Institute
Information Technology Association of America
Institute of Electrical and Electronics Engineers
MentorNet
National Action Council for Minorities in Engineering
National Association of Manufacturers
National Consortium for Graduate Degrees for Minorities in Science and
    Engineering
National Council of Teachers of Mathematics

National Society of Black Physicists
Partnership for Public Service
Project Kaleidoscope
RAND
Sigma Xi
Society for Advancement of Chicanos and Native Americans in Science
Women in Engineering Programs and Advocates Network

Appendix C
Summit Agenda
Pan-Organizational Summit on the
U.S. Science and Engineering Workforce

*All Sessions to take place in the National Academies' building at
2101 Constitution Avenue, NW, Washington, DC*

NOVEMBER 11, AUDITORIUM

2:30   Opening remarks—GUIRR Co-Chair William H. Joyce,
CEO Hercules

2:40   Challenges to the Community (Federal Session I)
NASA—Sam Armstrong, Senior Adviser to the Administrator
National Aeronautics and Space Administration
DEd—Susan Sclafani, Counselor to the Secretary of Education
Department of Education
DOE—Peter Faletra, Assistant Director, Science Education,
Office of Science
Department of Energy
DOC—John F. Sargent, Senior Technology Policy Analyst
Department of Commerce

3:20   Position papers, Group I
BEST—John Yochelson, President
Building Engineering and Science Talent
NCTM—Johnny Lott, President
National Council of Teachers of Mathematics
SACNAS—Maria Elena Zavala, President
Society for Advancement of Chicanos & Native Americans in Science
IRI —James Clovis, Head, Precollege Education Subcommittee
Industrial Research Institute

Panel Discussion with Presenters

4:15   Break

4:25   Position papers, Group II
       NACME—Daryl Chubin, Sr. Vice President, Policy and Research
       National Action Council for Minorities in Engineering
       ETS—Kurt Landgraf, President & CEO
       Educational Testing Service
       Sigma Xi—W. Frank Gilmore, President
       Sigma Xi, the Scientific Research Society
       WEPAN—Jan Rinehart, President
       Women in Engineering Programs and Advocates Network
       Alfred P. Sloan Foundation—Michael Teitelbaum, Director,
          S&E Workforce

       Panel Discussion with Presenters

5:35   Challenges to the Community (Federal Session II)
       NSF— Judith Ramaley, Assistant Director, Education &
          Human Resources
       National Science Foundation
       DOT— Joseph S. Toole, Associate Administrator for
          Professional Development
       Department of Transportation

6:00   Reception (all), **Rotunda**

6:20   Dinner (GUIRR members and invited speakers/designated
       presenters only)
       Members' Room
       Robert Reich, Secretary of Labor, Clinton Administration

NOVEMBER 12, AUDITORIUM

7:00   Continental Breakfast

7:50   Opening remarks—GUIRR Co-Chair Marye Anne Fox,
       Chancellor, North Carolina State University

8:00   Position papers, Group IV
       The National Academies—Wm. A. Wulf, President, National
          Academy of Engineering

The National Academies
AAAS—Shirley Malcom, Director, Education & Human Resources
American Association for the Advancement of Science
ASEE Engineering Dean's Council—David Wormley, Dean,
College of Engineering, Penn State University
American Society of Engineering Education
Business-Higher Education Forum—Dr. Constantine Papadakis,
President, Drexel University
Business-Higher Education Forum

Panel Discussion with Presenters

9:00 Position papers, Group V
GEM Consortium—Saundra Johnson, Executive Director
National Consortium for Graduate Degrees for Minorities in Science
AIChE—Dianne Dorland, President-Elect
American Institute of Chemical Engineers
ASCE—Tom Lenox, Sr. Managing Director
American Society for Civil Engineers
IEEE-USA—LeEarl Bryant, President
Institute of Electrical and Electronics Engineers

Panel Discussion with Presenters

10:00 Break

10:15 Position papers, Group VI
Project Kaleidoscope—Jeanne Narum, Director
Project Kaleidoscope
ASME—Susan Skemp, President
American Society of Mechanical Engineers
ASBMB—Stephen Dahms, Executive Director, CSUPERB
American Society for Biochemistry and Molecular Biology

Panel Discussion with Presenters

11:15 Position papers, Group VII
RAND—Bill Butz, Senior Economist
RAND Corporation
AIP—James H. Stith, Vice President, Physics Resources
American Institute of Physics
NSBP—Keith Jackson, President
National Society of Black Physicists

Council on Competitiveness— Amy Kaslow, Senior Fellow
Council on Competitiveness

Panel Discussion with Presenters

12:15 Lunch, **Lecture Room and Great Hall**
Shirley Jackson, President, Rensselaer Polytechnic Institute,
"Envisioning a 21st Century Science and Engineering Workforce"

1:00 Position papers, Group VIII
ASTRA—Mary Good, Chair
Alliance for Science and Technology Research in America
CPST— Eleanor Babco, Executive Director
Commission on Professionals in Science and Technology
ITAA— Harris Miller, President & CEO
Information Technology Association of America
MentorNet—Carol Muller, President & CEO
MentorNet

Panel Discussion with Presenters

2:00 Position papers, Group IX
NAM—Phyllis Eisen, Vice President Manufacturing Institute
National Association of Manufacturers
Global Alliance—Yolanda George, Co-Director
Global Alliance
PPS—Joan Timoney, Vice President, Programs
Partnership for Public Service
Coalition of the Concerned—Sam Armstrong
Coalition of the Concerned

Panel Discussion with Presenters

3:00 Break

3:15 Summary, Points of Agreement and Disagreement among
Presented Positions
GUIRR Co-Chair Marye Anne Fox, Chancellor, North Carolina
State University

3:30 Q&A / Discussion of the Way Ahead

3:50 Adjourn

Appendix D
National Academies Publications on the
U.S. Science and Engineering Workforce

Achieving High Educational Standards for All: Conference Summary. Timothy Ready, Christopher Edley Jr., and Catherine E. Snow. Washington, DC: National Academy Press, 2002.

Addressing the Nation's Changing Needs for Biomedical and Behavioral Scientists. Committee on National Needs for Biomedical and Behavioral Scientists. Washington, DC: National Academy Press, 2000.

Advisor, Teacher, Role Model, Friend: On Being a Mentor to Students in Science and Engineering. Committee on Science, Engineering, and Public Policy. Washington, DC: National Academy Press, 1997.

Attracting Science and Mathematics Ph.D.'s to Secondary School Education. Committee on Attracting Science and Mathematics Ph.D.'s to Secondary School Teaching. Washington, DC: National Academy Press, 2000.

Building a Diverse Work Force. Scientists and Engineers in the Office of Naval Research. Committee to Study Diversity in the Scientific and Engineering Work Force of the Office of Naval Research. Washington, DC: National Academy Press, 1997.

Building a Workforce for the Information Economy. Committee on Workforce Needs in the Information Economy. Washington, DC: National Academy Press, 2001.

Careers in Science and Engineering: A Student Planning Guide to Grad School and Beyond. Committee on Science, Engineering, and Public Policy. Washington, DC: National Academy Press, 1996.

Diversity in Engineering: Managing the Workforce of the Future. Committee on Diversity in the Engineering Workforce. Washington, DC: National Academy Press, 2002.

Educating Teachers of Science, Mathematics, and Technology: New Practices for the New Millennium. Committee on Science and Mathematics Teacher Preparation. Washington, DC: National Academy Press, 2000.

Enduring Knowledge for Changing Times. Center for Education. Washington, DC: National Academy Press, 2001.

Enhancing the Postdoctoral Experience for Scientists and Engineers. Committee on Science, Engineering, and Public Policy. Washington, DC: National Academy Press, 2000.

Evaluating and Improving Undergraduate Teaching in Science Technology Engineering and Mathematics. Marye Anne Fox and Norman Hackerman. Washington, DC: National Academy Press, 2002.

Forecasting Demand and Supply of Doctoral Scientists and Engineers. Office of Scientific and Engineering Personnel. Washington, DC: National Academy Press, 2000.

From Scarcity to Visibility. Gender Differences in the Careers of Doctoral Scientists and Engineers. Panel for the Study of Gender Differences in the Career Outcomes of Science and Engineering Ph.D.'s.Washington, DC: National Academy Press, 2001.

Myths and Tradeoffs: The Role of Tests in Undergraduate Admissions. Alexandra Beatty, M.R.C. Greenwood, and Robert L. Linn. Washington, DC: National Academy Press, 1999.

Trends in the Early Careers of Life Scientists. Board on Biology. Washington, DC: National Academy Press, 1998.

Improving Mathematics Education: Resources for Decision Making. Steve Leinwand and Gail Burrill. Washington, DC: National Academy Press, 2001.

Improving the Recruitment, Retention, and Utilization of Federal Scientists and Engineers. Alan K. Campbell, Stephen J. Lukasik, and Michael G. H. McGeary. Washington, DC: National Academy Press, 1993.

Learning and Understanding: Improving Advanced Study of Mathematics and Science in U.S. High Schools. Jerry P. Gollub, Meryl W. Bertenthal, Jay B. Labov, and Philip C. Curtis. Washington, DC: National Academy Press, 2002.

Measuring the Science and Engineering Enterprise. Committee to Assess the Portfolio of the Division of Science Resources Studies of NSF. Washington, DC: National Academy Press, 2000.

NASA's Education Programs: Defining Goals Assessing Outcomes. Committee on NASA Education Program Outcomes. Washington, DC: National Academy Press, 1994.

Preparing for the Workplace: Charting a Course for Federal Postsecondary Training Policy. Janet S. Hansen. Washington, DC: National Academy Press, 1994.

Research in Education. Richard J. Shavelson and Lisa Towne. Washington, DC: National Academy Press, 2002.

Reshaping the Graduate Education of Scientists and Engineers. Committee on Science, Engineering, and Public Policy. Washington, DC: National Academy Press, 1995.

Review of the U.S. Department of Defense Air, Space, and Supporting Information Systems Science and Technology Program. Committee on Review of the U.S. Department of Defense Air and Space Systems Science and Technology Program. Washington, DC: National Academy Press, 2001.

Technically Speaking: Why All Americans Need to Know More about Technology. Committee on Technology Literacy. Washington, DC: National Academy Press, 2002.

Transforming Undergraduate Education in Science, Mathematics, Engineering, and Technology. Committee on Undergraduate Science Education. Washington, DC: National Academy Press, 1999.

Who Will Do the Science of the Future? A Symposium on Careers of Women in Science. Committee on Women in Science and Engineering. Washington, DC: National Academy Press, 2000.

Women in the Chemical Workforce: A Workshop Report to the Chemical Sciences Roundtable. Chemical Sciences Roundtable. Washington, DC: National Academy Press, 2000.

The Knowledge Economy and Postsecondary Education. Patricia Albjerg Graham and Nevzer G. Stacey. Washington, DC: National Academy Press, 2002.

Transitions in Work and Learning: Implications for Assessment. Alan Lesgold, Michael J. Feuer, and Allison M. Black. Washington, DC: National Academy Press, 1997.

Trends in Federal Support of Research and Graduate Education. Stephen A. Merrill. Washington, DC: National Academy Press, 2001.